Welcome to Bermuda

Just a two-hour flight from most East Coast U.S. cities, Bermuda is one quick getaway that feels worlds away. Tranquil and prosperous, this island nation of pastel houses and manicured gardens also displays a deep British heritage with crisp colonial architecture. A comfortable climate provides year-round opportunities for outdoor recreation on pink-sand beaches, at championship golf courses, and in cerulean waters. Add excellent, varied shopping and dining, and it's easy to see why this small-in-size country looms large on many itineraries.

TOP REASONS TO GO

★ **Beaches:** Sand and sea come together in beautiful pink and blue crescents.

★ **Island Culture:** A rich heritage of British traditions with a calypso twist.

★ **Shopping:** Boutiques, galleries, and upscale department stores in walkable districts.

★ **Dining:** Superb independent and resort restaurants serve Bermudian and global cuisine.

★ **Water Sports:** Warm, clear waters are perfect for diving, snorkeling, boating, and more.

★ **Golf:** Greens designed by the greats include cliff-top holes and expansive ocean vistas.

Contents

MAPS

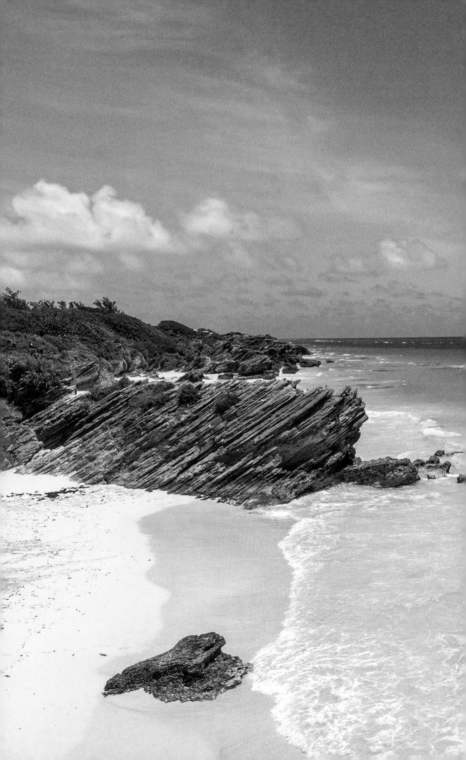

Chapter 1

EXPERIENCE BERMUDA

15 ULTIMATE EXPERIENCES

Bermuda offers terrific experiences that should be on every traveler's list. Here are Fodor's top picks for a memorable trip.

1 Relax on a Pink Beach

With a gently-curving crescent of pink sand lapped by turquoise waters and backed by uncluttered South Shore Park, Horseshoe Bay Beach is the perfect spot to swim, play, and soak up the sun. *(Ch. 4)*

2 Stroll St. George's Village

In Bermuda's oldest settlement you can step into
St. Peter's Anglican church and wander alleys lined
with traditional shops, pubs, and cottages. *(Ch. 5)*

3 Charter a Boat

There are 120 tiny islands scattered around Bermuda's
shores. Rent your own boat or charter one for a scenic
tour of the surrounding coves, lagoons, and islets.

4 Sleep in a Luxurious Hotel

No high-rises here, just elegant beachfront resorts and inland sanctuaries. Choose among luxurious hotels, cottage colonies, and flower-filled guesthouses.

5 Catch Cup Match Fever

A spirited two-day celebration, the annual Cup Match Cricket Festival is the highlight of Bermuda's summer calendar with plenty of Bermudian food and music. *(Ch. 2)*

6 Explore Underwater Treasures

The superior water clarity here affords divers and snorkelers technicolor views of coral and marine life, underwater caves, and shallow wrecks.

7 Go on a Glowworm Tour

From May through October, bioluminescent glowworms light up the shallow waters around the island two days after each full moon and can be seen on regular cruises. *(Ch. 2)*

8 Shop Fashionable Front Street

High-end retail dominates the island's shopping scene. The lack of sales tax provides a bit of savings for a vacation splurge on quality clothing, jewelry, and more. *(Ch. 7)*

9 Get Lost Along the Railway Trail

Escape to this car-free trail for walkers, joggers, and cyclists. It spans the island end-to-end, overlooking rocky coastlines and passing through green countryside. *(Ch. 2)*

10 Tee Off at an Ocean-View Course

On courses designed by the world's best golf architects, pros and high-handicappers alike are treated to sweeping ocean vistas and landscaping with spectacular blooms.

11 Bermuda Aquarium, Museum & Zoo

BAMZ brings Bermuda's undersea habitat up close with a towering 140,000-gallon tank. Also on display is area wildlife, including more than 300 birds, reptiles, and mammals. *(Ch. 6)*

12 Visit the Dockyard

Formerly a British military stronghold, the Dockyard is now home to museums, forts, water activities, a craft market, and great shops and eateries. *(Ch. 7)*

13 Sample a Rum Swizzle

Two must-have Bermudian cocktails, the Rum Swizzle and the Dark 'n' Stormy, share a secret weapon: Gosling's Black Seal Rum, loved by locals since 1806.

14 Whale-watching

Humpback whales migrate north past the island during the months of March and April, and they love to put on a show. You can see them from land or on a cruise. *(Ch. 2)*

15 Tour Crystal Caves

Easy to explore, the impressive underground passage has long stalactites and thin limestone straws above, and stalagmites in clear emerald pools below. *(Ch. 6)*

WHAT'S WHERE

1 City of Hamilton and Pembroke Parish. The city of Hamilton, in the heart of Pembroke, is a bustling little capital referred to as "town" by locals. Along with major historic sites, Hamilton has the broadest array of restaurants, shops, bars, and museums.

2 Central Parishes. Paget Parish, adjoining Pembroke to the south, is best known for its enviable selection of south-shore beaches and Paget Marsh and the Bermuda Botanical Gardens. Sleepy Devonshire Parish, adjoining Pembroke to the east, is the geographical center of the island, but most travelers merely pass through it. Serious sports enthusiasts are the exception, because the National Sports Centre, National Equestrian Centre, Bermuda Squash Racquets Association, and Ocean View Golf Course are all there. Warwick has Bermuda's longest beach; Warwick Long Bay Beach is rarely crowded, even in peak season. Southampton is home to Horseshoe Bay, the most popular pink-sand beach.

3 St. George's Parish. Air travelers first touch down in St. George's in the East End, just as the

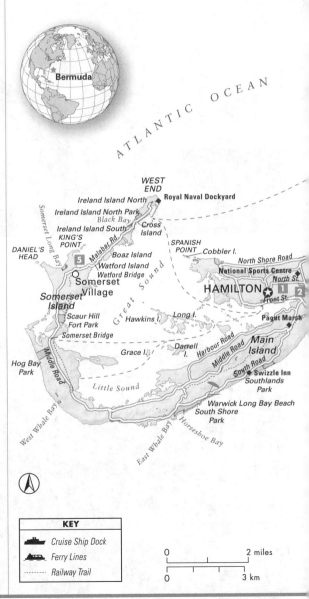

ATLANTIC OCEAN

Bermuda

WEST END
Royal Naval Dockyard
Ireland Island North
Ireland Island North Park
Black Bay
Cross Island
Ireland Island South
KING'S POINT
SPANISH POINT   Cobbler I.
Malabar Rd.
DANIEL'S HEAD
Somerset Long Bay
Boaz Island
North Shore Road
5
Watford Island
Watford Bridge
National Sports Centre
North St.
Somerset Village
HAMILTON
1 2
Front St.
Somerset Island
Great Sound
Hawkins I.
Long I.
Paget Marsh
Scaur Hill Fort Park
Darrell I.
Main Island
Somerset Bridge
Grace I.
Harbour Road
Middle Road
Hog Bay Park
Little Sound
South Road
Swizzle Inn
Southlands Park
Middle Road
Warwick Long Bay Beach
South Shore Park
West Whale Bay
East Whale Bay
Horseshoe Bay

KEY
🚢 Cruise Ship Dock
⛴ Ferry Lines
⋯⋯⋯ Railway Trail

0 — 2 miles
0 — 3 km

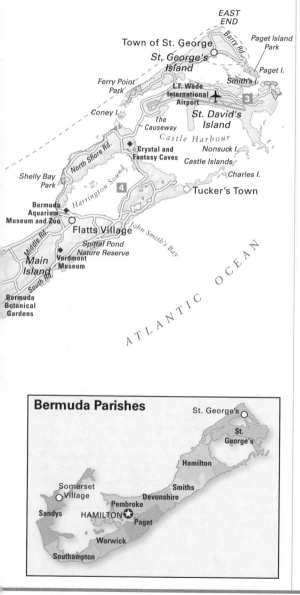

EAST
END

Town of St. George   Paget Island
Park
St. George's
Island   Paget I.

Ferry Point   Smith's I.
Park   L.F. Wade
International
Airport   3

Coney I.   *St. David's*
The   *Island*
Causeway
Castle Harbour
Crystal and
Fantasy Caves   Nonsuck I.
Castle Islands

Shelly Bay   Charles I.
Park
4   *Tucker's Town*

North Shore Rd.
Harrington Sound
Bermuda
Aquarium
Museum and Zoo   O
Flatts Village   *John Smith's Bay*
Middle Rd.   Spittal Pond
Nature Reserve
Main   Verdmont
Island   Museum
South Rd.
Bermuda
Botanical
Gardens   *A T L A N T I C*   *O C E A N*

Bermuda Parishes   St. George's O

St.
George's

Hamilton

Somerset   Smiths
O Village   Devonshire
Pembroke
Sandys   HAMILTON
Paget
Warwick
Southampton

crew of the *Sea Venture* did in 1609. Their shipwreck kick-started Bermuda's settlement, and the town is today a UNESCO World Heritage site.

4 **Eastern Parishes.** In the East End you'll also find Hamilton Parish (not the city of Hamilton), home to the Bermuda Aquarium, Museum & Zoo, the Crystal and Fantasy Caves, Shelly Bay Park, and the infamous Swizzle Inn. In Smith's Parish, which borders Harrington Sound, you'll find Spittal Pond Nature Reserve, the Verdmont Museum, and John Smith's Bay.

5 **West End.** At the farthest West End tip in the parish of Sandys (pronounced *Sands*) is Bermuda's single largest tourist attraction: the Royal Naval Dockyard. A former British bastion, the complex has been converted to house the National Museum of Bermuda, Dolphin Quest, and Snorkel Park Beach, plus shops and restaurants. You'll also find Cross Island, home of the America's Cup Village during the 35th America's Cup, which took place in 2017. Just outside of Dockyard is Somerset Village, with a handful of shops and the Somerset Country Squire Restaurant.

Bermuda Today

Bermuda has always been a land of adventure. Since it was first discovered by Europeans in 1503, explorers and castaways have sought their fortune on the island. Today's adventurers head to Bermuda for water sports, golf, and scooter riding. Great shopping, pink sand, and spas provide retreat for those in search of relaxation. While the island's tourism struggled to stay relevant after the 2008 worldwide recession, the development of the Bermuda Tourism Authority in 2014 has injected fresh life into the island, including attracting larger events such as the 2017 America's Cup, and a focus on travelers looking for genuine cultural experiences. Hotel developments, such as the St. Regis in St. George's, are on the horizon and will add more value to the island, particularly in the East End where a lack of hotel rooms has made it harder for the area to recover from the downturn in tourism. Thankfully the international business sector remains stable, and in true Bermudian spirit, locals continue to smile as they enjoy the island's rich natural bounty.

TRANSPORTATION CHALLENGES

While the island has a decent public transportation infrastructure, during summer months the buses, in particular, can get overcrowded, especially with beachgoers, and strikes by unionized workers are not unheard of, causing disruption. Bermuda has no real competitive ride-sharing services like Uber, and taxis can sometimes be difficult to come by, especially later in the evening. You can generally find taxi lines at the airport, on Front Street in Hamilton, and at major hotels, but it's worth getting friendly with your driver and scoring contact details if you intend to travel by taxi during your stay.

A MIX OF CULTURES

Bermuda's British-ness is obvious, from driving on the left side of the road, to afternoon tea, to wig-wearing lawyers strolling to court. The national sports are cricket and football, there are "bobbies on the beat" (police officers on foot), and red letterboxes on street corners. But don't let that make you think this is just a little Britain, especially these days. Bermudians are very proud of their island culture, which, along with British heritage, also mixes deep African and Caribbean roots; this is particularly evident during national holidays. Whether locals are dancing along to the drumbeat of the Gombeys or eating fish cakes on hot cross buns with peas and rice on Good Friday, there is an authentic feel to Bermuda's cultural mix.

PRICES ARE HIGH

The World Bank rates Bermuda as one of the most affluent countries in the world, and it won't take long to understand why. Start saving your dollars for Bermuda's high cost of living. Hotel accommodations are expensive, a bag of groceries costs more than $50, and gasoline is three times more expensive than in the United States. That being said, budget travelers shouldn't write off Bermuda. The iconic beaches are free, and taking public transportation will keep daily spending low. There are more casual restaurants and cafés popping up, particularly in the city of Hamilton, that make eating out a little more affordable. Also note that free walking tours are offered in Hamilton and St. George's, the Bermuda Botanical Gardens has free entry, and the Gibbs Hill Lighthouse is a bargain at just $2.50.

ROAD SAFETY

Bermuda has very few large, open roads, and driving on the left can be tricky for some tourists. With that said, it's important to weigh how comfortable you are driving a moped before you decide to rent one. In addition to issues related to the narrow, winding roads, other drivers are not the most courteous, even to tourists, and often pass; this is especially true of motorbike riders who speed and weave through traffic. Bermuda has several laws governing the size and quantity of vehicles on the road. Only Bermudians or full-time residents are allowed driver's licenses, and even then they can have only one car per household on this densely populated island. However, visitors are now able to rent small electric vehicles, no bigger than mopeds but with covered roofs and four wheels. These have proven to be much safer than the traditional moped.

TIMES ARE CHANGING

Bermuda's underlying culture is very conservative and heavily Christian, boasting one of the highest ratios of churches per capita in the world. There is some resistance to change (it was only in 2013 that the ban on Sunday liquor sales was lifted) from some of the most conservative citizens, but with the majority of the younger generation going overseas for school and work, there's now a greater openness and acceptance of people from all backgrounds. Although the government fought against legalizing same-sex marriage, as of 2019 it was legal on the island. There are still some vocal opponents, but the response to Bermuda's first Pride Parade in 2019 was overwhelmingly supportive and welcoming, particularly by the business community.

A RELATIVELY SAFE ISLAND

Bermuda is relatively safe compared with similar destinations, but petty crime is still an issue. Thieves often target tourists who leave unattended bags at beaches and valuables in unsecured rooms or in moped baskets. It's worth taking certain precautions to avoid any unwanted incidents. In particular, make sure to lock away all valuables in hotel rooms, keep windows and doors locked—especially in the evenings—and make sure to keep your belongings secure when you're riding a moped or enjoying a dip at the beach.

Natural Wonders in Bermuda

CRYSTAL AND FANTASY CAVES

Most of Bermuda's 150-some limestone caves are not easily seen, but these two were opened to the public because of their particular beauty and also the enterprising business acumen of the Wilkinson family, who turned them into attractions at the beginning of the 20th century.

WALSINGHAM NATURE RESERVE

The highlight of these 12 acres is the spectacular blue grotto for which the park is named, fed with water from the surrounding caves. Nearby is Tom Moore's Tavern, the longest-surviving restaurant on Bermuda, which has served diners in its 17th-century building for over 100 years.

THE TIDES AT FLATTS BRIDGE

Harrington Sound is as calm as a lake. But near the western end, Flatts Bridge, which connects Hamilton Parish and Smith's Parish, spans a narrow inlet with a particularly strong tidal current, making for a spectacular show as the waters rush underneath.

HORSESHOE BAY

If you're a sun seeker, there's no better place to enjoy Bermuda's pink sand than at the famous Horseshoe Bay. Although the beach is busy and bustling (especially on days when cruise ships are in port), if you venture east, there is plenty of room to stretch out and enjoy the generally calm water and soft pink sand Bermuda is known for. A restaurant with gear rentals, restrooms, and showers is near the main entrance.

COOPER'S ISLAND NATURE RESERVE

Cooper's Island offers unspoiled and virtually empty beaches since they are not accessible to motorized vehicles, requiring a quarter-mile walk. A NASA facility here recently re-opened, but 12 acres of surrounding nature reserve include magnificent views of Castle Harbour, a salt marsh, and a wildlife observation tower.

WARWICK LONG BAY BEACH

As the name suggests, Warwick Long Bay is one of the longest beaches on the island, but it tends to be quieter than nearby Horseshoe Bay. What it lacks in amenities, it makes up for in unspoiled beauty, with tide pools, beautiful walking trails, and a nearby playground. It's a popular snorkeling spot in the summer, when a small stand pops up to rent gear.

Horseshoe Bay

HOG BAY PARK

Hog Bay Park offers absolutely unspoiled views of the south shore, with some of the island's most varied shades of blue from its shallow shoreline. You'll pass rural agricultural land before the paths open up to a steep coastal track that takes you down to mostly rocky shore, where you may find a beach during low tide. The Railway Trail can be accessed from the parking lot.

ADMIRALTY PARK

Thrill seekers will find Admiralty Park, near Spanish Point in Pembroke Parish, the perfect spot to challenge their cliff-jumping skills. If cliff-jumping is not your thing, Clarence Cove offers a small, secluded beach with calm waters for wading, caves to explore, and walking trails to the remains of the Admiralty House.

BOTANICAL GARDENS

A quiet spot perfect for an easy stroll, the Botanical Gardens is part manicured lawns, part wild abandon. A particularly untamed wonder is the grove of giant banyan trees along the southwestern edge. But there's also a well-kept maze and the sensory gardens, which inspired writer Michael Ondaatje's book *In the Skin of a Lion*.

SPITTAL POND NATURE RESERVE

One of Bermuda's more dramatic coastal locations is ideal for those who want to enjoy a bit of trekking. With over 60 acres to explore, the coastal paths here offer some of the most breathtaking views on the island (and even the potential to spot whales in March and April.

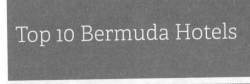

Top 10 Bermuda Hotels

THE REEFS

The rooms at The Reefs, which is owned and operated by a local family, run along a limestone cliff with unrivaled views over the south shore. An on-site, private beach is a highlight. Three restaurants make it easy for you to spend all your days on the property.

THE LOREN AT PINK BEACH

One of Bermuda's newest hotels, the Loren brings a modern, urban feel to the south shore. The property where the classic Pink Beach Club cottage colony once stood has been re-imagined with a sleek, modern design that firmly emphasizes its proximity to the ocean. Every room has a large private terrace or balcony to take full advantage of the stunning vistas.

ROSEDON HOTEL

Surrounded by lush tropical gardens mere steps from the city center, the Rosedon Hotel was originally built as a private home in 1906. The landscaped gardens and lounges around the pool make the property feel removed from central Hamilton. Rooms are spacious and decorated with island-inspired details, including four-poster beds.

CAMBRIDGE BEACHES RESORT & SPA

One of Bermuda's original cottage colonies, Cambridge Beaches is remote but alluring, providing one of the only exclusive, adult-only options on Bermuda for those looking to really get away from it all. Luckily, the Dockyard is a short taxi ride away, with ferries to Hamilton and St. George's.

POMPANO BEACH CLUB

Pompano Beach Club, with its perfectly framed water views, has been lovingly run by the same family for over 60 years. The hotel takes pride in its warm, personalized service and is chock-full of amenities (including a private beach) that make it particularly well-suited to families.

ROSEWOOD BERMUDA

Spreading across 240 acres and offering views of tranquil Castle Harbour and the iconic south shore, the Rosewood sits amongst the luxurious Tucker's Town homes of the rich and famous, and the well-appointed hotel makes it easy to feel like you are hobnobbing with some of the area's well-heeled residents.

HAMILTON PRINCESS & BEACH CLUB

One of the oldest hotels on the island, "The Pink Palace" first opened its doors in 1885. It retains its Bermudian charm but has been infused with a new vibrancy. Guests also have full access to a private beach club on Bermuda's famous south shore, 20 minutes away.

THE FAIRMONT SOUTHAMPTON, BERMUDA RESORT

If you are looking for a family-friendly resort with the feel of an all-inclusive, the Fairmont ticks all the boxes. The towering pink hotel sits on a verdant hillside that sprawls across nearly 100 acres and offers views over both the ocean and islands, including Gibbs Hill Lighthouse.

GROTTO BAY BEACH RESORT BERMUDA

Offering one of the only all-inclusive experiences on the island, Grotto Bay Beach Resort Bermuda is just a five-minute drive from the airport. Lush tropical gardens lead down to a private pink-sand beach and a spa built inside a 500,000-year-old cave. Guests have a choice of three restaurants on site to indulge their other appetites.

THE ROYAL PALMS

On the outskirts of the city of Hamilton, The Royal Palms's garden setting is a peaceful alternative to some of Bermuda's larger, more sprawling properties. With only 32 rooms, the boutique hotel gets top marks by creating personalized service, and many guests return year after year.

Bermuda's 10 Best Restaurants

WATERLOT INN

The Waterlot continues to be one of Bermuda's best steak houses, offering great food in a refined and elegant setting. Inside the former manor house, service is attentive, and the wait staff are personable and knowledgeable. Don't skip the restaurant's signature Caesar salad, prepared tableside.

TOM MOORE'S TAVERN

Originally built as a private home in 1652, Tom Moore's Tavern became a restaurant almost 100 years ago, making it the oldest-surviving eating establishment on Bermuda. It's well known for its take on sweet classics, including crêpes Suzette prepared tableside and a daily soufflé that's worth the wait.

HARRY'S

Named to honor the Cox family's patriarch, Harry's feels like a restaurant straight from the *Mad Men* era. The Harry's Classic—a shrimp cocktail, iceberg wedge salad, 14-ounce New York strip steak, and a slice of cheesecake—reinforces that notion, though daily specials may be more inventive.

ASCOTS

For romantics and foodies alike, this restaurant in the Royal Palms Hotel offers an old-world setting but a much more modern take on Mediterranean cuisine infused with Bermudian flavors (with artful presentations), all from chef Edmund Smith. In addition to fresh seafood, you can have veal chops or roast duck.

MARCUS'

Inside the stylish Hamilton Princess & Beach Club, a former ballroom has been infused with a fresh island vibe highlighting the views of Hamilton Harbour, not to mention a menu by celebrity chef Marcus Samuelsson, who offers both his signature dishes (chicken and waffles, anyone?) but also fish chowder bites and Bermudian-style jerk chicken. The ambience is buzzy, especially on Sunday during the popular Champagne Brunch.

BOLERO BRASSERIE

Tucked away above Hamilton's bustling Front Street, Bolero Brasserie is an intimate restaurant dimly lit with deep red walls, quirky artwork, and a menu of Continental favorites and some vegetarian choices from chef Jonny Roberts. A popular balcony overlooking the hubbub makes this restaurant the perfect spot to people watch.

Marcus'

DEVIL'S ISLE

A small, contemporary café offers a communal table, where you may meet some locals while you dine on locally sourced and mostly organic salads, bowls, burgers, and a few entrees that include salmon and grilled chicken. Don't miss having a cup of the company's delightful, locally roasted coffee.

SEASIDE GRILL

Seaside Grill is a simple take-out counter on the north shore, but it makes one of the best fish sandwiches on the island, an iconic Bermudian staple made from piles of freshly caught, crispy fish between thick-cut homemade bread, spread with tartar sauce. It's not only delicious but is one of the island's Instagram-worthy meals. You can also have your fish grilled as an entree.

PORT O' CALL

The sophisticated Port O' Call on Hamilton's busy Front Street offers a menu focused on fresh, local seafood, which is delivered daily, though not always from Bermudian waters. Leave room for the restaurant's creamy, light cheesecake for dessert. On Fridays, the bar and patio turn into a happy hour hot spot. It's perfect for a business lunch or romantic dinner.

TEMPEST BISTRO

Wait to hear the daily specials for both lunch and dinner before deciding on your meal at the harborside Tempest Bistro, which offers great views of St. George's Harbor. They are usually the highlight since the menu's focus is on whatever fresh seafood might be available that day.

Bermuda with Kids

WHAT TO SEE AND DO

Bermuda is generally seen as a destination for honeymooners and baby boomers, but it's also a great place for families, with plenty of kid-friendly attractions. The water at the south-shore beaches can get a little rough (and those beaches can get crowded), but there are various kid-friendly beaches, including Clearwater Beach, Turtle Bay Beach, and Shelly Bay Beach.

The **Bermuda Aquarium, Museum & Zoo** tops many family itineraries thanks to cute critters and engaging displays that include walk-through enclosures, supersize fish tanks, a tidal touch pool, and a glass-enclosed beehive. BAMZ also offers thrice-daily seal feedings and docent-led weekend activities that are equal parts entertainment and education, plus a fun outdoor play area where little ones can make discoveries at their own pace.

You can introduce your offspring to still more animals at the Dockyard's **National Museum of Bermuda,** where sheep graze on the upper grounds (their job is to keep the grass well mowed); nearby, bottlenose dolphins interact with participants in the various Dolphin Quest Bermuda programs. Marine life awaits next door, too, at the affordable **Snorkel Park Beach,** where you can see over 50 varieties of fish, not to mention anemone, sea cucumber, and various coral. Kayaks, paddle boats, Jet Skis and even underwater scooters can be rented here.

One of the best family beaches in Bermuda is Shelly Bay Beach, known for its sandy bottom and shallow, calm water. The park is popular for picnics under the shade trees, swimming, and the large playground just behind the beach, which attracts local kids on weekends and school holidays.

Though they're not as tourist oriented, Bermuda's other fortresses attract youngsters as well. **Fort St. Catherine's** 17th-century ramparts and spooky underground passages set the perfect stage for playing make-believe. There are also some cool bonus features (among them an arsenal of antique weapons and replica crown jewels) that can help keep the gang entertained on those rare rainy days.

Elsewhere, families can go underground at **Crystal and Fantasy Caves,** where guides point out formations that look like familiar skylines and spacecraft; or go underwater at the **Bermuda Underwater Exploration Institute,** where you can experience deep-sea diving in a simulator pod. The upwardly mobile, meanwhile, can climb 185 steps to the top of **Gibbs Hill Lighthouse,** the highest spot in Bermuda.

The **Bermuda National Gallery** is surprisingly family-friendly as well. It runs a number of special programs aimed directly at youngsters and provides drawing stations where they can create their own masterpieces.

At night, the popular **Harbour Nights** festival in Hamilton (every Wednesday from May through September) offers an array of Bermudian-style street food, including fish sandwiches, patties, and more from booths along several streets. **Warwick Lanes** in Warwick Parish offers family bowling in the late afternoon and evening, as well as a good on-site restaurant.

WHERE TO EAT AND STAY

Kids will have to forgo their favorite fast food on Bermuda because the island is essentially a franchise-free zone; however, there are a number of family-friendly options. **La Trattoria** in the city of Hamilton is the casual Italian-food spot with some of the best options for kids, and it's a fun spot for adults as well. **Pizza House,** which allows kids to design their own pizza, has three outlets across the island, while **Paraquet** offers American-style diner food in Paget Parish.

A few select hotels, among them the **Fairmont Southampton, Elbow Beach Resort,** and **Grotto Bay Beach Resort,** go the extra mile for families. The Fairmont Southampton has kid-friendly menus and a real year-round kids' club with activities scheduled each day. Elbow Beach Resort has less impressive kids' activities, but it too offers babysitting. Grotto Bay Beach Resort has facilities designed for families with small children, as well as a summer kids' program. The enclosed bay, fish-feeding aquarium, two underground caves with supervised exploring, and the kiddie pool beside the larger pool put parents at ease when their children hit the water. **Pompano Beach Club** has an arcade room, table games, and a kids' pool.

Smaller properties (with smaller price tags) are also excellent choices for families with children. Try **Clairfont Apartments,** which offers one-bedrooms close to the south-shore beaches and a three-minute walk from a large playground. Renting homes suitable for hosting children has also become a popular option, often through sites like **Airbnb.** This can be an attractive choice because these places are often cheaper than a hotel and provide a little more room to spread out. Having a kitchen will also be an advantage when trying to please picky palates.

A RESOURCE FOR PARENTS

Little Longtails If you don't want to lug all your kids' extras on vacation, Little Longtails will deliver the essentials, including car seats, cribs, and strollers, to your hotel or vacation rental. The company, run by two mothers, also stocks kids' toys, books, and beach items. They can even arrange to deliver groceries to your accommodations through their Kiddie Concierge. ☎ *441/707–7658* ⊕ *www. littlelongtails.com.*

Weddings and Honeymoons

Bermuda is a popular wedding destination because of its secluded pink beaches, easy access from the United States, well-established infrastructure that includes English-speaking wedding personnel, and its remarkably high romance quotient (the island even has an honest-to-goodness Lovers' Lane).

THE DETAILS

License. You must send a Notice of Intended Marriage form to the **Bermuda Registry General** (☎ 441/297–7739 ⊕ www.registrygeneral.gov.bm) within three months of your intended wedding date. A fee of $353 must accompany the form. A Marriage Certificate costs $65 and can be applied for at the same time. The notice is then published in the local newspaper. There is a waiting period of 15 days, and if no formal objection is raised, the license (valid for three months) will be issued.

The Perfect Backdrop. The obvious choices for a Bermuda destination wedding are right on the beach or on one of the stunning cliff-tops looking down over the turquoise water. Some hotels have beachfront or graden gazebos. Historic properties like the World Heritage Centre in St. George's or Fort Hamilton are also popular.

Dress. Although most brides go for wedding gowns, dress at Bermuda weddings tends to be casual. Grooms often wear linen pants and short-sleeved shirts. Guests dress smart-casual. Bare feet on the beach are a must.

Local Customs. Bermudians serve two wedding cakes; the groom's cake is plain, often a pound cake, and the multitier bride's cake is a dark fruitcake. The bride and groom walk hand in hand beneath a Bermuda moongate—an archway made of limestone and coral usually found at the entrance to gardens. It's said that all who do so are assured everlasting luck.

THE BIG DAY

Most larger resorts have their own wedding planners, but the island also has independent wedding planners.

Bermuda Bride Nikki Begg is internationally renowned for delivering breathtaking Bermuda destination weddings. ☎ 441/295–8697 ⊕ www.bermudabride.com.

The Bridal Suite Bermuda The knowledgeable wedding consultants here will work tirelessly to create the most unforgettable day of your life. ☎ 441/707–1318 ⊕ www.bridalsuitebermudaweddings.com.

THE HONEYMOON

Cambridge Beaches Resort & Spa. Sunsets, candlelit dinners, and beautiful scenery are all at this adults-only resort, which offers the ultimate pampering experience.

Elbow Beach Resort. This cottage colony with lush gardens welcomes its honeymooners with a bottle of bubbly. There are beautiful beachfront cottages, and the spa has couples' treatment rooms.

The Loren at Pink Beach. An escape does not get much more private or luxe than at the island's chicest hotel, which has 45 oceanfront suites set on 8 coastal acres. Book a couples' spa treatment in rooms overlooking the Atlantic.

The Reefs Resort & Club. The cliffside luxury resort has breathtaking views. You'll get champagne and chocolate-covered strawberries on your arrival, and you can book a gourmet dinner right on the beach.

Rosewood Bermuda. The beautiful resort's rooms all have stunning views, but a suite is worth the splurge.

TRAVEL SMART

Updated by
Melissa Fox

★ **CAPITAL:**
Hamilton

☗ **POPULATION:**
60,828

🗨 **LANGUAGE:**
English

$ **CURRENCY:**
Bermudian dollar; pegged
to the U.S. dollar

☏ **AREA CODE:**
1 441

⚠ **EMERGENCIES:**
911

🚗 **DRIVING:**
On the left

⚡ **ELECTRICITY:**
120v/60 cycles; plugs are
U.S. standard two- and
three-prong

⊘ **TIME:**
Atlantic Daylight Time (ADT),
1 hour ahead of New York

⊕ **WEB RESOURCES:**
www.gotobermuda.com
www.bermuda.com
www.bermuda4u.com

✈ **AIRPORT:**
L. F. Wade International
Airport (BDA)

BERMUDA

⊛Hamilton

ATLANTIC
OCEAN

Know Before You Go

BERMUDA IS CLOSER THAN YOU THINK

Flying time to Bermuda from most East Coast cities is about 2 hours, and you can fly nonstop from Atlanta, Baltimore, Boston, Miami, Newark (EWR), New York City (JFK), and Philadelphia, and seasonally from Charlotte and Washington, D.C.

YOUR DOLLARS ARE GOOD HERE

The Bermudian dollar is on par with the U.S. dollar, and the two currencies are used interchangeably, so you'll have no need to change any money. (While you can use American money anywhere, change is often given in Bermudian currency.) Try to avoid accumulating large amounts of local money, though, because it's difficult to change back (local banks are usually quite accommodating). ATMs are plentiful but usually dispense only Bermudian dollars (other than HSBC, which tends to offer both U.S. and Bermudian dollars). But an increasing number of venues will accept credit cards, even for small items.

IT'S A ZIKA-FREE ZONE

The Zika virus has never been reported in Bermuda, even as it's become endemic in much of the Caribbean, because the Aedes aegypti mosquito (the most typical carrier) is not endemic to the country. Bermuda has relatively few mosquitoes and very few reported cases of mosquito-borne illnesses. So far in 2019, one imported case of dengue has been confirmed in Bermuda, but none seems to have originated in the country (three other cases of imported dengue were suspected but not confirmed).

BRING YOUR PASSPORT

U.S. citizens arriving by air and sea to Bermuda need a valid passport, though cruise-ship passengers on closed-loop cruises (those departing and arriving in the same U.S. port) need only have proof of citizenship and identity (a government-issued photo ID and a birth certificate with a raised seal). You can fill out your Bermuda Arrival Card online before you leave (⊕ *www.bermudaarrivalcard. com*); just remember to print it out and bring it with you to show the Bermuda immigration officials. On your return to the U.S., you'll clear customs and immigration in Bermuda before you board your flight (and Global Entry is supported).

IT'S A LITTLE FORMAL

As a rule of thumb, Bermudians dress more formally than most Americans. In the evening, some of the more upscale restaurants and hotel dining rooms require men to wear a jacket and tie and women to dress comparably, so bring a few dressy outfits. But increasingly venues are more accepting of the trend toward "smart casual." In this case, women should be fine with slacks or a skirt and a dressy blouse or sweater. Bermudian men often wear Bermuda shorts (and proper knee socks) with a jacket and tie for formal events and business meetings.

THE CLIMATE IS NOT TROPICAL

Unlike the Caribbean, Bermuda is not a tropical destination. It's climate is subtropical, which means it's not nearly as reliably warm (nor as hot) as the islands to the south. In the summer, temperatures rarely exceed 90 degrees, and in the winter they rarely go below 65 degrees. Water temperatures rarely go below 65 degrees in the winter, nor above 83 degrees in the summer. Bermuda is affected by the occasional hurricane, but direct hits are rare.

IT'S NOT ACTUALLY AN "ISLAND"

Bermuda is not a single island; rather, it's an archipelago of 7 main islands and some 170 other named islets and rocks. The main island is called "Bermuda," but the official name of the country is "The Bermuda Islands."

ONLY A FEW ANIMALS ARE INDIGENOUS

While humans have introduced many new animal and plant species

to Bermuda, only two vertebrates are believed to be indigenous, the Bermuda skink (a lizard) and the diamondback terrapin (a turtle). Five bat species pre-dated humans in Bermuda, but all are found in the eastern United States and are thought to have flown to Bermuda from there. Several species of sea turtles lay their eggs on Bermuda beaches, and several bird species are found there, but the country's national bird, the Bermuda petral, was thought to have gone extinct in the 1620s; however, it was rediscovered in 1951. A ground-nesting bird, it's the second-yrarest seabird in the world.

VISITORS CANNOT RENT CARS

Famously, Bermuda does not allow tourists to rent cars. Consequently (and because taxis are so expensive), scooters have been popular among tourists for decades. However, increasingly crowded roads mean that driving a scooter or moped can be a fairly dangerous proposition for the unskilled rider. You can, however, rent a Renault Twizy, a tiny, two-seat electric vehicle that's less than four feet wide, or one of several similar microcars. Although charging is free, keep in mind that renting one of these will set you back at least $100 per day. A cheaper alternative is a bus pass, which costs $62 per week (but many buses don't run after 7 pm).

BERMUDA IS EXPENSIVE

While flights to Bermuda can cost well under $300 round trip, both dining and lodging prices on Bermuda are high. The cheapest meal will likely cost at least $20; the cheapest AirBnB apartment is at least $100 per night. But high-end restaurants can easily top $100 per person, and an "inexpensive" hotel room costs about $275 per night (double that for a high-end resort). Take-out from restaurants can be cheaper than sit-down meals (and you can at least save on gratuities and drinks). You can cut your lodging budget by about 40% by visiting in the off-season, which is sun-kissed yet cool and ideal for tennis, golf, and shopping.

Getting Here and Around

It's easy to get to Bermuda by air from the United States, and the price is cheaper than it once was, as more discount airlines have added flights from major East Coast hubs.

✈ Air

Flying time to Bermuda from most East Coast cities is about 2 hours; from Toronto, 3 hours; and 7 hours from London Gatwick.

Nonstop service to Bermuda is available year-round on major airlines from Atlanta, Baltimore, Boston, Miami, Newark (NJ), New York City, Philadelphia, Toronto, and London, and seasonally from Charlotte and Washington, D.C.

Most flights arrive around noon, making for particularly long waits to get through immigration; however, British Airways flights and a couple of American Airlines flights from New York arrive in the evening.

U.S. passengers clear customs and immigration when leaving Bermuda, so they are treated as domestic travelers upon landing in the United States. Global Entry is supported.

AIRPORTS

Bermuda's gateway is L. F. Wade International Airport (BDA), formerly Bermuda International Airport, on the East End of the island. It's approximately 9 miles from Hamilton (30-minute cab ride), 13 miles from Southampton (40-minute cab ride), and 17 miles from Somerset (50 minutes by cab). The town of St. George's is about a 15-minute cab ride from the airport.

■TIP→ **Ask the local tourist board about hotel and local transportation packages that include tickets to major museum exhibits or other special events.**

AIRPORT TRANSFERS

Taxis, available outside the arrivals gate, are the usual and most convenient way to leave the airport. The approximate fare (not including tip) to Hamilton is $35; to St. George's, $21; to south-shore hotels, $50; and to Sandys (Somerset), $80. A surcharge of $1 is added for each piece of luggage stored in the trunk or on the roof. Fares are 25%–50% higher between midnight and 6 am and all day on Sunday and public holidays. Fifteen percent is an acceptable tip.

CEO Transport Ltd. has a range of vehicles available to transport guests to hotels and guesthouses. Prices range from $20 for shared shuttle service up to $220 for a VIP Meet and Greet Service in a luxury sedan.

⬤ Boat

The Bermuda Ministry of Transport maintains excellent, frequent, and on-time ferry service from Hamilton to Paget and Warwick (the pink line), Somerset and the Dockyard in the West End (the blue line), Rockaway in Southampton (the green line), and on weekdays in summer only, the Dockyard and St. George's (the orange line).

A one-way adult fare from Hamilton Paget or Warwick is $3.50; to Somerset, the Dockyard, or St. George's, $5. The last departures are from Hamilton at 8 pm. Sunday ferry service is limited and ends around 6 pm. You can bring a bicycle on board free of charge, but you'll pay $4.50 extra to take a motor scooter to Somerset or the Dockyard. Motor scooters are not allowed on the pink line. Discounted one-, two-, three-, four-, and seven-day passes are available for use on both ferries and buses. They cost $19, $31.50, $44, $48.50, and $62,

respectively. Monthly passes are also available. The helpful ferry operators can answer questions about routes and schedules and can even help get your bike on board. Schedules are published online, posted at each landing, and also available at the Ferry Terminal, Central Bus Terminal, Visitor Services Centres, and most hotels, as well as at post offices.

🚌 Bus

Bermuda's pink and blue buses travel the island from east to west. To find a bus stop outside Hamilton, look for either a stone shelter or a pink or blue pole. For buses heading to Hamilton, the pole is pink; for those traveling away from Hamilton, the pole is blue. Remember to wait on the proper side of the road. Driving in Bermuda is on the left. Bus drivers will not make change, so purchase tickets or discounted tokens or carry plenty of coins.

In addition to public buses, private minibuses serve St. George's. The minibus fare depends on the destination, but you won't pay more than $5 or $6. Minibuses, which you can flag down, drop you wherever you want to go in this parish. They operate daily from about 7:30 am to 11 pm. Smoking is not permitted on buses.

Bermuda is divided into 14 bus zones, each about 2 miles long. Within the first three zones, the rate is $3.50 (coins only). For longer distances, the fare is $5. If you plan to travel by public transportation often, buy a booklet of tickets (15 14-zone tickets for $37.50, or 15 three-zone tickets for $25). You can also buy a few tokens, which, unlike tickets, are sold individually. In addition to tickets and tokens, there are one-, two-, three-, four-,

and seven-day passes ($19, $31.50, $44, $48.50, and $62, respectively). Monthly passes are also available. All bus passes are good for ferry service and are available at the Central Bus Terminal. Tickets and passes are also sold at many hotels and guesthouses.

Hamilton buses arrive and depart from the Central Bus Terminal on Washington Street, near City Hall. An office here is open weekdays from 7:15 am to 7 pm, Saturday from 7:30 am to 6 pm, and Sunday and holidays from 8:30 am to 5:30 pm; it's the only place to buy money-saving tokens.

Buses run about every 15 minutes, except on Sunday, when they usually come every half hour or hour, depending on the route. Bus schedules are available at the bus terminal in Hamilton and at many hotels. The timetable also offers an itinerary for a do-it-yourself, one-day sightseeing tour by bus and ferry. Upon request, the driver will be happy to tell you when you've reached your stop. Be sure to greet the bus driver when boarding—it's considered rude in Bermuda to ask a bus driver a question, such as the fare or details on your destination, without first offering a greeting.

🚗 Car

You cannot rent a car in Bermuda. The island has strict laws governing overcrowded roads, so even Bermudians are only allowed one car per household. A popular, albeit somewhat dangerous, alternative is to rent mopeds or scooters, which are better for negotiating the island's narrow roads. If driving a scooter is not your idea of a good time, there are options. With cockpit-style seats, a centrally located steering wheel, and foot pedals, the two-person Renault

Getting Here and Around

Twizys from Current Vehicles are not only safer than mopeds, they're affordable and fun to drive. These mini electric cars are less than 4 feet wide, which makes them the perfect size for Bermuda's narrow roads, and have a range of up to 80 km (50 miles) on a single charge. Explore the island in style, comfort, and emission-free good conscience. Book in advance and pick up your Twizy at one of three locations: the Loren, Hamilton Princess & Beach Club, or Fairmont Southampton. For your convenience, Current Bermuda has installed dedicated charging facilities across the island at partnering hotel properties. Find a list on their website. ⊕ *www.currentvehicles. com/charging-network.*

Another, safer rental alternative to motor scooters has been introduced to the island by Bermuda Rental Car Ltd. While traditional-size car rentals are out of the question, Oleander Cycles has introduced a rental service offering electric vehicles that seat up to four people and provide much-needed air-conditioning for those hot summer days spent cruising one end of the island to the other.

🏍 Scooter

Because car rentals are not allowed in Bermuda, you might decide to get around by moped or scooter. Bermudians routinely use the words *moped* and *scooter* interchangeably, even though they're different. You must pedal to start a moped, and it carries only one person. A scooter, on the other hand, which starts when you put the key in the ignition, is more powerful and holds one or two passengers.

■ TIP➔ **Think twice before renting a moped, as accidents occur frequently and are occasionally fatal.** The best ways to avoid

mishaps are to drive defensively, obey the speed limit, remember to stay on the left-hand side of the road—especially at traffic circles—and avoid riding in the rain and at night.

Helmets are required by law. Mopeds and scooters can be rented from cycle companies by the hour, the day, or the week. They will show first-time riders how to operate the vehicles. Rates vary, so it's worth calling several liveries to see what they charge. Single-seat scooter rentals cost $55–$75 per day or from about $200–$250 per week. Some liveries tack a mandatory insurance-and-repair charge on top of the bill, whereas others include the cost of insurance, breakdown service, pickup and delivery, and a tank of gas in the quoted price. A $20 deposit may also be charged for the lock, key, and helmet. You must be at least 16 and have a valid driver's license to rent. Major hotels have their own cycle liveries, and all hotels and most guesthouses will make rental arrangements.

Riding a motor scooter for the first time can be disconcerting wherever you are. Here you have the added confusion that Bermudians drive on the left. In addition, though the posted speed limit is 35 kph (about 22 mph), the unofficial speed limit is actually closer to 50 kph (31 mph; and many locals actually travel faster than that). At most rental shops, lessons on how to ride a motor scooter are perfunctory at best—practice as much as you can before going on the main road and beware of unusual traffic patterns such as double-laned roundabouts. Though many tourists can and do rent motor scooters, the public transportation system (ferries and buses) is excellent and should not be ruled out.

The Bermudian slang dictionary *Bermewjan Vurds* defines "road rash" (grazes received from sliding along Bermuda's

roads in an accident) as "a skin disease common amongst tourists brave enough to rent mopeds."

GASOLINE
Gas for cycles runs from $3 to $4 per liter, but you can cover a great deal of ground on the full tank that comes with the wheels. Gas stations will accept major credit cards. It's customary to tip attendants—a couple of dollars is adequate.

PARKING
On-street parking bays for scooters are plentiful and easy to spot. What's even better is they're free!

ROAD CONDITIONS
Roads are narrow, winding, and full of blind curves. Whether driving cars or scooters, Bermudians tend to be quite cautious around less-experienced visiting riders, but crowded city streets make accidents all the more common. Local rush hours are weekdays from 7:30 am to 9 am and from 4 pm to 6 pm. Roads are often bumpy, and they may be slippery under a morning mist or rainfall. Street lamps are few and far between outside the cities, so be especially careful driving at night.

ROADSIDE EMERGENCIES
The number for Bermuda's emergency services is ☎ 911. Scooters are often stolen, so to be safe you should always secure your scooter with the provided lock and carry the number of your hire company with you. Also, don't ride with valuables in your bike basket, as you are putting yourself at risk of theft. Passing motorists can grab your belongings and ride off without you even knowing it.

RULES OF THE ROAD
The speed limit is 35 kph (22 mph), except in the UNESCO World Heritage site of St. George's, where it is a mere 25 kph (about 15 mph). The limits, however, are not very well enforced, and the actual driving speed in Bermuda hovers around 50 kph (31 mph). Police seldom target tourists for parking offenses or other driving infractions. Drunk driving is a serious problem in Bermuda, despite stiff penalties. The blood-alcohol limit is 0.08. The courts will impose a $1,000 fine for a driving-while-intoxicated infraction, and also take the driver off the road for at least one year. There is also a law that forbids use of a mobile phone while driving a scooter.

🚗 Taxi
Taxis are the fastest and easiest way to get around the island; unfortunately, they are also the most costly and can take a long time to arrive. Four-seater taxis charge $7.90 for the first mile and $2.75 for each subsequent mile. Between midnight and 6 am, and on Sunday and holidays, a 25%–50% surcharge is added to the fare. There's a $1 charge for each piece of luggage stored in the trunk or on the roof. Taxi drivers accept only American or Bermudian cash, but not bills larger than $50, and they expect a 15% tip. You can phone for taxi pickup, but you may wait while the cab navigates Bermuda's heavy traffic, so don't hesitate to hail a taxi on the street. Another option is Hitch, a local booking app to arrange transportation on demand. The app is available for both Android and Apple devices. ⊕ www.hitch.bm.

For a personalized taxi tour of the island, the minimum duration is three hours, at $50 per hour for one to four people and $70 an hour for five or six, excluding tip.

Essentials

Activities

Long before your plane touches down in Bermuda, the island's greatest asset becomes breathtakingly obvious—the crystal-clear, aquamarine water that frames the tiny, hook-shaped atoll.

So clear are Bermuda's waters that in 1994 the government nixed a local scuba-diving group's plan to create a unique dive site by sinking an abandoned American warplane in 30 feet of water off the island's East End, fairly close to the end of the airport's runway. The government feared that the plane would be easily visible from above—to arriving passengers— and could cause undue distress. It's the incredible clarity of the water that makes Bermuda one of the world's greatest places for exploratory scuba diving and snorkeling, especially among the age-old shipwrecks off the island. The presence of these sunken ships is actually one of Bermuda's ironies—as translucent as the water is, it wasn't quite clear enough to make the treacherous reefs visible to the hundreds of ship captains who have smashed their vessels on them through the centuries.

Thanks to Bermuda's position near the Gulf Stream, the water stays warm year-round. In summer the ocean is usually above 80°F, and it's even warmer in the shallows between the reefs and shore. In winter the water temperature only occasionally drops below 70°F, but it seems cooler because the air temperature is usually in the mid-60s. There's less call for water sports December through March, not because of a drop in water temperature but because of windy conditions. The wind causes rough water, which in turn creates problems for fishing and diving boats, and underwater visibility is often clouded by sand and debris.

Whether it's renting a glass-bottomed kayak for a gentle paddle over the reefs, taking a motorboat for a spin, or spending an adrenaline-filled afternoon wakeboarding, getting out on the water is an essential part of the Bermuda experience. In high season, mid-April through mid-October, fishing, diving, and yacht charters fill up quickly.

Bermudians take their onshore sports seriously, too. Cricket and soccer are the national sports, but road running, golf, field hockey, rugby, and a host of other activities get their share of love. Bermudian soccer stars, such as former Manchester City striker Shaun Goater, have delighted crowds in British and U.S. leagues through the years, and Bermudian sailors hold their own in world competition, as do runners, equestrians, and swimmers. Tennis is quite a big deal here, too, and with 70 courts packed into these 21.6 square miles (56 square km), it's hard to believe there's room left for horseback riding, biking, running, and golf.

BIKING

The best and sometimes only way to explore Bermuda's nooks and crannies— its little hidden coves and 18th-century tribe (side) roads—is by bicycle or motor scooter. Arriving at the small shore roads and hill trails, however, means first navigating Bermuda's rather treacherous main roads. They are narrow, with no shoulders, and often congested with traffic (especially near Hamilton during rush hours). Fortunately, there's another, safer option for biking in Bermuda: the Railway Trail, a dedicated cycle path blissfully free of cars.

Despite the traffic, bicycle racing is a popular sport in Bermuda, and club groups regularly whir around the island on evening, weekend, and early-morning training rides. Be prepared for some

tough climbs—the roads running north and south across the island are particularly steep and winding—and the wind can sap even the strongest rider's strength, especially along South Shore Road in Warwick and Southampton Parishes. Island roads are no place for novice riders. Helmets are strongly recommended on pedal bikes (it's illegal to ride without them on a motor scooter), and parents should think twice before allowing preteens to bike here.

Information on local races or on how to meet up with fellow cyclists for regular group rides is available on the Bermuda Bicycle Assocation website, ⊕ *www. bermudabicycle.org.* The Winner's Edge bike shop on Front Street in Hamilton is also a good source of information about the local cycling scene; visit its website at ⊕ *www.winnersedge.bm.*

In Bermuda bicycles are called pedal or push bikes to distinguish them from the more common motorized two-wheelers, which are also called bikes. Some of the cycle liveries around the island rent both, so make sure to specify whether you want a pedal or motor bike. If you're sure you want to bicycle while you're in Bermuda, try to reserve rental bikes a few days in advance. Rates are around $40 a day, though the longer you rent, the more economical your daily rate. You may be charged an additional $30 or so for a repair waiver and for a refundable deposit.

★ **Bermuda Railway Trail**
BICYCLING | Running intermittently along the length of the old Bermuda Railway (old "Rattle 'n' Shake"), this trail is scenic and restricted to pedestrian and bicycle traffic. You can enter and exit the trail at several signposted points. One lovely route starts at Somerset Bridge and ends 2½ miles later near Mangrove Bay. You can take your bike onto the ferry for a

ride from Hamilton or St. George's to the Somerset Bridge stop. From there, bike to the bridge on the main road, turn right, and ride uphill for about 50 yards until you reach the sign announcing "Railway Trail." The segment has spectacular views of the Great Sound. Toward the end of the trail segment, you are on Beacon Hill Road opposite the bus depot. Here you can turn around and head back to Somerset Bridge, or, for refreshment, turn left and ride to the main road, and make a sharp right turn to find Mangrove Bay and several pubs. In Hamilton Parish, a 740-foot bridge allows walkers, joggers, and bikers to pass between Crawl Hill and Coney Island. Because parts of the Railway Trail are isolated and not well lit, plan your excursions for daytime hours.

BIRD-WATCHING
Forty species of warblers have been spotted in Bermuda, especially in the casuarina trees along the south shore and West End. Other omnipresent species include kiskadees, swifts, cuckoos, flycatchers, swallows, thrushes, kingbirds, and orioles. Bird conservation is a big deal in Bermuda. You can see bluebird boxes on every island golf course, which act as safe nesting sites for this jeopardized species, threatened by development and the invasive sparrow.

The largest variety of birds can be spotted during fall migration, when thousands of birds pass overhead, stop for a rest on their way south, or spend the winter on the island. You might spot the rare American avocet or the curlew sandpiper. In spring look for brightly colored Central and South American birds migrating north. The white-tailed tropic bird, a beautiful white bird with black markings and a 12- to 17-inch-long tail (locals call it a "longtail"), is one of the first to arrive. Summer is the quietest season for bird-watching in Bermuda. Late migrants,

Essentials

like the barn swallow and chimney swift, pass by, and if you check the ponds you may see the occasional shorebird.

Bermuda Audubon Society

BIRD WATCHING | The society's excellent *A Birdwatching Guide to Bermuda,* by president Andrew Dobson, published by the Arlequin Press, has maps, illustrations, and descriptions of birds and their habitats. It also sells a special DVD featuring the history and conservation of the East End's Nonsuch Island. Several birding events are organized throughout the year, including the Christmas Bird Count—Bermuda averages over 80 species per count, although 250 species have been recorded. You can find a listing of the Audubon Society's events on its website as well as a bird-watching checklist. Birders may also be interested in David Wingate's successful efforts to repopulate the native cahow bird population via artificial burrows on Nonsuch Island. ☎ *441/238–8628* ⊕ *www.audubon.bm.*

BOATING

Bermuda is gorgeous by land, but you should take to the water to fully appreciate its beauty. You can either rent your own boat or charter one with a skipper. There are literally scores of options to suit all tastes, from champagne cruises at sunset to cruise and kayak ecotours.

More than 20 large power cruisers and sailing vessels, piloted by local skippers, are available for charter. Primarily 30 to 60 feet long, most charter sailboats can carry up to 30 passengers, sometimes overnight. Meals and drinks can be included on request, and a few skippers offer dinner cruises for the romantically inclined. Rates generally range from $500 to $750 for a three-hour cruise, or $800 to $1,500 for a full-day cruise, with additional per-person charges for large groups. Where you go and what you do—exploring, swimming, snorkeling,

cruising—is usually up to you and your skipper. Generally, however, cruises travel to and around the islands of the Great Sound. Several charter skippers advertise year-round operations, but the off-season schedule can be haphazard. Skippers devote periods of the off-season to maintenance and repairs or close altogether if bookings lag. Be sure to book well in advance; in the high season, do so before you arrive on the island.

CRICKET

Cricket is one of the favorite pastimes on this sports-mad island, a fact that was seen with the national celebrations that followed Bermuda's qualification for the Cricket World Cup in 2007. Bermuda is the smallest country ever to make the finals of the competition, and its cricketeers are treated as heroes in their homeland. The island's cricket season runs from April through September; check the Bermuda Cricket Board's website (⊕ *www.cricket.bm*) for information.

FISHING

Bermuda's proximity to the deep ocean makes it one of the best places in the world for deep-sea fishing. Many of the International Fishing Association's world-record catches were hauled in a few miles off the Bermuda coastline. July and August is marlin season, and anglers from all over the world come to the island in a bid to try to hook monster blue marlin in excess of 1,000 pounds. Deep-sea fishing is not just for the experts, though. Most charter companies are happy to teach amateurs how to hook and reel in a catch—whether it's tuna, wahoo, or even marlin. Some of the charter fishers let you keep your catch, but they're not obliged to do so. Many of the fishers rely on sales to restaurants to bolster their businesses, so unless it's a good day they might not give much away. And don't be surprised to find fish

you pulled out of the ocean that day on the menu in one of Bermuda's many restaurants that evening. As well as deep-sea fishing, shore fishing is also popular, while some fishers trawl inside the reefs. If you've got the cash, there's no substitute for the thrill of the open ocean. Scores of operators are on the island, about 20 of which are regularly out on the water. A full list is available at ⊕ www.gotobermuda.com/sportfishing. Prices vary depending on the size and quality of the boat.

Three major reef bands lie at various distances from the island. The first is anywhere from ½ to 5 miles offshore. The second, the Challenger Bank, is about 12 miles offshore. The third, the Argus Bank, is about 30 miles offshore. As a rule, the farther out you go, the larger the fish—and the more expensive the charter.

Most charter-fishing captains go to the reefs and deep water to the southwest and northwest of the island, where the fishing is best. Catches over the reefs include snapper, amberjack, grouper, and barracuda. Of the most sought-after deepwater fish—marlin, tuna, wahoo, and dolphinfish—wahoo is the most common, dolphinfish the least. Trawling is the usual method of deepwater fishing, and charter-boat operators offer various tackle setups, with test-line weights ranging from 20 pounds to 130 pounds. The boats, which range from 31 feet to 55 feet long, are fitted with gear and electronics to track fish, including depth sounders, global-positioning systems, loran systems, video fish finders, radar, and computer scanners.

Half-day and full-day charters are offered by most operators, but full-day trips offer the best chance for a big catch because the boat has time to reach waters that are less often fished. Rates are about $900 per boat for half a day (four hours),

$1,300 per day (eight hours). Request more information about chartering a fishing boat at Visitor Services Centres in Hamilton, the Dockyard, or St. George's.

The principal catches for shore fishers are pompano, bonefish, and snapper. Excellent sport for saltwater fly-fishing is the wily and strong bonefish, which hovers in coves, harbors, and bays. Among the more popular spots for bonefish are West Whale Bay and Spring Benny's Bay, which have large expanses of clear, shallow water protected by reefs close to shore. Good fishing holes are plentiful along the south shore, too. Fishing in the Great Sound and St. George's Harbour can be rewarding, but enclosed Harrington Sound is less promising. Ask at local tackle shops about the latest hot spots and the best baits. You can also make rental arrangements through your hotel or contact **H2O Sports** (☎ 441/234–3082, ⊕ www.h2osportsbermuda.com).

GOLF

Golf is an important facet of sporting life in Bermuda, where golf courses make up nearly 17% of the island's 21.6 square miles (56 square km). The scenery on the courses is quite often spectacular, with trees and shrubs decked out in multicolor blossoms against a backdrop of brilliant blue sea and sky. The layouts may be shorter than what you're accustomed to, but they're remarkably challenging, thanks to capricious ocean breezes, daunting natural terrain, and the clever work of world-class golf architects.

Of the six 18-hole courses and one 9-hole layout on Bermuda, four are championship venues: Belmont Hills, the Mid Ocean Club, Port Royal, and Tucker's Point. All are well maintained, but you should not expect the springy bent grass fairways and fast greens typical of U.S. golf courses. The rough is coarse Bermuda grass that will turn your club in

Essentials

your hands. Most clubs have TifEagle or Tifdwarf greens—finer-bladed grasses that are drought-resistant and putt faster and truer than Bermuda grass. Because the island's freshwater supply is limited, watering is usually devoted to the greens and tees, which means the fairways are likely to be firm and give you lots of roll. Expect plenty of sand hazards and wind—*especially* wind.

Many courses overseed with rye grass sometime between late September and early November to maintain color and texture through the cooler winter months. Some courses use temporary greens, whereas others keep their regular greens in play during the reseeding process. This makes for inaccurate putting situations, so if you're visiting in fall, call ahead to find out the condition of the greens. Though all courses now have carts, there's often a "cart path only" rule in force to protect the fairways; expect to do some walking.

Many Bermudian tracks have holes on the ocean or atop seaside cliffs. They're wonderfully scenic, but the wind and that big natural water hazard can play havoc with your game.

All courses in Bermuda have dress codes: long pants or Bermuda (knee-length) shorts and collared shirts for both men and women. Denim is not allowed. ■TIP→ **Bermudian men always wear color-coordinated knee-high socks with their shorts on other occasions, but it's okay to go bare-legged on the golf course.**

Courses in Bermuda are rated by the United States Golf Association (USGA), just as they are in the United States, so you can tell at a glance how difficult a course is. For example, a par-72 course with a rating of 68 means that a scratch golfer (one who usually shoots par) should be four under par for the round.

High handicappers should score better than usual, too.

Reserve tee times before you leave home or ask your hotel concierge to do so as soon as you arrive. This is especially necessary to access the private courses. "Sunset" tee times, available at lower greens fees, generally start at 3 pm, but call ahead to be sure.

Bermuda Golf Association

GOLF | The association stages a variety of tournaments beginning in January each year. Overseas entrants are actively encouraged, with the Goodwill Tournament in December the main competition for overseas golfers. ✉ *Victoria Place Bldg., 31 Victoria St., Hamilton* ☎ *441/295–9972* ⊕ *www.bermudagolf. org.*

HORSEBACK RIDING

Because most of the land on Bermuda is residential, opportunities for riding through the countryside are few. The chief exception is South Shore Park, between South Shore Road and the Warwick beaches. Sandy trails, most of which are open only to walkers or riders, wind through stands of dune grass and oleander and over coral bluffs.

KITEBOARDING

Also known as kite surfing, this is one of the newest and fastest-growing extreme sports in the world. It involves using a large power kite to drag a small surfboard along the water. If you're interested in giving it a try, check out Island Winds Bermuda to hook up with local instructors or rent equipment. If extreme sports are not your thing, the sight of the giant kites dipping and rising in the breeze is still an awesome spectacle if you're walking along Elbow Beach on a windy day.

RUGBY

Bermuda's rugby season runs from September to April.

World Rugby Classic

RUGBY | Since the late 1970s, Bermuda has played host to the World Rugby Classic, an epic gathering that brings together top players from arond the world, now retired, for a week of hard-hitting rugby and harder-hitting partying. The event is hugely popular among Bermudians and the international business community. Now held in early to mid-November, the Classic allows fans of the sport to see some of their favorite players from years past. ⊠ *Bermuda National Sports Centre, 65 Roberts Ave.* ☎ *441/295–6574 inquiries, 441/295–8085 Bermuda National Sports Centre* ⊕ *www.worldrugby.bm* ✉ *From $25 per day to $100 for 5-day pass.*

RUNNING AND WALKING

Top runners flock to the island in January for the Bermuda International Race Weekend, which includes a marathon and 10-km (6-mile) races. Many of the difficulties that cyclists face in Bermuda—hills, traffic, and wind—also confront runners. Be careful of traffic when walking or running along Bermuda's narrow roads—most don't have shoulders.

Runners who favor firm pavement are happiest along the **Railway Trail** *(see Bicycling)*, a former train route, one of the most peaceful stretches of road in Bermuda.

If you like running on sand, head for the **south shore beaches** *(see Beaches)*. The trails through South Shore Park are relatively firm. A large number of serious runners can be seen on Horseshoe Bay and Elbow Beach early in the morning and after 5 pm. Another good beach for running is half-mile-long (1-km-long) Warwick Long Bay, the island's longest uninterrupted stretch of sand. The sand is softer here than at Horseshoe and Elbow, so it's difficult to get good footing, particularly at high tide. By using South Shore Park trails to skirt the coral bluffs, you can create a route that connects several beaches. Note that the trails can be winding and uneven in places.

SAILING AND YACHTING

Bermuda has a worldwide reputation as a yacht-racing center. The sight of the racing fleet, with brightly colored spinnakers flying, is striking even if it's difficult to follow the intricacies of the race. The racing season runs from March to November. Most races are held on weekends in the Great Sound, and several classes of boats usually compete. You can watch from Spanish Point and along the Somerset shoreline. Anyone who wants to get a real sense of the action should be on board a boat near the racecourse. The Argo Gold Cup race is in October, and International Race Week is at the end of April or beginning of May. In June in alternating years, Bermuda serves as the finish point for oceangoing yachts in three major races starting in the United States. Bermuda also took the international spotlight as the host of the 35th America's Cup in June 2017.

Outfitters like **Blue Hole Watersports** and **H2O Sports** *(see Fishing)* have a range of craft to rent and also offer lessons for beginners.

SCUBA DIVING

Bermuda has all the ingredients for classic scuba diving—reefs, wrecks, underwater caves, a variety of coral and marine life, and clear, warm water. Although you can dive year-round (you will have to bring your own gear in winter, when dive shops are closed), the best months are May through October, when the water is calmest and warmest. No prior certification is necessary, and novices can expect to dive in water up to 25 feet deep after several hours of instruction. Many hotels, including Grotto Bay Beach Resort and Fairmont Southampton, offer discounted

Essentials

scuba rates or Dive and Stay packages that enable guests to learn the basics in a pool, on the beach, or off a dive boat, and then experience a reef or wreck dive.

The easiest day trips involve exploring the south-shore reefs that lie inshore. Be sure to bring an underwater camera as these reefs may be the most dramatic in Bermuda. The ocean-side drop-off exceeds 60 feet in some places, and the coral is so honeycombed with caves, ledges, and holes that opportunities for discovery are pretty much infinite. Despite concerns about dying coral and dwindling fish populations, most of Bermuda's reefs are still in good health. No one eager to swim with multicolor schools of fish or the occasional barracuda will be disappointed. ■TIP→ **In the interest of preservation, the removal of coral is illegal and subject to hefty fines.**

Dive shops around Bermuda prominently display a map of the outlying reef system and its wreck sites. Only 38 of the wrecks from the past three centuries are marked. They're the larger wrecks that are still in good condition. The nautical carnage includes some 300 wreck sites—an astonishing number—many of which are well preserved. As a general rule, the more recent the wreck or the more deeply submerged it is, the better its condition. Most of the well-preserved wrecks are to the north and east, and dive depths range between 25 feet and 80 feet. Several wrecks off the western end of the island are in relatively shallow water, 30 feet or less, making them accessible to novice divers and even snorkelers.

SNORKELING

The clarity of the water, the stunning array of coral reefs, and the shallow resting places of several wrecks make snorkeling in the waters around Bermuda—both inshore and offshore—particularly worthwhile. You can snorkel year-round, although a wet suit is advisable for anyone planning to spend a long time in the water in winter, when the water temperature can dip into the 60s. The water also tends to be rougher in winter, often restricting snorkeling to the protected areas of Harrington Sound and Castle Harbour. Underwater caves, grottoes, coral formations, and schools of small fish are the highlights of these areas.

Some of the best snorkeling sites are accessible only by boat. As the number of wrecks attests, navigating around Bermuda's reef-strewn waters is no simple task, especially for inexperienced boaters. If you rent a boat yourself, stick to the protected waters of the sounds, harbors, and bays, and be sure to ask for an ocean-navigation chart. These charts point out shallow waters, rocks, and hidden reefs.

For trips to the reefs, let someone else do the navigating—a charter-boat skipper or one of the snorkeling-cruise operators. Some of the best reefs for snorkeling, complete with shallow-water wrecks, are to the west, but where the tour guide or skipper goes often depends on the tide, weather, and water conditions. For snorkelers who demand privacy and freedom of movement, a boat charter (complete with captain) is the only answer, but the cost is considerable—expect to pay upward of $550 for three hours and up to six people. By comparison, half a day of snorkeling on a regularly scheduled cruise generally costs $65 to $85, including equipment and instruction.

SNORKELING SITES
Clearwater Beach and Turtle Bay

SNORKELING | FAMILY | On the southeastern coast of the island and bordered by L. F. Wade International Airport, Clearwater Beach and adjacent Turtle Bay are local snorkeling favorites for the calm surf and

sea turtle sightings. Changing facilities are by the playground at Clearwater, and Gombey's Bar offers snacks and beverages. Adjacent Cooper's Island Nature Reserve is also home to several other beautiful spots to enjoy local sea life, including Long Bay, a 5- to 10-minute stroll from the gates at the end of Turtle Bay. ⊠ *Cooper's Island Rd.* Ⓜ *Bus 6 from St. George's; check with driver if bus makes this stop.*

John Smith's Bay

SNORKELING | The popular snorkeling spot off the south shore of Smith's Parish has several reefs close to the shore as well as the added safety of a lifeguard overseeing the beach. Beware, this site occasionally experiences rip currents. ⊠ *South Shore Rd.*

Tobacco Bay

SNORKELING | FAMILY | A beautiful bay tucked in a cove near historic Fort St. Catherine's beach offers wonderful snorkeling, public facilities, and equipment rentals, and there's a snack bar near the shore. This site is the most popular in St. George's, often hosting concerts, parties, and other events; it can get crowded. To get here from the Town of St. George, follow signs up the hill past the Unfinished Church and over the hill. The walk is about 15–20 minutes. ⊠ *9 Coot's Pond Rd., St. George's* ⊕ *www.tobaccobay.bm.*

Warwick Long Bay

SNORKELING | On the south shore in Warwick, this ½-mile (1-km) of beach—considered the longest on the island—is usually secluded and quiet. It's the perfect spot to check out Bermuda's underwater life without bumping into any other snorkelers. You'll have plenty of room to explore, and there's an inner reef very close to the shore. Visitors should exercise caution here, as strong winds and a steep drop-off at the beach make the surf a bit tricker to traverse. A concessions stand is open during summer months. ⊠ *South Shore Rd.* Ⓜ *Bus 7 from Hamilton or Dockyard.*

West Whale Bay

SNORKELING | Tiny West Whale Bay, off the western shore near the Port Royal Golf Course in Southampton, is quiet and usually uncrowded, and a good spot for snorkeling. You can also explore the history of the West Whale Bay Fort and Battery, catch the local sunset (without the crowds), or view the humpback whales that pass by the island on their annual migration at the end of winter and beginning of spring. The beach disappears during high tide, though, so check tide times first. ⊠ *Whale Bay Rd.* Ⓜ *Bus 7 or 8 from Hamilton or Dockyard.*

SOCCER

Football (soccer) season runs from September through April in Bermuda. One of Bermuda's two national sports, football is massively popular among Bermudians, who often crowd matches in the evening and on weekends. You can watch local action in various age divisions battle it out on fields around the island, or enjoy a cold pint of beer while cheering on your favorite international team at one of Hamilton's popular watering holes: **The Docksider Pub & Restaurant** or **Flanagan's Outback Sports Bar.**

Bermuda Football Association

SOCCER | The association is in charge of player development, scheduling, and league regulations. For more details on soccer in Bermuda and to view photographs from past events, visit the BFA's website. ☎ *441/295–2199* ⊕ *www. bermudafa.com.*

TENNIS

Bermuda has one tennis court for every 600 residents, a ratio that even the most tennis-crazed countries would find difficult to match. Many are private,

Essentials

but the public has access to more than 70 courts in 20 locations. Courts are inexpensive and seldom full. Hourly rates for nonguests are about $15 to $20. You might want to consider bringing along a few fresh cans of balls, because balls in Bermuda cost $6 to $8 per can—two to three times the rate in the United States. Among the surfaces used in Bermuda are Har-Tru, clay, cork, and hard composites, of which the relatively slow Plexipave composite is the most prevalent. Despite Bermuda's British roots, the island has no public grass court.

Wind, heat (in summer), and humidity are the most distinct characteristics of Bermudian tennis. From October through March, when daytime temperatures rarely exceed 80°F, play is comfortable throughout the day. In summer the heat radiating from the court (especially hard courts) can make play uncomfortable between 11 am and 3 pm, so some clubs take a midday break. Most tennis facilities offer lessons, ranging from $30 to $60 for 30 minutes of instruction, and racket rentals for $4 to $10 per hour.

Bermuda Lawn Tennis Association

TENNIS | Established in 1964, the association is the governing body for tennis in Bermuda and hosts all the important tennis events on the island. The BLTA headquarters are at the popular W. E. R. Joell Tennis Stadium, a short taxi ride from the city of Hamilton. Visit the website for an up-to-date calendar of tournaments and events. ✉ W. E. R. Joell Tennis Stadium, 2 Marsh Folly Rd. ☎ 441/296–0834 ⊕ www.blta.bm.

YOGA

Bermuda caught the yoga bug from its North American neighbors in the late '90s, and has since embraced the trend, especially within the local community of health-conscious working professionals. Many gyms around the island, including

Magnum Power Force Gym, Flatts Fitness, and Court House, offer regular weekly classes with tourist-friendly non-member rates.

Yoga Bermuda

AEROBICS/YOGA | A community of yoga instructors representing a range of practices from across the island created Yoga Bermuda, dedicated to advancing yoga among locals and visitors alike. Visit the website to get up-to-date information on yoga-related events and activities, as well as to find drop-in classes or book private lessons for the duration of your stay. ⊕ www.yogabermuda.com.

WHALE-WATCHING

During March and April the majestic humpback whales pass Bermuda as they migrate north to summer feeding grounds. Watching these giant animals as they leap out of the ocean is an awe-inspiring spectacle. You can see them from Elbow Beach or West Whale Bay on a clear day, if you're prepared to wait. But if you want to get a close-up view, you can book a tour with an operator like **Fantasea Diving & Watersports** (⊕ fantasea.bm) or spring for a private offshore charter.

🏖 Beaches

Bermuda's south-shore beaches are more scenic than those on the north side, with fine, pinkish sand and limestone dunes topped with summer flowers and Bermuda crabgrass. The water on the south shore does get a little rougher when the winds are from the south and southwest, but mainly the pale-blue waves break at the barrier reefs offshore and roll gently onto the sandy shoreline. Because the barrier reefs break up the waves, surfing has not really taken off in Bermuda, though many locals—especially children—love to

bodysurf at Horseshoe Bay. Kitesurfing is also becoming increasingly popular. Most Bermudian beaches are relatively small compared with ocean beaches in the United States, ranging from about 15 yards to a half mile or so in length. In winter, when the weather is more severe, beaches may erode—even disappear—only to be replenished as the wind subsides in spring.

Before beginning your adventure, pick up the pocket-size map of Bermuda available for free in all Visitor Services Centres and most hotels. Complete with bus and ferry information, the guide shows beach locations and how to reach them. You can also download maps, brochures, and transportation timetables from the Bermuda Tourism Authority's website at ⊕ *www.gotobermuda.com/ official-visitor-guides.*

Few Bermudian beaches offer shade, but some have palm trees and thatched shelters. The sun can be intense, so bring a hat and plenty of sunscreen. You can rent umbrellas at some beaches, but food and drink are rare, so pack snacks and lots of water.

🍴 Dining

What's incredible about the Bermuda restaurant scene isn't so much the number or quality of restaurants, but the sheer variety of cuisines represented on the menus, especially considering that Bermuda is such a tiny island. It hosts a medley of global cuisines—British, French, Italian, Portuguese, American, Caribbean, Indian, Chinese, and Thai— reminders of Bermuda's history as a colony.

Many superior independent and resort restaurants attract a constant and steady stream of internationally acclaimed chefs,

assuring that the latest techniques and trends are menu regulars. At the same time, virtually all restaurant menus list traditional Bermudian dishes and drinks, so you have the opportunity to taste local specialties at almost any meal.

As you might expect, methods are not all that's imported. Roughly 80% of Bermuda's food is flown or shipped in, most of it from the United States. This explains why restaurant prices are often higher here than on the mainland.

Nevertheless, there are a number of delicious local ingredients that you should look for. At the top of the list is extraordinary seafood, like lobster (best during September through March), crab, oysters, mussels, clams, red snapper, rockfish, tuna, and wahoo. Additionally, many chefs work with local growers to serve fresh seasonal fruits and vegetables, such as potatoes, carrots, leeks, tomatoes, corn, broccoli, and Bermuda onions (one of the island's earliest exports); and in the fruit department, strawberries, cherries, bananas, and loquats (small yellow fruit used for preserves). Imports notwithstanding, Bermudian cuisine really begins and ends with local ingredients and traditional preparations, and therein lies the island's culinary identity.

While in Bermuda, try to eat like a local and put a couple of traditional dishes to the test. In this seafood paradise, favorite dishes include mussel pie, shark hash, and codfish and bananas. As for soups, you can go for fish chowder, conch chowder, or traditional Portuguese black-eyed bean soup. Don't forget to kick back and relax after your meal with a rum swizzle, a Black and Coke (made with Gosling's Black Seal Rum), or a Dark 'n' Stormy. Ginger beer—which is quite different from ginger ale—remains the island's most popular soda for the kids.

Essentials

MEALS AND MEALTIMES

Unless otherwise noted, the restaurants listed in this guide are open daily for lunch and dinner.

A word of warning to those who are used to eating out late: it can be difficult to find a place that serves food after 10 pm. Your last options are a burger van called Jorjays, usually open late into the night on Front Street in Hamilton, or island-famous Ice Queen, a tiny fast-food joint on South Shore Road just outside of Hamilton, which serves burgers, fries, and a plethora of other favorites until 5 am every day. Apart from a handful of benches, Ice Queen offers no seating.

RESERVATIONS

Reservations are always a good idea. We mention them only when they're essential or not accepted. Book as far ahead as you can and reconfirm when you arrive, especially in high season. Many restaurants close—or curtail hours or days of service—in the off-season, so call ahead before setting out for lunch or dinner.

WHAT TO WEAR

Bermuda has had a reputation for strict sartorial standards, but most of the mid-price restaurants are much more casual these days. In many of the pubs and bars in town, you would not be out of place in shorts and a T-shirt. It's a different story in more upscale restaurants, often attached to hotels. Even when not required, a jacket for men is rarely out of place. In our restaurant reviews we mention dress only when men are required to wear either a jacket or a jacket and tie.

WINE, BEER, AND SPIRITS

Bermuda's two national drinks, the Dark 'n' Stormy (dark rum and ginger beer) and the rum swizzle (a mixed fruit cocktail with dark and light rum), both rely on the locally produced Gosling's Rum. These drinks are everywhere—so watch out! The only locally produced beers are available at Frog & Onion Pub in Dockyard, and a few restaurants carry locally produced On De Rock brews. Otherwise, available beers are fairly standard North American and European brands, and wines are plentiful. Liquor can't be bought from a liquor store after 9 pm any day of the week.

Arguably, the the Dark 'n' Stormy is one of Bermuda's most popular exports, and this simple concoction has shown up on menus around the world. Get it wrong, though, and you may face the consequences: The Gosling family, the magnates behind island favorite Gosling's Rum, have five live trademarks with the U.S. Patent and Trademark Office that defend their age-old recipe.

MENU INFORMATION

Restaurant and menu guides are available at any Visitor Services Centre. The island's telephone directory also publishes a good selection of restaurant menus.

PRICES

Much harder to swallow than a delicious Bermuda fish chowder are the prices of dining out. Bermuda has never sought a reputation for affordability, and restaurants are no exception. A few greasy spoons serve standard North American fare (and a few local favorites) at a decent price, but by and large you should prepare for a bit of sticker shock. Don't be surprised if dinner for two with wine at one of the very top places puts a $200–$300 dent in your pocket. A 17% service charge is almost always added to the bill "for your convenience."

SMOKING

Smoking is banned in all restaurants and bars.

WHAT IT COSTS in U.S. Dollars			
$	$$	$$$	$$$$
RESTAURANTS			
under $21	$21–$30	$31–$40	over $40

✚ Health

The most common types of illnesses are caused by contaminated food and water. If you have problems, mild cases of traveler's diarrhea may respond to Imodium (known generically as loperamide) or Pepto-Bismol. Be sure to drink plenty of fluids; if you can't keep fluids down, seek medical help immediately.

Infectious diseases can be airborne or passed via mosquitoes and ticks and through direct or indirect physical contact with animals or people. Mosquito-borne viruses are a rare occurrence in Bermuda, but as the Zika virus is common on islands in the Caribbean, visitors are still urged to take the necessary precautions. Some illnesses, including Norwalk-like viruses that affect your digestive tract, can be passed along through contaminated food. Speak with your physician and/or check the Centers for Disease Control or World Health Organization websites for health alerts, particularly if you're pregnant, traveling with children, or have a chronic illness.

SPECIFIC ISSUES IN BERMUDA

Sunburn and sunstroke are legitimate concerns if you're traveling to Bermuda in summer. On hot, sunny days, wear a hat, a beach cover-up, and lots of sunblock. These are essential for a day on a boat or at the beach. Be sure to take the same kind of precautions on overcast summer days—some of the worst cases of sunburn happen on cloudy afternoons when sunblock seems unnecessary.

Drink plenty of water and, above all, limit the amount of time you spend in the sun until you become acclimated.

The Portuguese man-of-war occasionally visits Bermuda's waters, so be alert when swimming, especially in summer or whenever the water is particularly warm. This creature is recognizable by a purple, balloonlike float sack of perhaps 8 inches in diameter, below which dangle 20- to 60-inch tentacles armed with powerful stinging cells. Contact with the stinging cells causes immediate and severe pain. Seek medical attention right away: a serious sting can send a person into shock. In the meantime—or if getting to a doctor will take a while—treat the affected area liberally with vinegar. Ammonia is also an effective antidote to the sting. Although usually encountered in the water, Portuguese men-of-war may also wash up on the shore, usually among nests of seaweed. If you spot one on the beach, steer clear, as the sting is just as dangerous out of the water.

More recently, divers have encountered the highly poisonous lionfish, which is not a native of the waters. Swimmers will be extremely unlikely to come into contact with one, while divers should just exercise caution around the creatures, which are not aggressive unless provoked.

🛏 Lodging

Few places in the world boast the charm of Bermuda's curvaceous, colorful shoreline. It's a boon, then, that the lagoons, coves, and coasts, as well as its inland sanctuaries, are filled with equally colorful, alluring places to stay. But wherever you opt to stay, you are never far away from picture-perfect water views.

Essentials

The quintessential accommodation on the island is a pink cottage amid manicured gardens and coral-stone pathways. Terraced whitewashed roofs (designed to capture rainwater) sit atop walls of pinks, peaches, and pastels, looking like cakes of ice cream in pink-wafer sand. Add a waterfront setting, and voilà—the lure of Bermuda.

If you find yourself craving a beachfront resort, and you can afford it, several places offer quality right-on-the-sand stays; another handful are a stone's throw away from the beach. The island is blessed with clean, well-maintained public beaches that are easily reached by bus and aren't far from any point on the island.

Hamilton has many sophisticated lodging choices, but vacationers looking for beachfront relaxation will be disappointed in the beachless capital city. In fact, all noteworthy beaches are on the southern side of the island. With only a couple of exceptions, beachfront lodging choices are along a 7-mile stretch of coast that runs along the central to western tail of the island, west from Paget to Warwick, Southampton, and Sandys. Lodging choices on the north coast of the island are often on glittering Hamilton Harbour or have deepwater access to the Atlantic, but not beaches.

Bermuda is a land of cottage colonies, cliff-top apartments, and beachfront resort hotels. Hidden along small parish roads, however, you can also find family-run, flower-filled guesthouses and simple, inexpensive efficiencies. In fact, with the exception of the Fairmont Southampton, and the tall but unobtrusive larger main building at Elbow Beach, there are no high-rises in Bermuda. And nowhere do neon signs sully the landscape. Indeed, many of Bermuda's lodging properties are guesthouses, identifiable only by small, inconspicuous signs or plaques.

Those who prefer bed-and-breakfasts will have no problem finding quaint retreats with local attention.

FACILITIES

The number and quality of facilities vary greatly according to the size and rates of the property. Resort hotels are the best equipped, with restaurants, pools, beach clubs, gyms, and (in the case of Fairmont Southampton and Rosewood Bermuda) a golf course. Cottage colonies also typically have a clubhouse with a restaurant and bar, plus a pool or private beach, and perhaps a golf course. Each cottage has a kitchen, and housekeeping services are provided. Small hotels usually have a pool, and some have a restaurant or guest-only dining room, but few have fitness facilities or in-room extras like minibars. Efficiencies or housekeeping apartments almost always come with a kitchen or kitchenette. Some properties have pools, but you may have to take the bus or a scooter to get to the beach. Even the smallest property can arrange sailing, snorkeling, scuba, and deep-sea fishing excursions, as well as sightseeing.

Assume that all lodgings listed are equipped with private bathrooms and air-conditioning unless we say otherwise.

APARTMENT AND VILLA RENTALS

If you want a home base that's roomy enough for a family, consider renting a private house or apartment. Furnished rentals can save you money, especially if you're traveling with a group.

Airbnb (⊕ *www.airbnb.com*) has really taken off on the island, and it's by far the cheapest way to stay in Bermuda. There are rooms and entire homes for rent all across the island, with a decent number of centrally located places, which is great because there aren't *that* many hotel options near Hamilton. And, of

course, you can save money by cooking and eating in. Bermuda also has several well-regarded property management and rental services.

PRICES

Rates at Bermuda's luxury resorts are comparable to those at posh hotels in New York, London, and Paris. A 9.75% government occupancy tax plus a tourism fee are tacked on to all hotel bills, and a service charge is levied. Some hotels calculate the service charge as 10% of the bill, whereas others charge a per-diem amount. There's a mandatory 17% service charge for food and beverage bills and some resorts add a resort fee. The only way to be sure of your final hotel bill is to call ahead to confirm rates. Virtually every hotel on the island offers at least one vacation package—frequently some kind of honeymoon special—and many of these are extraordinarily good deals.

You can shave about 40% off your hotel bill by visiting Bermuda in low or shoulder seasons. Because temperatures rarely dip below 60°F in winter, the low season (November through March) is ideal for tennis, golf, and shopping.

When pricing accommodations, always ask what's included. Most lodgings offer a choice of meal plans, several with "dine-around" privileges at other island restaurants.

Prices in the hotel reviews are the lowest cost of a standard double room in high season, excluding taxes, service charges, and meal plans. Prices for rentals are the lowest per-night cost for a one-bedroom unit in high season.

WHAT IT COSTS in U.S. Dollars

	$	$$	$$$	$$$$
HOTELS				
	under $201	$201– $300	$301– $400	over $400

$ Money

The Bermudian dollar is on par with the U.S. dollar, and the two currencies are used interchangeably. Other non-Bermudian currency must be converted. You can use American money anywhere, but change is often given in Bermudian currency. Try to avoid accumulating large amounts of local money, which is difficult to exchange for U.S. dollars in Bermuda (local banks are usually quite accommodating, though) and expensive to exchange in the United States. ATMs are plentiful, as are the number of venues that will accept credit cards, even for small items.

Since Bermuda imports everything from cars to cardigans, prices are high. At an upscale restaurant, for example, you're bound to pay as much for a meal as you would in a top New York, London, or Paris restaurant: on average, $60 to $80 per person, $120 with drinks and wine. There are cheaper options, of course; the island is full of coffee shops and cafés, where you can eat hamburgers and french fries with locals for about $15. The same meal at a restaurant costs about $25.

Prices here are given for adults. Substantially reduced fees are almost always available for children, students, and senior citizens.

Essentials

	NEIGHBORHOOD VIBE	PROS	CONS
Hamilton and Pembroke Parish	The heart of the island, where business and pleasure, locals and tourists mix. Fine dining, historic sites, and popular entertainment.	Convenient shopping and dining within walking distance; easily accessible public transportation hub; bustling nightlife.	Can be busy and noisy in evenings and on weekends; far from beaches.
Central Parishes	Quaint island charm a short trip from Hamilton.	Quiet and peaceful residential areas; close to parks, walking trails, and many of the island's most popular beaches.	Unless you're near a bus stop, transportation is necessary to reach beaches or local restaurants. Walking can be hazardous as there are few sidewalks in this area.
St. George's	Bermuda's first city is a treasure trove of the island's colonial history.	Walking distance from popular beaches and historic sites; quiet and laid-back.	Sleepy town shuts down early; few restaurants and limited options for night-time entertainment; transportation required to get to and from Hamilton; expensive taxi ride.
Eastern Parishes	The true Bermuda exists among the colorful cottages and friendly smiles of the locals living outside Hamilton.	Accommodations are more reasonably priced; easier access to local golf courses and several important sights like Crystal and Fantasy Caves and the Bermuda Aquarium, Museum & Zoo.	Personal transportation is necessary in order to get around on your own; dining options are limited, and there is no delivery.
West End	The tip of the "fish-hook"; rest and relaxation are never closer than when you're in the West End of Bermuda.	Excellent opportunities to explore the many forts and military installations; access to the bustling Dockyard; great local shopping opportunities and sports.	Far from Hamilton; restaurants and bars are fewer and close early; personal transportation recommended.

Item	Average Cost
Cup of Coffee	$3
Glass of Wine	$11
Glass of Beer	$8
Sandwich	$10
One-Mile Taxi Ride in Hamilton	$10
Museum Admission	Free–$20

ATMS AND BANKS

ATMs are found all over Bermuda, in shops, arcades, supermarkets, the airport, and two of the island's banks. Both HSBC Bermuda and the Bank of Butterfield are affiliated with the Cirrus and Plus networks. Note that both banks' ATMs only accept personal identification numbers (PIN) with four digits. Some ATMs will dispense U.S. dollars; it's worth noting or asking in advance. Typical withdrawal amounts are multiples of $20 up to $100. ATM robberies are a rarity in Bermuda, but if you're concerned, Reid Street and Front Street—which have the most banks—are Hamilton's busiest, and hence safest, places to withdraw cash.

CREDIT CARDS

Most Bermudian shops and restaurants accept credit and debit cards. The most widely accepted cards are MasterCard, Visa, and American Express.

🍸 Nightlife

Bermudians love to drink. That's the title of a popular local song, and it hits the nail right on the head. Yes, the island that gave the world the Dark 'n' Stormy and the rum swizzle might not have the largest selection of hot spots in which to party the night away, but what Bermuda lacks in venues it makes up for in attitude.

Tourists, expats, and locals all mix together to create a melting-pot social scene, especially on Friday night—the unofficial party day for just about everyone living on the Rock. The vibe is civilized but still fun and friendly, and if you're not sure where you want to go, just ask around; people will be more than happy to give you their thoughts—they might even buy you a drink!

Hamilton is the island's central nightlife hub, with a smattering of decent bars and clubs featuring live music and drink promotions. Outside the city there's a thriving nightlife scene within the hotels. In summer, weekly cruises and beach bashes add to the party scene.

Bermuda has a long tradition of producing superb jazz artists (among other genres), so be sure to check event listings when you arrive to see if you can catch some local musicians. As a general rule, both men and women tend to dress smart casual for clubs. That said, only a few clubs in Hamilton have an actual dress code of no flip-flops or tank tops (and it's not always enforced). Pubs and clubs begin to fill up around 10 or 11.

🧳 Packing

As a rule of thumb, Bermudians dress more formally than most Americans. In the evening, some of the more upscale restaurants and hotel dining rooms require men to wear a jacket and tie and women to dress comparably, so bring a few dressy outfits. But increasingly venues are more accepting of the trend toward "smart casual." In this case, women should be fine with slacks or a skirt and a dressy blouse or sweater. Bermudian men often wear Bermuda shorts (and proper knee socks) with a jacket

Essentials

and tie for formal events and business meetings.

During the cooler months, bring lightweight woolens or cottons that you can wear in layers to accommodate varieties of weather. A lightweight jacket is always a good idea. Regardless of the season, pack a swimsuit, a beachwear cover-up, sunscreen, and sunglasses, as well as a raincoat (umbrellas are typically provided by hotels). Comfortable walking shoes are a must. If you plan to play tennis, be aware that many courts require proper whites and that tennis balls in Bermuda are extremely expensive. Bring your own tennis balls if possible.

Bermuda-bound airlines commonly accept golf-club bags in lieu of a piece of luggage, but there are fairly stringent guidelines governing the maximum amount of equipment that can be transported without an excess baggage fee. The general rule of thumb is one covered bag containing a maximum of 14 clubs, 12 balls, and one pair of shoes.

🛂 Passport

U.S. citizens arriving by air and sea to Bermuda need a valid passport, though cruise-ship passengers on closed-loop cruises (those departing and arriving in the same U.S. port) need only have proof of citizenship and identity (a government-issued photo ID and a birth certificate with a raised seal).

🎭 Performing Arts

If you prefer culture with your rum concoctions, there's plenty to do. City Hall in Hamilton provides a venue for visiting artists on an ad hoc basis. Dramatic productions take place across a variety of venues—anywhere from a hotel auditorium to the back of a Front Street pub.

Bermuda's arts scene is concentrated in a number of art galleries—the Masterworks Museum in the Bermuda Botanical Gardens, City Hall in Hamilton, and the Bermuda Arts Centre in Dockyard are the best known—a handful of performance venues, and a few gathering spots, like Rock Island Coffee on Reid Street in Hamilton. For dramatic and musical performances, the Earl Cameron Theatre, the Mid-Ocean Amphitheatre at the Fairmont Southampton, and the Ruth Seaton James Auditorium at CedarBridge Academy host the country's best, including Bermuda Festival events.

For a rundown of what's hot and happening in Bermuda, pick up the Bermuda Calendar of Events brochure at any Visitor Services Centre. The free monthly *Bermuda.com* guide also lists upcoming island events and can be accessed online at ⊕ *www.bermuda.com*. *Bermuda*, another free magazine, describes arts, nightlife venues, and dining info and can be found in tourist shops and at the ferry terminal; it's also available digitally at ⊕ *issuu.com/bermudaexploreparadise*. It's also a good idea to check ⊕ *www. bdatix.com* or ⊕ *www.premiertickets-global.com* for upcoming show information. And to prove there's plenty to do in Bermuda (if you know where to look), the Nothing To Do In Bermuda website is updated regularly (⊕ *www.nothingtodoin-bermuda.com*).

Because the arts scene in Bermuda is so casual, many events and performers operate on a seasonal or part-time basis. Your best bet is to check with your hotel or City Hall for current offerings. Old-school bulletin boards in coffee shops are also good places to check for upcoming events.

🛍 Shopping

If you're accustomed to shopping in Neiman Marcus, Saks Fifth Avenue, and Bergdorf Goodman, the prices in Bermuda's elegant shops won't bother you. The island is a high-end shopping haven; designer clothing and accessories, from Max Mara to Coach, tend to be sold at prices comparable to those in the United States but at least without the sales tax.

That doesn't mean bargain hunters are out of luck in Bermuda. Crystal, china, watches, and jewelry are often less expensive here and sometimes even on par with American outlet-store prices. Perfume and cosmetics are often sold at discount prices, and there are bargains to be had on woolens and cashmeres in early spring, when stores' winter stocks must go. The island's unforgiving humidity and lack of storage space mean sales are frequent and really meant to sweep stock off the shelves.

Art galleries in Bermuda attract serious shoppers and collectors. The island's thriving population of artists and artisans—many of whom are internationally recognized—produces well-regarded work, from paintings, photographs, and sculpture to miniature furniture, handblown glass, and dolls. During your gallery visits, look for Bruce Stuart's abstract paintings, Graeme Outerbridge's vivid photographs of Bermudian architecture and scenery, and Chesley Trott's slim wood and bronze sculptures. If you just want to look, you can marvel at Graham Foster's 1,000-square-foot mural titled *Hall of History* in Dockyard, depicting ships, farmers, and more.

Bermuda-made specialty comestibles include rum and rum-based liqueurs, delicious local honey, and delectable loquat jam, which you can find in most grocery stores. Nearly every restaurant and pantry in Bermuda contains a bottle of Sherry Peppers Sauce from Outerbridge Peppers Ltd., and these essential condiments make tasty gift additions to home pantries. The original line of products has expanded to include Bloody Mary mix, pepper jellies, and barbecue sauce, and all can be found in grocery stores on the island.

BUSINESS HOURS

Shops are generally open Monday to Saturday from 9 to 5 and closed on Sunday, although some shops and supermarkets are open from 1 to 6 on Sunday. From April to October some of the smaller Front Street shops in Hamilton stay open late and on Sunday. The shops in the Clocktower Mall at the Royal Naval Dockyard are usually open from Monday to Saturday 9 to 6 (11 to 4 in winter) and Sunday 10 to 6. Some extend their hours around Christmas. Almost all stores close for public holidays.

CUSTOMS
Bermuda Customs

It's illegal to export shipwreck artifacts or a Bermuda-cedar carving or item of furniture that's more than 50 years old without a special permit from Bermuda Customs. ⊠ *Customs House, 40 Front St., Hamilton* ☎ *441/295–4816* ⊕ *www.gov.bm/department/customs.*

DUTY FREE

The duty-free shop at the airport sells liquor, perfume, cigarettes, rum cakes, and other items. You can also order duty-free spirits at some of the liquor stores in town, and the management will make arrangements to deliver your purchase to your hotel or cruise ship. If you choose to shop in town rather than at the airport, it's best to buy liquor at least 24 hours before your departure, or by 9:30 on the day of an afternoon departure, in order to allow time for delivery. With liquor, it pays to shop around, because prices vary.

Essentials

Grocery stores usually charge more than liquor stores. U.S. citizens age 21 and older who have been out of the country for 48 hours are allowed to bring home 1 liter of duty-free liquor.

KEY DESTINATIONS

Department stores such as A. S. Cooper & Sons and Gibbons Company in Hamilton are excellent one-stop shopping destinations, but you may have more fun exploring the boutiques on Front and Reid streets and streets branching off them. For crafts, head to the Royal Naval Dockyard, where you can find artisans' studios and a permanent craft market. The Town of St. George has a bit of everything, including lots of small, unique boutiques, where you can find the perfect island outfit or a Bermuda-cedar model of a famous ship.

SHOPPING DISTRICTS

Hamilton has the greatest concentration of shops in Bermuda, and Front Street is its pièce de résistance. Lined with small, pastel-colored buildings, this most fashionable of Bermuda's streets houses sedate department stores and snazzy boutiques, with several small arcades and shopping alleys leading off it. A smart canopy shades the entrance to the 55 Front Street Group, which houses Crisson's. Modern Butterfield Place has galleries and boutiques.

St. George's Water Street, Duke of York Street, Hunters Wharf, and Somers Wharf are the sites of numerous renovated buildings that house branches of Front Street stores, as well as artisans' studios. Historic King's Square offers little more than a couple of T-shirt and souvenir shops.

In the West End, Somerset Village has a few shops, but they hardly merit a special shopping trip. The Clocktower Mall, however, in a historic building at the Royal Naval Dockyard, has a few more shopping opportunities, including branches of Front Street shops and specialty boutiques. The Dockyard is also home to the Craft Market, the Bermuda Arts Centre, and the Jon Faulkner Gallery, formerly Bermuda Clayworks.

$ Taxes

Hotels add a 9.75% government occupancy tax to the bill, and most add a 10% service charge or a per-diem dollar equivalent in lieu of tips. Other extra charges sometimes include a 5% "energy surcharge" (at small guesthouses) and a 17% service charge (at most restaurants).

A $35 airport-departure tax and an $8.25 airport-security fee are built into the price of your ticket, as is a 16-passenger facility charge, whereas cruise lines collect $60 in advance for each passenger, again, normally included in the price of the ticket.

$ Tipping

Tipping in Bermuda is fairly similar to tipping in the United States. A service charge of 10% (or an equivalent per-diem amount), which covers everything from baggage handling to maid service, is added to your hotel bill, though people often still tip a few extra dollars. Most restaurants tack on a 17% service charge; if not, a 17% tip is customary (more for exceptional service).

Tipping Guidelines for Bermuda

Bartender	$1 to $3 per round of drinks, depending on the number of drinks
Bellhop	$2 per bag, depending on the level of the hotel
Dive Instructor	5% to 10% of the total trip
Gas Station Attendant	$2
Grocery Bagger	$1 to $2 a bag
Hotel Maid	$10 at lower-end accommodations, $20 at higher-end accommodations
Porter at Airport	$1 per bag
Taxi Driver	15%, but round up the fare to the next dollar amount
Waiter	17%; nothing additional if a service charge is added to the bill

Embassy/Consulate

The U.S. consulate in Bermuda is near Hamilton, east of the city center.

Visa

U.S. citizens do not need a visa to enter Bermuda for a period less than 90 days.

Visitor Information

Have all your questions answered about what it's like to be a visitor to Bermuda by getting in touch with the island's Tourism Authority (⊕ www.gotobermuda. com). The government-run department can offer help and advice on the best places to stay and visit. The Bermuda tourism website lists Visitor Services Centres around the island and also offers lots of travel deals and has a calendar of events so you can plan your days and nights with the locals. If you are heading to St. George's in the East End, the St. George's Foundation (⊕ www.stgeorgesfoundation.org) can help you find your way around the Old Town.

When to Go

Low Season: Low season is November through March, when the pace on the island is even slower than it normally is. Average temperatures typically range from 55°F at night to the high 60s in the early afternoon.

Shoulder Season: The shoulder seasons in October and April offer good weather for outdoor pursuits, though the beaches can get chilly. Hotel rates are cheaper, and the island remains lively.

High Season: Summer is high season in Bermuda, from May through September, when island temperatures are the warmest. The island teems with activity, and the events calendar is full.

On the Calendar

Bermuda is a year-round destination with an active events calendar, so we've highlighted the top annual offerings. For more options, consult **The Bermuda Tourism Authority** (☎ 800/237–6832 or 441/296–9200 ⊕ www.gotobermuda.com). Local publications like the free, widely distributed tourist magazine **The Bermuda. com Guide** provide a monthly overview, while the island's newspaper, the **Royal Gazette** (⊕ www.royalgazette.com), typically highlights upcoming events in print and online. Further info can be found at ⊕ www.bermuda.com, ⊕ www.bernews. com, and ⊕ Bermynet.com.

January

Bermuda Festival of the Performing Arts. Since 1976 the Bermuda Festival of the Performing Arts, the largest of its kind on the island, has featured international performers. Plays, ballets, chamber orchestras, and jazz jams are staged over two months at The Earl Cameron Theatre and other venues. Lunchtime concerts, book readings, and crafts workshops are also not to be missed. ☎ 441/295–1291 ⊕ www.bermudafestival.org.

Bermuda International Race Weekend. On your mark! Bermuda International Race Weekend kicks off the third weekend of the month. The event begins Friday night with the Front Street Mile. It also includes a marathon, half marathon, and a 10-km (6-mile) charity walk. Top runners participate, but most races are open to all. ⊠ Bermuda National Athletics Association, 48 Cedarparkade, Hamilton ☎ 441/296–0951 ⊕ www.bermudarace-weekend.com.

Bermuda Regional Bridge Tournament. The decades-old Bermuda Regional Bridge Tournament attracts more than 400 players from both home and abroad. Sanctioned by the American Contract Bridge League, the round-robins are an elegant, exciting, and unique event hosted at the Fairmont Southampton resort the last week of January. ⊕ www.bermudaregional.com.

Members' Photography Show. At the annual Members' Photography Show, held during the end of the month in the Bermuda Society of Arts gallery, you can see the work of local amateur and professional photographers, including many underwater shots. ⊠ City Hall, 17 Church St., Hamilton ☎ 441/292–3824 ⊕ www.bsoa. bm.

Mid Atlantic Athletic Club Races. This club hosts many middle- to long-distance running events at various locations across the island throughout the year. The main attraction is the annual Fairmont to Fairmont, a 7.2-mile (11.6-km) race that challenges participants to make the trek from the Hamilton Princess (managed by Fairmont) to the Fairmont Southampton. The Renaissance 10 Miler and Team Challenge in March and the Fidelity 5k in June are also popular. ☎ 441/239–4803 ⊕ www.maac.bm.

March

Bermuda International Film Festival. This top-notch festival is a celebration of independent films from all over the world. A full week of springtime screenings takes place at City Hall in Hamilton. Tickets are sold for individual films as well as for workshops and seminars. Festival parties are also popular, as Hamilton mimics—for a few days at least—the glamour of Sundance, minus the fancy cars. ☎ 441/293–3456 ⊕ www.biff.bm.

March and April

Bermuda All Breed Championship Dog Shows and Obedience Trials. The event draws dog lovers from far and wide to the Bermuda Botanical Gardens in Paget each spring and again in October. In addition, the International Dog Events Association (IDEA) hosts agility events every January and April. ☎ 441/295–6696 ⊕ www.dogtrainingclubbda.org ⊕ www. bermudakennelclub.com.

Bermuda Men's and Ladies' Match Play Championships. The island golf association swings into gear with the Bermuda Men's and Ladies' Match Play Championships. Both are played at the exclusive Mid Ocean Club in Tucker's Town. ☎ 441/295–9972 ⊕ www.bermudagolf. org.

Good Friday. Good Friday is a public holiday and traditionally a kite-flying day. Bermudians usually make special Bermuda kites out of tissue paper, glue, and wooden sticks, and celebrate with fish cakes on hot cross buns.

Palm Sunday Walk. The Palm Sunday Walk is an annual 5- to 8-mile (8- to 13-km) stroll sponsored by the Bermuda National Trust. Following a different route each year, the event allows thousands of walkers to access private properties that would otherwise be off-limits. ☎ 441/236–6483 ⊕ www.bnt.bm.

Zoom Around the Sound. Zoom Around the Sound, an annual 7.2-mile (12-km) trip around Harrington Sound sponsored by the Bermuda Zoological Society, invites walkers, joggers, runners, bikers, and rollerbladers to go the distance. It's a fundraiser for the Bermuda Aquarium, Museum & Zoo. ☎ 441/293–2727 ext. 2130 ⊕ www.bamz.org.

April

Agricultural Exhibition. Much like a state fair, Bermuda's Agricultural Exhibition fosters a fun, educational environment with a variety of livestock competitions, horticultural displays, and homemade, farm-fresh food contests. This three-day event at the Bermuda Botanical Gardens typically runs the third weekend in April and is great for kids. ☎ 441/236–4812 ⊕ bermudaexhibition.com.

Butterfield Bermuda Grand Prix. Cyclists gear up for the Butterfield Bermuda Grand Prix. Bermuda's biggest bike race of the year focuses on amateur and junior riders, both from the island and elsewhere. The events, spread over three days, include timed trials, road races, and hair-raising criterium. ⊕ www. bikesignup.com/Race/BM/Various/ BermudaGrandPrix.

Legends of Squash. The well-attended Legends of Squash tournament attracts some of the best players in the sport. The event is organized by the Bermuda Squash Racquets Association and held at the end of April. ☎ 441/292–6881 ⊕ www.bermudasquash.com.

Peppercorn Ceremony. At the end of April every year, members of St. George's Masonic Lodge pay their rent on the Old State House with great pomp and circumstance during the Peppercorn Ceremony. A single peppercorn is solemnly passed over to the mayor in a stylish (if somewhat surreal) display that includes a march by the Bermuda Regiment. See the website for current information about the date and other details. ☎ 441/297–1532 ⊕ peppercornbda.com.

On the Calendar

April and May

International Invitational Race Week.
Regatta season gets off to a roaring start with International Invitational Race Week, hosted by the illustrious Royal Bermuda Yacht Club in late April and early May. Since 1937 it has pitted Bermuda's top sailors against the best of the rest in keel boat and dinghy-class races on the Great Sound. ✉ *Royal Bermuda Yacht Club, 15 Point Pleasant Rd., Hamilton* ⊕ *www.regattanetwork.com/event/18033.*

May

Bermuda End-to-End. On the first Saturday in May, Bermuda End-to-End lets you get exercise and meet residents while raising money for charity. The full 24-mile walking course mostly follows the Railway Trail, but alternate routes (including ones for swimmers, bicyclists, boaters, and equestrians) are also available. ☎ *441/292-6992* ⊕ *www.bermudaend-toend.bm.*

Bermuda Half Marathon Derby. Held on Bermuda Day (May 24), a public holiday, the race brings thousands of locals and visitors, who line the edges of the 13.1-mile (21-km) course. Even if you aren't a runner, it's great fun to watch. There's also the annual Heritage Day parade, complete with Gombeys, baton twirlers, floats, and musicians, in Hamilton afterward. The procession starts at 1:30 pm from Bernard Park, finishing on Front Street several hours later. ☎ *441/737-0046* ⊕ *www.bermudamarathon.bm.*

Bermuda Heritage Month. May is Bermuda Heritage Month, when a host of commemorative, cultural, and sporting activities are scheduled. The climax is Bermuda Day (May 24), a public holiday that includes a parade around Hamilton, a cycling race, and dinghy races in St. George's Harbour. Traditionally, this is also the first day that locals swim, swearing the water is too cold earlier in the year—though most visitors don't seem to mind. ☎ *441/292-1681* ⊕ *communityand-culture.bm/pages/heritage-month.*

Bermuda Horse & Pony Association Spring Show. Horse lovers can watch a range of equestrian events at the two-day Bermuda Horse & Pony Association Spring Show, which is held at the National Equestrian Centre or the Botanical Gardens in early May. ☎ *441/505-3815* ⊕ *www.bef.bm.*

Bermuda Senior Stroke Play Championship. Open to women over 50 and men over 55, the Bermuda Senior Stroke Play Championships are hosted at the stunning Belmont Hills Golf Course. Challenging water hazards, a dramatic landscape, and panoramic views of Hamilton Harbour await. ☎ *441/295-9972* ⊕ *www.bermudagolf.org.*

May and June

Open Houses & Gardens Event. Prepare to go green with envy. Tuesday afternoons in May and June, the Garden Club of Bermuda leads to-die-for tours through private properties during its yearly Open Houses & Gardens Event. These walkabouts offer a rare glimpse into unique architectural and horticultural landmarks at the peak of the island's growing season. ☎ *441/234-2455* ⊕ *www.garden-clubbermuda.org.*

June

Annapolis Bermuda Ocean Race. First held in 1979, the 753-mile (1,212-km) Annapolis Bermuda Ocean Race sets sail from Maryland in even-numbered years.

Hosted by the Royal Hamilton Amateur Dinghy Club, it attracts competitors from all over the world. ⊕ *www.bermudaoceanrace.com*.

Bermuda Amateur Stroke Play Championships. The championships are hosted by Port Royal Golf Course in Southampton. The exciting 52-hole event treats competitors to over 6,842 manicured yards and picturesque ocean views. ☎ *441/295–9972* ⊕ *www.bermudagolf.org*.

Bermuda Anglers Club International Light Tackle Tournament. Founded in 1937, the Bermuda Anglers Club has been hosting their International Light Tackle Tournament since 1967. Teams of three anglers are invited to try their hands at reeling in a variety of billfish, tuna, marlin, and more. ⊕ *www.ilttbermuda.com*.

Bermuda Triathlons. The Bermuda Triathlon Association holds these sporting events about once a month from April to October. The events are of various lengths and combine a swim, a cycling leg, and a run. The BTA also hosts sprint series throughout summer months. Many of the events take place at Clearwater Beach in St. David's or at Harrington Sound Dock. ⊕ *www.bermudatriathlon.com*.

Harbour Nights. This street festival featuring Bermudian artists, crafts, Gombey dancers, face painting, and the like takes place every Wednesday night from May to September on Front, Queen, and Reid streets in the city of Hamilton. The carnival encompasses a larger area in downtown Hamilton and features live entertainers and rides for the kids. ⊕ *www.bermudachamber.bm/harbour-nights*.

Marion–Bermuda Cruising Yacht Race. Intrepid yacht sailors travel 645 miles (1,038 km) from Plymouth County, Massachusetts, during the biennial Marion–Bermuda Cruising Yacht Race co-hosted

by the Royal Hamilton Amateur Dinghy Club. It's a prestigious, uniquely Bermudian event that takes place in odd-numbered years. ☎ *441/236–2250* ⊕ *www.marionbermuda.com*.

Newport Bermuda Race. Seasoned yacht sailors chart a challenging 635-mile (1,022-km) course from Rhode Island to St. David's Lighthouse during the biennial Newport Bermuda Race. One of the sailing world's preeminent blue-water events, it's held mid-June in even-numbered years and is hosted by the Royal Bermuda Yacht Club. ☎ *441/295–2214* ⊕ *www.bermudarace.com*.

July

Bermuda Triple Crown. The island keeps reeling in top-notch anglers with the back-to-back billfish tournaments that make up the Bermuda Triple Crown. First up is the Bermuda Billfish Blast, followed by the Bermuda Big Game Classic and the Sea Horse Anglers Club Billfish Tournament. As if we needed an excuse to get salty! ⊕ *www.bermudatriplecrown.com*.

July and August

Cup Match Cricket Festival. The festival is a spirited two-day celebration centered on the match between rival Somerset and St. George's cricket clubs. (Locals sport red and navy if they're Somerset fans, dark blue and light blue if they're St. George's fans.) The highlight of Bermuda's events calendar, it's scheduled for the Thursday and Friday before the first Monday in August, in conjunction with two public holidays: Emancipation Day and Somers Day. The location of the match alternates annually between Somerset Cricket Club in Sandys Parish and St. George's Cricket Club in St. George's Parish. ☎ *441/234–0327, 441/297–0374*.

On the Calendar

September

Bermuda Mixed Foursomes Amateur Golf Championship. The championship is a two-day, 36-stroke play competition for couples at Turtle Hill Golf Club in Southampton. ⊠ *Turtle Hill Golf Club, 101 South Rd.* ☎ *441/295–9972* ⊕ *www. bermudagolf.org.*

International Sand Sculpture Competition. Bermuda's fine pink sand is put to good use during Horseshoe Bay's one-day International Sand Sculpture Competition, typically held on the Saturday before Labor Day. Teams of up to six people are encouraged to get creative and build the craziest sculptures possible on a 15-by-15-foot patch of beach. Prizes are awarded in seven categories, including Families, Professionals, and Tourists. ☎ *441/505–7822* ⊕ *www.sandcastle.bm.*

October

Argo Group Gold Cup. The weeklong Argo Group Gold Cup sees match-race skippers (America's Cup competitors among them) vie for the titular trophy and a $100,000 purse. Races are in Hamilton Harbour, and the Royal Bermuda Yacht Club opens its doors for the event, making this one especially appealing to spectators. ☎ *441/295–2214* ⊕ *www. argogroupgoldcup.com.*

Bermuda International Dog Show. The two-day dog show is an exciting outdoor event that draws handlers and owners from the United States, Canada, and Bermuda. Teams perform various courses using signals to meet challenging performance requirements—barking is allowed! ⊕ *www.bermudakennelclub. com.*

November

Reconvening of Parliament. On the first Friday in November, the Reconvening of Parliament kicks off when the governor, in full regalia, arrives at Hamilton's Cabinet Building in a horse-drawn landau. His Speech from the Throne (detailing new policies and initiatives) usually begins around 11 am, so arrive by 10:15 to secure a good spot. ⊠ *Sessions House, Church St., Hamilton* ☎ *441/292–7408* ⊕ *www.parliament.bm.*

Remembrance Day. Remembrance Day is a public holiday held in memory of fallen soldiers from Bermuda and its allied nations. A parade with Bermudian, British, and U.S. military units; the Bermuda Police; and war-veterans' organizations takes place on November 11 on Front Street in Hamilton, and commemorative wreaths are laid at the Cenotaph near the Cabinet Building.

Santa Claus Parade. Father Christmas visits Front Street in the Santa Claus Parade, usually held the last week of November. The energy level is high as Santa cruises through Hamilton, accompanied by marching bands, majorettes, Bermuda Gombeys, and floats.

World Rugby Classic. During the World Rugby Classic, former international players from around the globe again represent their respective countries in matches at the Bermuda National Sports Centre in Devonshire Parish. Afterward, fans can mix with the players in a "tavern tent" behind the touchline. ☎ *441/295–6574* ⊕ *www.worldrugby.bm.*

December

Annual Christmas Walkabout in St. George's. The annual walkabout in St. George's is an early-evening event hosted by the Bermuda National Trust. Properties specially decked out for the holiday season open their doors to the public. Choir concerts, Christmas-themed readings, and eggnog sipping are also on the agenda. ☎ 441/236–6483 ⊕ www.bnt.bm.

Bermuda Goodwill Tournament. Foursomes made up of professional and amateur golfers swing into action during the Bermuda Goodwill Tournament for a week of camaraderie and golf at the Mid Ocean Golf Club. First held in 1922, it's the world's oldest pro-am competition, and spectators are invited to watch the event for free. ☎ 441/295–4640 ⊕ www. bermudagoodwillgolf.com.

Boxing Day. Following Commonwealth tradition, Bermuda makes December 26 a public holiday: Boxing Day. Pugilists need not apply, but many other sporting activities—like harness racing and motocross competitions—are scheduled, and Gombey troupes mark the day by dancing in the streets.

Christmas Boat Parade. Every other year the Christmas Boat Parade sees decorated vessels of every size and description float through Hamilton Harbour. The event, which can draw 20,000 spectators, usually takes place on the second Saturday of December and is topped off by fireworks. It is held in odd-numbered years.

Great Itineraries

Bumming Around Bermuda: Sea, Sand, and Sights

DAY 1: HORSESHOE BAY

Chances are you came for that legendary pink sand, so don't waste any time finding it. Spend the day bouncing from beach to beautiful beach along the south shore (Bus 7 bus will get you there and back from the city of Hamilton), or just choose one and settle in. Our top pick is the flagship beach at **Horseshoe Bay,** a gently curving crescent lapped by turquoise water and backed by South Shore Park. It does get crowded here—but for good reason. Unlike most Bermudian beaches, Horseshoe Bay has lifeguards (in season), changing rooms, and on-site food, drink, and beach-gear rentals available at **Rum Bum Beach Bar.** There's also a protected inlet, dubbed Horseshoe Baby Beach, which is perfect for young children. Looking for something more private? Picturesque trails through the park will lead you to secluded coves like Stonehole and Chaplin bays. When the sun goes down—and you have sand in every crevice—stroll over to the lively **Henry VIII Pub and Restaurant** for an evening bite.

DAY 2: THE TOWN OF ST. GEORGE

Founded in 1612, **St. George's** qualifies as one of the oldest towns in the Western Hemisphere and deserves a place on any traveler's itinerary. This UNESCO World Heritage site has a smattering of worthwhile museums, including the Bermuda National Trust Museum at the Globe Hotel and Tucker House. Historic buildings such as St. Peter's Church also should not be missed. Organized walks and road train tours cover the highlights. Yet the real delight here is simply wandering the walled lanes and quaint alleys lined with traditional shops, pubs, and cottages. All those roads eventually lead to **King's Square,** where you can try out the replica stocks. Nearby is another device formerly used to punish unruly folk—the seesaw-like ducking stool—which serves as the focal point for reenactments starring the Town Crier and a wet wench. (These are staged at 12:30 pm May through October, Monday through Thursday and Saturday; other months on Wednesday and Saturday only.) If you have time, continue your history lesson outside St. George's at **Fort St. Catherine,** a hilltop defense built in the 17th century. Stop for a swim just below it in snug Achilles Bay or at **Fort St. Catherine Beach,** then cap the day back in town with a meal at the **White Horse Pub & Restaurant** on the water's edge.

DAY 3: THE CITY OF HAMILTON

Since there's a little bit of everything here, you can plot a course according to your individual tastes. Shoppers should make a beeline for the **Front Street** area to spend a few hours in the stores and galleries. Prefer sightseeing? Pick up a brochure for a self-guided tour at the Visitor Services Centre (VSC). Outside the city, visit **Fort Hamilton**: it's a must for history buffs and a great spot for photo ops. Alternatively, you can investigate sunken treasure and seashells without ever getting wet at the **Bermuda Underwater Exploration Institute** (about a 15-minute walk from the city center), or get out on the water itself. Excursion options from Hamilton range from archipelago tours and glass-bottom-boat trips to low-cost ferry rides. Afterward, gear up to see Hamilton by night. Pubs and clubs start filling around 10 pm, leaving plenty of time for dinner at one of the area's surprisingly diverse restaurants.

DAY 4: THE DOCKYARD

Once a military stronghold and now a magnet for tourists, the **Royal Naval Dockyard** offers a full day of history with a side of shopping and adventure. Its centerpiece is the **National Museum of Bermuda,** where you can find exhibits on whaling, sailing, shipbuilding, and shipwrecks set within an imposing stone fortress. Once you've taken in the stunning views from the ramparts, head to the **Old Cooperage.** This former barrel-making factory is the perfect place to stock up on unique souvenirs, because it houses both the Bermuda Craft Market (perhaps the island's best-stocked, best-priced craft outlet) and the Bermuda Arts Centre (a high-end co-op with gallery and studio space). After lunch in an area eatery, join one of the educational in-water programs offered by **Dolphin Quest** at the Keep Pond, or swim right next door at the inexpensive **Snorkel Park Beach.** Spring through fall, adrenaline junkies can Jet Ski with H2O Sports. For a more placid on-the-water experience, take the slow, scenic ferry to Somerset Island and disembark at Watford Bridge. From there, explore quiet Somerset Village before sitting down for dinner at the **Somerset Country Squire,** a traditional tavern overlooking Mangrove Bay.

DAY 5: GO GREEN

While dedicated duffers spend at least one day putting the island's top greens, neophytes can get into the swing of things at the **Bermuda Golf Academy.** Other essential "greens" include the **Bermuda Botanical Gardens** and **Paget Marsh Nature Reserve,** both near the city of Hamilton. The former is a Victorian venue with formal flowerbeds and subtropical fruit orchards; the latter a 25-acre tract that covers five distinct ecosystems (including primeval woodlands that contain the last surviving stands of native palmetto and cedar). From November to May, **Spittal Pond Nature Reserve,** on Bermuda's south shore, is a major draw for bird-watchers, thanks to the 30-odd species of waterfowl that stop here; in April it attracts whale-watchers hoping to spy migrating humpbacks from the preserve's oceanfront cliffs. You can access more "undiscovered" spots by traversing all or part of the **Bermuda Railway Trail.** With its lush greenery and dramatic lookouts, this 18-mile recreational route is best seen on foot or by pedal bike. If you like packaged excursions, **Fantasea Bermuda** has a surf-and-turf deal that combines a shoreline cruise with a guided cycle tour along the trail, and a cool-down swim at a Somerset beach.

Best Tours

ECOTOURS

Hidden Gems of Bermuda Limited. Ashley Harris of this island ecotour company takes people cliff jumping or cave swimming in some of the more off-the-beaten-path locations across the island. Go with the group or book a special tour. ⊠ *Dockyard* ☎ *441/236–1300* ⊕ *www. bermudahiddengems.com* ✉ *From $100 per person for 5 hours.*

GARDEN AND WILDLIFE TOURS

Bermuda Botanical Gardens. Free 90-minute guided tours of the Bermuda Botanical Gardens depart from the visitor center Wednesday, Thursday, and Friday at 10:30 am, weather permitting. Buses stop outside the gardens by the King Edward Memorial Hospital entrance. ⊠ *169 South Shore Rd.* ☎ *441/236–5902* Ⓜ *Buses 1, 2, and 7.*

Byways Bermuda. The company offers personalized off-the-beaten-path tours of Bermuda that focus on nature and history. ☎ *441/535–9169* ⊕ *www.bermudabyways.com* ✉ *$100 for 6-hour tour and lunch.*

Garden Club of Bermuda. The club of Bermuda offers a unique tour of visiting local gardens. ☎ *441/295–3661* ⊕ *www. gardenclubbermuda.org* ✉ *$100 for 4 people, $25 for each additional person.*

HISTORICAL AND SOCIAL TOURS

Bermuda Lecture & Tours. These tours are run by witty British transplant Tim Rogers, who has lived in Bermuda for more than a decade. Rogers leads exceptional walks (and seated talks) about various Bermuda topics that other historians or guides sticking to their textbooks may be hesitant to discuss. His humorous and conversational tours cover intriguing historical material on piracy, local ghosts and lore, and the island's more interesting geologic and architectural features.

Special group rates are also available. ☎ *441/234–4082* ✉ *trogers@northrock. bm* ✉ *90-minute walking tour $80 per couple, $10 extra for each additional person.*

Bermuda Tourism Authority *(BTA).* The BTA publishes brochures with self-guided tours of Hamilton, St. George's, the West End, and the Railway Trail. Available free at all Visitor Services Centres and at hotels and guesthouses, the brochures also contain detailed directions for walkers and cyclists as well as historical notes and anecdotes. The BTA also coordinates walking tours of Hamilton, St. George's, Spittal Pond Nature Reserve, the Royal Naval Dockyard, and Somerset. The tours of Hamilton and St. George's, as well as most of the Royal Naval Dockyard tours, take in historic buildings, while the Spittal Pond and Somerset tours focus on the island's flora. ☎ *441/296–9200* ⊕ *www. gotobermuda.com* ✉ *Free.*

Segway Tours of Bermuda. The company offers daily historical tours of the Royal Naval Dockyard aboard a Segway—an electric two-wheel vehicle. The machines are the only vehicles that can tour the National Museum of Bermuda. Sites include the Clocktower Mall, Casemates Prison, the Victualling Yard, the Glassblowing and Rum Cake Factory, and the Sail Loft. The 90-minute tour includes a brief orientation to the vehicle. ⊠ *Dockyard* ☎ *441/236–1300* ⊕ *www.segway. bm* ✉ *$80 for 90-minute tour.*

TAXI AND MINIBUS TOURS

For an independent tour of Bermuda, a taxi is a good but more expensive alternative to a group tour. A blue flag on the hood of a cab indicates that the driver is a qualified tour guide. These cabs can be difficult to find, but most of their drivers are friendly and entertaining—they

sometimes bend the truth for a good yarn—and well informed about the island and its history. Ask your hotel to arrange a tour with a knowledgeable driver.

Cabs seat four or six, and the legal rate for island tours (minimum three hours) is $50 per hour for one to four passengers and $70 per hour for five to seven passengers. Two children under 12 equal an adult.

Bee-Line Transport Ltd. ☎ *441/293–0303, 441/504–7375 after hours* ⊕ *www.beelinetransportltd.com.*

Bermuda Island Taxi. ☎ *441/295–4141* ⊕ *www.ridebermuda.com.*

Destination Bermuda Ltd. ✉ *Hamilton* ☎ *441/292–2325* ⊕ *www.destinationbermuda.bm.*

Contacts

✈ Air

AIRLINES Air Canada.
☎ 888/247–2262 ⊕ www.
aircanada.com. **American
Airlines.** ☎ 800/433–7300
⊕ www.aa.com. **British
Airways.** ☎ 800/247–9297
⊕ www.britishairways.
com. **Delta Airlines.**
☎ 800/221–1212 for U.S.
reservations, 800/241–
4141 for international
reservations ⊕ www.
delta.com. **JetBlue.**
☎ 800/538–2583 ⊕ www.
jetblue.com. **United.**
☎ 800/864–8331 for U.S.
and Canada reservations
⊕ www.united.com.
WestJet. ☎ 888/937–8538
⊕ www.westjet.com.

**AIRPORT INFORMATION L.
F. Wade International Airport
(BDA).** ⊠ 3 Cahow Way
☎ 441/293–2470 ⊕ www.
bermudaairport.com.

**AIRPORT TRANS-
FERS Bermuda Island
Taxi.** ☎ 441/295–4141
⊕ www.ridebermuda.
com. **BTA Dispatching Ltd.**
☎ 441/296–2121 ⊕ www.
btadispatching.bm. **CEO
Transport Ltd.** ☎ 441/234–
4366, 855/859–6454 U.S.
toll-free ⊕ www.limober-
muda.com. **First Step Taxi
Service.** ☎ 441/735–7151.

⚓ Boat

**CONTACTS Ministry of
Transport, Department of
Marine and Ports Services.**
☎ 441/295–4506 Hamilton
Ferry Terminal ⊕ www.
marineandports.bm.

🚌 Bus

**CONTACTS Public Transport
Bermuda.** ☎ 441/292–
3851 ⊕ www.gov.bm/
bus-routes-and-maps.

🚗 Car

**CONTACTS Bermuda Rental
Car Ltd..** ☎ 441/236–2453
⊕ bermudarentalcar.com.
Current Vehicles. ⊕ www.
currentvehicles.com.

🛏 Lodging

**CONTACTS Bermuda
Rentals.** ⊕ www.bermuda-
rentals.com . **BermudaG-
etaway.** ⊕ www.bermud-
agetaway.com . **Coldwell
Banker JW Bermuda Realty.**
☎ 441/292–1793 ⊕ www.
vacationhomesbermuda.
com. **White Roof B&B.** ⊠ 4
Fort Hill ☎ 441/234–2050
⊕ whiteroofbnb.com.

🛵 Scooter

**RENTAL COMPANIES
Elbow Beach Cycles Ltd.**
⊠ Elbow Beach Resort,
60 South Shore Rd.
☎ 441/296–2300 ⊕ www.
elbowbeachcycles.com.
Oleander Cycles. ⊠ 6
Valley Rd., off Middle Rd.
☎ 441/236–2453 ⊕ www.
oleandercycles.bm. **Smatt's
Cycle Livery Ltd.** ⊠ 74
Pitts Bay Rd., Hamilton
☎ 441/295–1180 ⊕ www.
smattscyclelivery.com.

🚕 Taxi

**CONTACTS Bermuda Island
Taxi.** ☎ 441/295–4141
⊕ www.ridebermuda.
com. **BTA Dispatching
Ltd..** ☎ 441/296–2121
⊕ www.btadispatching.
bm. **First Step Taxi Service.**
☎ 441/735–7151.

🇺🇸 Embassy/Consulate

**CONTACTS U.S. Consulate
General in Bermuda.** ⊠ 16
Middle Rd. ☎ 441/295–
1342 ⊕ bm.usconsulate.
gov.

📍 Visitor Information

**CONTACTS Bermuda
Tourism Authority.** ⊠ 22
Church St., Hamilton
☎ 441/296–9200 in Ber-
muda, 800/237–6832 from
the U.S. ⊕ www.gotober-
muda.com. **St. George's
Foundation.** ⊠ Admiral's
Walk, 16 Water St., St.
George's ☎ 441/297–8043
⊕ www.stgeorgesfounda-
tion.org.

Chapter 3

CITY OF HAMILTON AND PEMBROKE PARISH

Updated by
Robyn Bardgett

⊙ Sights	🍴 Restaurants	🛏 Hotels	🛍 Shopping	🍸 Nightlife
★★★★☆	★★★★★	★★★★☆	★★★★★	★★★★★

3

ISLAND SNAPSHOT

TOP EXPERIENCES

■ **Front Street shopping:** The City of Hamilton has Bermuda's largest, most fashionable collection of shops, and Front Street, with its candy-colored shop fronts, is the best place to start.

■ **Views from Fort Hamilton:** This is the best place to take in great views of the entire city and beyond.

■ **Harborside dining:** Watch boats zoom across the harbor as you dine or sip something cold at one of the bars or restaurants lining Front Street.

■ **Admiralty House Park:** Just a short drive outside Hamilton, check out the trails or even take the plunge off the rocky cliffs into the water at this park.

■ **Bermuda Underwater Exploration Institute:** On the way into the city, stop here for a deeper look into the mysteries of the ocean surrounding Bermuda.

■ **Hamilton nightlife:** Sunset drinks on a harborside patio, a late-night pub crawl, and local music events are all options in Bermuda's nightlife hub.

GETTING HERE

The City of Hamilton is Bermuda's hub for transportation, and buses from places as far apart as Dockyard and St. George's arrive at the main bus terminal here. Ferries from points west, including Dockyard and Paget, arrive at the Hamilton Ferry Terminal. Tickets and passes are available from the main terminals and are interchangeable on both the ferry and buses. The city is easily walkable; however, there are parking spaces for mopeds dotted between spaces for cars, as well as charging stations for mini electric rental cars.

PLANNING YOUR TIME

You can buzz through Hamilton in a few hours, but plan to give it a day if you want to visit some of the museums, Fort Hamilton, and the Bermuda Underwater Exploration Institute. Serious shoppers should set aside another half day to browse around the shops, and do give yourself time to have a meal or drink by the harbor.

QUICK BITES

■ **Devil's Isle.** Sip a freshly squeezed juice or nutritious smoothie at this trendy spot, which also has its own line of coffee, or try healthy options like the popular Harvest Bowl. ✉ 19 Burnaby St., Hamilton ☏ 441/292-3284 ⊕ www.devilsislecoffee.bm.

■ **Brew.** Bringing coffeehouse culture to Bermuda, Brew has great coffee (try the curlywurly frappé), a buzzy atmosphere, tasty food choices, and free Wi-Fi, plus good craft beer and wine selections for evenings. ✉ 53 Front St., Hamilton ☏ 441/542-2739.

■ **Bermy Eats.** Hidden along Chancery Lane off Front Street, this popular lunch spot offers fresh sandwiches, wraps, salads, and baked goods, plus great coffee and a Saturday-morning crepe breakfast the kids will love. ✉ 11 Chancery La., Hamilton ☏ 441/292-2353 ⊕ bermyeats.com.

■ **Dangelini's Cafe & Bakery.** Watch Hamilton come alive from the shade of a harbor-view table at this little spot next to the ferry terminal. You'll find hot and cold caffeinated concoctions as well as homemade pastries, scones, and muffins. ✉ 8 Front St., Hamilton ☏ 441/295-5272 ⊕ dangeliniscafe.com.

With a permanent resident population of 1,900 households, Hamilton doesn't qualify as a major metropolis; it's not even the largest town on the island. However, it has enough stores, restaurants, and offices to amp up the island's energy level.

Hamilton also has a thriving international business community (centered on financial and investment services, insurance, telecommunications, global management of intellectual property, shipping, and aircraft and ship registration) that lends it a degree of sophistication seldom found in so small a center. Locals refer to the City of Hamilton as "town," and "baka-town" describes the thriving North East Hamilton Economic Empowerment Zone, where you'll find a diverse range of food and shops. Outside the city, Pembroke Parish is mostly residential; still, make time to visit Fort Hamilton and the Bermuda Underwater Exploration Institute on the outskirts of town. And if you're looking for a place to take a dip without heading too far afield, spend some time exploring the small beach and cliffs for diving at Admiralty House Park.

◉ Sights

While the City of Hamilton is known for its shopping and business district, there are still some historical sights worth searching out around the parish, such as Fort Hamilton. In addition, the large number of parks in the city make a great place for some quiet reflection, particularly those like Albuoy's Point that overlook Hamilton Harbour.

★ Admiralty House Park

NATIONAL/STATE PARK | The park, site of the extravagant, now mostly demolished, home of a former admiral of the British Navy, has man-made caves to explore and trails with views of the north shore, but it's also notable as the perfect spot to attempt a favorite pastime of locals: cliff jumping. The cliffs are about 15–20 feet high, and the water below is deep and clear. Wear good water shoes, as the walk back up the cliffs can be a bit rocky. If you're less thrill seeker and more of a sun seeker, there's a small beach to relax off a calm cove and lagoon-like water to wade in. ⊠ 68 Spanish Point Rd., Hamilton.

Albuoy's Point

CITY PARK | For a ringside seat to the show of sailboats and passenger ferries zigzagging around the many islands that dot Hamilton Harbour, grab a bench beneath the trees at Albuoy's Point, a small waterside park. Nearby is the Royal Bermuda Yacht Club, founded in 1844 and granted the use of the term Royal by Prince Albert in 1845. Today luminaries from the international sailing scene hobnob with local yacht owners and business executives at the club's 1930s headquarters. If you're around between April and November, you might even catch one of the many club-sponsored racing events. ⊠ Hamilton ✛ Off Front St.

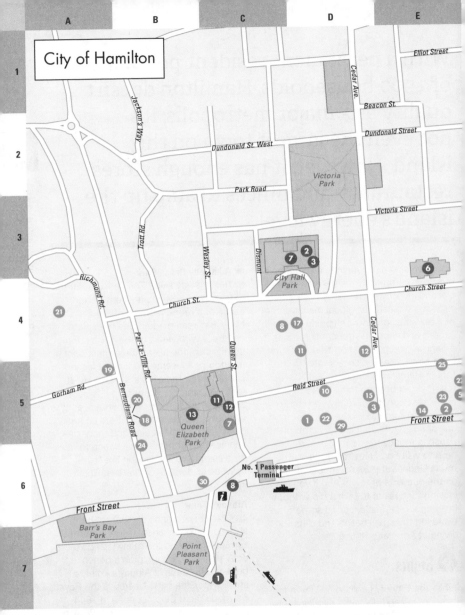

City of Hamilton

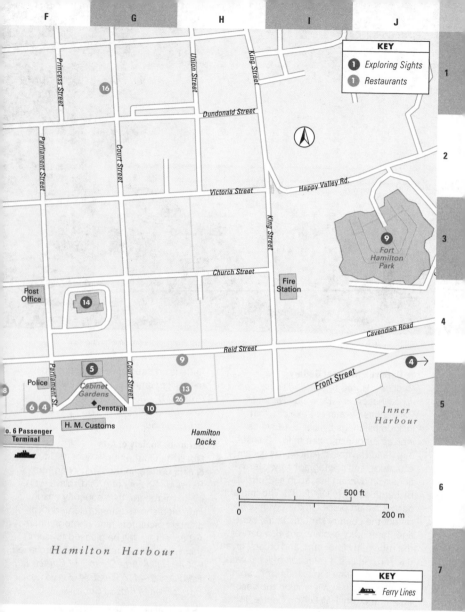

1 Exploring Sights

1 Restaurants

Fort Hamilton Park

Inner Harbour

Hamilton Docks

H. M. Customs

No. 6 Passenger Terminal

Hamilton Harbour

Cabinet Gardens

Cenotaph

Police

Post Office

Fire Station

0   500 ft
0   200 m

KEY

Ferry Lines

7 Bulli.Social **C5**

8 Buzz **C4**

9 Chopsticks **H5**

10 Coconut Rock and
Yashi Sushi Bar **D5**

11 The Cottage Café
& Bistro **D4**

12 Devil's Isle Cafe **D5**

13 The Docksider Pub &
Restaurant **H5**

14 Flanagan's Irish Pub **E5**

15 Hog Penny Pub **D5**

16 Jamaican Grill **G1**

17 La Trattoria **D4**

18 Little Venice **B5**

19 Lobster Pot &
Boat House Bar **A5**

20 L'Oriental **B5**

21 Mad Hatters **A4**

22 The Pickled Onion **D5**

23 Port O' Call **E5**

24 Portofino **B6**

25 The Red Carpet **E5**

26 Rosa's **H5**

27 Ruby Murrys **E5**

28 Streetwize **F5**

29 The Terrace **D5**

30 Utopia **B6**

Jumping off the cliffs into the ocean at Admiralty House Park is a popular pastime for the local kids.

★ Bermuda National Gallery

MUSEUM | Home to Bermuda's national art collection, the Bermuda National Gallery has permanent exhibits that include paintings by island artists as well as European masters like Gainsborough and Reynolds; African masks and sculpture; and photographs by internationally known artists, such as Bermudian Richard Saunders (1922–87). The fine and decorative art pieces in the collection reflect the country's multicultural heritage. Temporary exhibits are also part of the museum's program, and on any given day you can see a selection of local work along with a traveling exhibit from another museum. The gallery is on the second floor in the City Hall & Arts Centre, in the East Exhibition Room.

For a comprehensive look at the collections, join one of the free docent-led tours offered Thursday at 10 am (private ones can be arranged on request). Lectures and other programs are listed in the gallery's online calendar. Some of these are targeted specifically at children, and there is an interactive education space at the gallery entrance. ⊠ City Hall & Arts Centre, 17 Church St., 2nd fl., Hamilton ☎ 441/295–9428 ⊕ www.bng.bm 🖼 $5 ⊙ Closed Sun.

Bermuda Society of Arts

MUSEUM | On the upper floor of City Hall & Arts Centre, in the West Wing, the Bermuda Society of Arts displays work by its members. Its frequently changing juried shows attract talented local painters, sculptors, and photographers. Art collectors will be pleased to learn that many pieces may also be purchased. ⊠ City Hall & Arts Centre, 17 Church St., Hamilton ☎ 441/292–3824 ⊕ www.bsoa.bm 🖼 Free ⊙ Closed Sun.

★ Bermuda Underwater Exploration Institute (BUEI)

MUSEUM | FAMILY | The 40,000-square-foot Ocean Discovery Centre at the institute showcases local contributions to oceanographic research and undersea discovery. Highlights include the world-class shell collection amassed by resident Jack Lightbourn (three of the 1,000

species were identified by and named for Lightbourn himself) and a gallery honoring native-born archaeologist Teddy Tucker featuring booty from Bermudian shipwrecks. The equipment that made such discoveries possible is displayed, including a replica of the bathysphere William Beebe and Otis Barton used in their record-smashing 1934 dive. (Forget the Bermuda Triangle: the real mystery is how they descended a half mile in a metal ball less than 5 feet in diameter!) A more modern "submersible," Nautilus-X2, lets wannabe explorers take a simulated seven-minute trip to the ocean floor. Special events, like lectures, glowworm cruises, and whale-watching trips, are available for an added fee. The on-site Harbourfront restaurant is a lovely choice for lunch. ■TIP→ **Pedestrians may access the facility by following the sidewalk on the water side of Front Street. Motorists must drive out of town on Front Street, round the traffic circle, and exit at the lane signposted for the BUEI.** ⊠ *40 Crow La., Hamilton* ⊹ *Off E. Broadway* ☎ *441/292–7219* ⊕ *www.buei.bm* ⊠ *$15.*

Cabinet Building

GOVERNMENT BUILDING | The most rewarding time to visit the Cabinet Building, which was completed in 1841 and remodeled almost a century later, is during the formal opening of Parliament, traditionally held on the first Friday of November. His Excellency the Governor, dressed in a plumed hat and full regalia, arrives on the grounds in a landau drawn by magnificent black horses and accompanied by a police escort. A senior officer, carrying the Black Rod made by the Crown jewelers, next asks the speaker of the House, elected representatives, and members of the Senate chamber to convene. The governor then presents the Throne Speech from a tiny cedar throne dating from 1642. At other times of the year the Cabinet Building is open to the public every day except Tuesday. ⊠ *105 Front St., Hamilton* ☎ *441/292–5501*

⊕ *www.gov.bm* ⊠ *Free* ⊙ *Closed to the public Tues.*

Cathedral of the Most Holy Trinity

RELIGIOUS SITE | After the original Anglican sanctuary on this site was torched by an arsonist in 1884, Scottish architect William Hay was enlisted to design a replacement: true to his training, Hay erected a Gothic-style structure in the grand European tradition. Inside, the clerestory in the nave is supported by piers of polished Scottish granite; soaring archways are trimmed in stone imported from France; and the choir stalls and bishop's throne are carved out of English oak. The pulpit is modeled on the one in Hay's hometown cathedral (St. Giles in Edinburgh), and the whole thing is crowned by a copper roof that stands out among Bermuda's typical white-topped buildings.

Despite the European flourishes, Bermuda Cathedral still has a subtropical flair. After all, the limestone building blocks came from the Par-la-Ville quarry, and one of its loveliest stained-glass windows—the Angel Window on the east wall of the north transept—was created by local artist Vivienne Gilmore Gardner. ■TIP→ **After sauntering around the interior, you can climb the 155 steps of the church tower for a heavenly view of Hamilton and its harbor.** ⊠ *29 Church St., Hamilton* ☎ *441/292–4033* ⊕ *www.anglican.bm* ⊠ *Cathedral free; tower $3* ⊙ *Tower closed weekends.*

City Hall & Arts Centre

GOVERNMENT BUILDING | Set back from the street, City Hall contains Hamilton's administrative offices as well as two art galleries and a performance hall. Instead of a clock, its tower is topped with a bronze wind vane—a prudent choice in a land where the weather is as important as the time. The building itself was designed in 1960 by Bermudian architect Wilfred Onions, a champion of balanced simplicity. Massive cedar doors open onto an impressive lobby notable for its

A Good Walk in Hamilton

Any tour of Hamilton should begin on **Front Street**, a tidy thoroughfare lined with ice cream–color buildings, many with cheery awnings and ornate balconies. The Visitor Services Centre next to the Ferry Terminal at 8 Front Street is a good starting point. Continue west and swing down Point Pleasant Road to **Albuoy's Point** for a splendid view of Hamilton Harbour. Afterward, retrace your steps, passing the Ferry Terminal Building where passengers board boats for sightseeing excursions. (You can also depart from here on more affordable round-trip rides to the Dockyard and St. George's via the Sea Express ferry.) Stroll toward the intersection of Front and Queen streets, where you can see the Birdcage, a much-photographed traffic box named for its designer, Michael "Dickey" Bird.

Turn up Queen Street to see the 19th-century **Perot Post Office.** Just beyond it is the **Museum of the Bermuda Historical Society** and **Bermuda National Library.** Follow Queen Street away from the harbor to Church Street to reach the **City Hall & Arts Centre**, which houses the Bermuda National Gallery, the Bermuda Society of Arts, and a performing arts venue.

At the City Hall steps, turn east on Church Street and pass the Hamilton Bus Terminal. One block farther, the imposing **Cathedral of the Most Holy Trinity** looms up before you. Next, past the cathedral near the corner of Church and Parliament streets, you'll come to **Sessions House.** Keep going down Parliament to Front Street for a look at the **Cabinet Building** and, in front of it, the Cenotaph for fallen Bermudian soldiers. From here you might head back to Front Street for a leisurely stroll past (or into) the shops, then linger over lunch in one of the many cafés overlooking the harbor.

If you're up for a longer walk (about 15 minutes east from the Cenotaph) or are traveling by scooter or taxi, head to the **Bermuda Underwater Exploration Institute (BUEI). Fort Hamilton** is another worthwhile destination, though the road to it—north on King Street, then a sharp right on Happy Valley Road—is a bit too steep for casual walkers. The moated fort has gorgeous grounds, underground passageways, and great views of Hamilton and its harbor.

beautiful chandeliers and portraits of mayors past and present. To the left is the Earl Cameron Theatre, a major venue for concerts, plays, and dance performances. To the right are the civic offices. A handsome cedar staircase leads upstairs to two upper-floor art galleries, or you can take an elevator. ⊠ *17 Church St., Hamilton* ☎ *441/292–1234* ⊠ *Free.*

City of Hamilton Visitor Services Centre
INFO CENTER | Located next to the Ferry Terminal, the Visitor Services Centre is a good place to start when you're ready to explore the rest of Hamilton. The distinctive building was built out of repurposed shipping containers, and it's the place to pick up pamphlets and maps, to book tours and excursions, and to have your questions answered. Look for brochures for self-guided city walking tours. You can also purchase Bermuda-branded merchandise. On the top floor, the Birdcage has front-row harbor views and inventive cocktails from Twisted Spoon Cocktail Co. ⊠ *10 Front St., Hamilton* ☎ *441/261–2872* ⊕ *www.gotobermuda.com.*

Hamilton's Cathedral of the Most Holy Trinity offers great views of Hamilton from its tower.

★ Fort Hamilton

MILITARY SITE | FAMILY | This imposing, moat-ringed fortress has underground passageways that were cut through solid rock by Royal Engineers in the 1860s. Built to defend the West End's Royal Naval Dockyard from land attacks, it was outdated even before its completion, but remains a fine example of a polygonal Victorian fort. Even if you're not a big fan of military history, the hilltop site's stellar views and stunning gardens make the trip worthwhile. On Monday at noon, from November to March, bagpipes echo through the grounds as the kilt-clad members of the Bermuda Islands Pipe Band perform a traditional skirling ceremony. ■ **TIP→ Due to one-way streets, getting to the fort by scooter can be a bit challenging. From downtown Hamilton head north on Queen Street, turn right on Church Street, then turn left to go up the hill on King Street. Make a sharp (270-degree) right turn onto Happy Valley Road and follow the signs. Pedestrians may walk along Front Street to King Street.** ⊠ *Happy Valley Rd., Hamilton* ☎ *441/292–1234* ◎ *Free.*

Front Street

NEIGHBORHOOD | Running along the harbor, Hamilton's main thoroughfare bustles with small cars, motor scooters, bicycles, buses, the occasional horse-drawn carriage, and sometimes hordes of cruise-ship passengers. The prime attractions here are the high-class low-rise shops that line the street, but don't overlook small offshoots and alleyways like Chancery Lane, Old Cellar Lane, and the Walkers Arcade, where you'll stumble upon hidden-away boutiques. ⊠ *Hamilton.*

Museum of the Bermuda Historical Society/ Bermuda National Library

MUSEUM | Established in 1839, the library has a reference section with virtually every book ever written about Bermuda, as well as a microfilm collection of Bermudian newspapers dating back to 1784. Mark Twain admired the giant rubber tree that stands on Queen Street in the front yard of this Georgian house, formerly owned by postmaster William Bennett Perot and his family.

You may find yourself walking down a quiet lane almost anywhere in Hamilton, which is a city filled with parks and quaint back alleys.

To the left of the library entrance is the electic collection of Bermuda Historical Society's museum, chronicling the island's past through interesting—and in some cases downright quirky—artifacts. One display, for instance, is full of Bermudian silver dating from the 1600s. Check out the portraits of Sir George Somers and his wife, painted around 1605, and of William Perot and his wife that hang in the entrance hall. The museum offers limited-edition prints from its vast photographic archives. You can also pick up a free copy of the letter George Washington wrote in 1775; addressed to the inhabitants of Bermuda, it requests gunpowder for use in the American Revolution. Museum tours are by appointment. ✉ 13 Queen St., Hamilton ✛ Opposite Reid St. ☎ 441/299–0029 library, 441/295–2487 museum ⊕ www. bnl.bm 🎫 Free ☺ Museum and library closed Sun.

Perot Post Office

GOVERNMENT BUILDING | To some, this rather austere 1840s structure is simply a place to mail a letter, but to stamp collectors the Perot Post Office, named for Hamilton's first postmaster, is a veritable shrine. William Bennett Perot (1791–1871) was certainly a genial fellow: he would meet arriving steamers, collect the incoming mail, stash it in his beaver hat, and then stroll around Hamilton to deliver it, greeting each recipient with a tip of his chapeau. But it was his resourcefulness that made him most famous among philatelists. Tired of individually hand-stamping outgoing letters, Perot began printing stamps in 1848. Of the thousands he produced, only 11 still exist—and several of those are owned by Queen Elizabeth. If you'd like to get your hands on one, be prepared to dig deep. In 2005 a Perot-era one-penny stamp sold at auction for a record-breaking $244,000. ✉ 9 Queen St., Hamilton ☎ 441/292–9052 🎫 Free.

Queen Elizabeth Park (Par-la-Ville Park)

NATIONAL/STATE PARK | Next to the Perot Post Office is the Queen Street entrance to pretty Queen Elizabeth Park (there's another entrance on Par-la-Ville Road), which was officially renamed in 2012 to mark the Diamond Jubilee celebration of Queen Elizabeth II. Once postmaster William Perot's private garden, it has winding paths, luxuriant blooms, plentiful benches, and a photogenic Bermuda moongate. Long popular with people-watchers, it is now the site of the Bermuda National Library and Bermuda Historical Society Museum, too. The Bermuda National Gallery has created a sculpture garden in the park by installing several major outdoor works. On summer Saturdays you will find Gombey dancers entertaining visitors here. ⊠ *Queen St., Hamilton* ⊠ *Free.*

Sessions House and Jubilee Clock Tower

GOVERNMENT BUILDING | This eye-catching Italianate edifice, erected in 1819, is where the House of Assembly (Bermuda's lower house of Parliament) and the Supreme Court convene. The Florentine towers and colonnade, decorated with red terra-cotta, were added to the building in 1887 to commemorate Queen Victoria's Golden Jubilee. The Victoria Jubilee Clock Tower made its striking debut—albeit a few years late—at midnight on December 31, 1893. Bermuda's Westminster-style Parliament meets on the second floor, where the speaker rules the roost in a powdered wig and robe. (The island has approximately 14 times as many politicians per capita as Europe or North America, so maintaining order is no small feat.) Sartorial splendor is equally evident downstairs in the Supreme Court, where wigs and robes— red for judges, black for barristers—are again the order of the day. ■TIP➜ **You're welcome to watch the colorful proceedings: bear in mind, though, that visitors, too, are required to wear appropriate attire.** Call first to find out when parliamentary

What's in a Name? ⊙

Bermudians cultivated onions long before Americans colonists did. In fact, throughout the 19th century they were one of the island's major exports, and its people were so closely identified with the tear-inducing plant that anyone born and bred here came to be known as an "Onion." Though competition eventually put an end to the lucrative trade, this nickname for locals stuck.

sessions and court cases are scheduled. ⊠ *21 Parliament St., Hamilton* ☎ *441/292–7408 House of Assembly, 441/292–1350 Supreme Court* ⊕ *www. gov.bm* ⊠ *Free.*

🍴 Restaurants

Bermuda's capital city has the largest concentration of eateries within a stone's throw from one another. Fresh seafood is the highlight, as many restaurants receive daily catches from local fishermen. It's best to explore the food options on foot, as most are based in and around Front Street, and it won't take long to find something to satisfy your craving. Don't forget to stroll down the side streets and alleyways, as some of the best restaurants are tucked away out of sight. Many restaurants have balconies overlooking picturesque Hamilton Harbour, which makes this area a great spot for alfresco dining. Don't be surprised to see restaurant staff clearing away their tables and chairs around 10 pm, when the restaurants are transformed into clubs and the fun really begins.

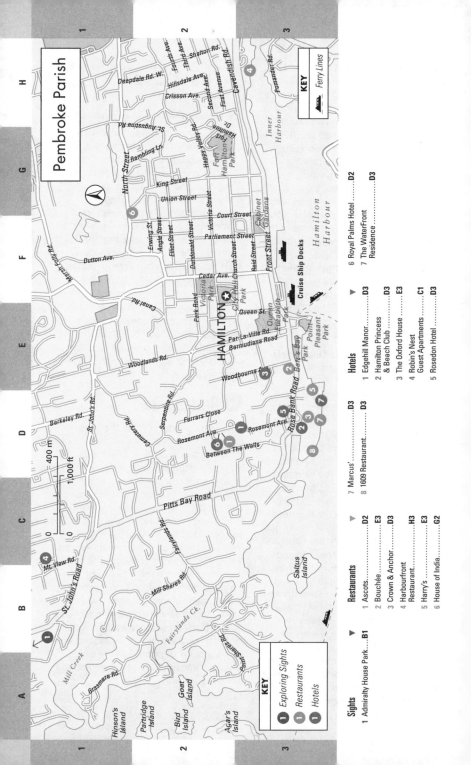

Pembroke Parish

Angelo's Bistro

$$ | ITALIAN | Located in a busy alleyway between Reid Street and Front Street, this unassuming eatery is a well-kept secret for great Italian food. The menu features island-inspired meat and seafood dishes, handmade pastas and warm focaccia, as well as a number of vegan and gluten-free options. **Known for:** varied menu with authentic Italian cuisine; alfresco courtyard dining; attentive owner and staff. $ *Average main: $25* ✉ *Walker Arcade, 12 Reid St., Hamilton* ☎ *441/232–1000* ☾ *Closed Sun.*

Ascots

$$$ | EUROPEAN | Housed in an elegant former mansion just outside downtown Hamilton and run under the exacting standards of owners Angelo Armano and Edmund Smith, Ascots has a creative and seasonal menu with offerings that incorporate fresh ingredients from local farmers and fisherfolk. Start off with the Bermuda fish cakes or the chilled banana soup with black rum—it's unusual but very popular—and move on to mains such as slow-cooked wild mushroom risotto, pan-seared snapper, and chargrilled rib-eye steak. **Known for:** exquisite food presentation; relaxed patio overlooking lush gardens; award-winning wine list. $ *Average main: $40* ✉ *Royal Palms Hotel, 24 Rosemont Ave.* ☎ *441/295–9644* ⊕ *www.ascots.bm* ☾ *Closed Sun. No lunch Sat.*

Astwood Arms

$$ | BRITISH | FAMILY | At this Victorian-style bar and restaurant renovated from a former jewelry shop, the menu lists traditional gastropub offerings including Scotch eggs and Balti chicken pie. It is also a surprisingly child-friendly spot, with a kids' menu that features mini burgers, fish fingers, and grilled chicken with peas. **Known for:** flatbreads and tacos as well as pub classics; impressive gin offerings; lively bar scene. $ *Average main: $24* ✉ *85 Front St., Hamilton* ☎ *441/292–5818* ⊕ *www.astwoodarms.bm.*

★ Barracuda Grill

$$$ | SEAFOOD | The tastefully decorated contemporary dining room—mahogany-framed chairs and banquettes, soft-gold lights over the tables—is reminiscent of sophisticated big-city restaurants, and the food (from both the sea and land) that comes to the table is created by a culinary team dedicated to excellence. Ease into your meal with a bowl of island-style fish chowder; for an entrée, try one of their classics, such as Bermuda rockfish or Boursin-stuffed beef tenderloin. **Known for:** daily locally caught fish; lively martini bar; creatively plated dishes. $ *Average main: $36* ✉ *5 Burnaby Hill, Hamilton* ☎ *441/292–1609* ⊕ *www.barracuda-grill.com* ☾ *No lunch weekends.*

Bermuda Bistro at the Beach

$ | AMERICAN | Despite what the name suggests, this restaurant is right in the heart of Hamilton, and a good place to savor the day's fresh fish special while enjoying an afternoon filled with people-watching and happy hour drink specials on the open-air patio. It's the ideal stop-off during a day of shopping, offering plentiful, inexpensive, and quick food—from a hearty three-course lunch to an afternoon snack, from burgers and sandwiches to salads and steaks. **Known for:** easygoing patio dining; weekend party atmosphere; open late at night. $ *Average main: $19* ✉ *103 Front St., Hamilton* ☎ *441/292–0219* ⊕ *www.thebeachbermuda.com.*

Bistro J

$$$ | BISTRO | Delivering prompt, impeccable service and outstanding value, this quiet spot offers fixed-price two- and three-course meals at lunch and dinner. Fresh pasta, seafood, and local produce are combined in an imaginative daily menu that's written on a large blackboard hanging on the wall. **Known for:** daily fixed-price menus; excellent wine selection; warm, relaxed atmosphere. $ *Average main: $35* ✉ *Chancery La., Hamilton*

✢ *Off Front St.* ☎ *441/296–8546* ⊕ *www. bistroj.bm* ⊙ *No lunch weekends. No dinner Sun.*

Bolero Brasserie

$$$ | BRASSERIE | The smartly dressed waitstaff, bustling atmosphere, and art-filled walls lend an authentic European feel to this beloved Front Street bistro. Owner and chef Johnny Roberts takes great pride in Bolero's frequently updated brasserie menu, featuring snails, ballotine of foie gras, roast rack of lamb, and even black pudding. **Known for:** seasonally inspired bistro menu; harbor-view balcony; reservations needed for lunch and dinner. ⑤ *Average main: $33* ✉ *95 Front St., Hamilton* ✢ *Entrance on Bermuda House La.* ☎ *441/292–4507* ⊕ *www. bolerobrasserie.com* ⊙ *Closed Sun. No lunch Sat.*

Bouchée

$$ | FRENCH | It's worth the walk west out of Hamilton to see why this charming French restaurant is a firm favorite with locals and tourists alike. Rise and shine with the extensive breakfast fare while enjoying the sophisticated-casual atmosphere and a morning pick-me-up cocktail, or go for dinner and try the catch of the day, usually rockfish or wahoo, cooked to your liking. **Known for:** reasonably priced breakfast fare; popular weekend brunch; French café atmosphere. ⑤ *Average main: $26* ✉ *75 Pitts Bay Rd., Hamilton* ✢ *Near Woodburne Ave.* ☎ *441/295–5759* ⊕ *www.bouchee.bm* ⊙ *No dinner Sun. or Mon.*

Bulli.Social

$ | AMERICAN | Bermuda's only gourmet burger restaurant spices up Hamilton's lunchtime scene with an array of creatively topped patties, poutines, and hot dogs. Enjoy the social buzz out back on the patio, which overlooks Queen Elizabeth Park and transforms into a lively happy hour hot spot on Friday and Saturday. **Known for:** slider combo; full bar and patio seating; smoked brisket and pork. ⑤ *Average main: $16* ✉ *7 Queen*

St., Hamilton ☎ *441/232–2855* ⊕ *www. bullisocial.com* ⊙ *Closed Sun.*

Buzz

$ | CAFÉ | With 10 venues across the island, Buzz is a cheap and cheerful café with a variety of made-to-order breakfast and lunch options. Inexpensive and convenient snacks, cold drinks, and plenty of healthy choices make this an essential spot to refuel. **Known for:** convenient grab-and-go snacks; vegetarian options; coffee and smoothies. ⑤ *Average main: $10* ✉ *Washington Mall, 20 Church St., Upper Level, Hamilton* ☎ *441/295–1979* ⊕ *www.buzzcafe.bm* ⊙ *No dinner.*

Chopsticks

$ | ASIAN | FAMILY | Locals and visitors alike come here for an extensive menu that includes Szechuan, Hunan, Cantonese, and Mandarin favorites. Top Chinese choices include the sesame chicken and the house specialty, Peking duck; for Thai tastes, try the *panang* red curry (a coconut milk-curry sauce). **Known for:** diverse Asian-fusion menu; convenient takeout; painted mural and indoor waterfall. ⑤ *Average main: $19* ✉ *88 Reid St., Hamilton* ☎ *441/292–0791* ⊕ *www.chopsticks.bm* ⊙ *No lunch weekends.*

Coconut Rock and Yashi Sushi Bar

$$ | ECLECTIC | Whether you're in the mood for shrimp tempura and sashimi served in a quiet room with black-lacquer tables and paper lanterns, or you're hankering for a salad and a steak surrounded by loud music videos, these adjoining restaurants can satisfy. Well hidden beneath Hamilton's main shopping street, the venue transforms into a lively cocktail destination at night, especially on weekends. **Known for:** varied international cuisine; after-work hangout for locals; the wait for tables is worth it. ⑤ *Average main: $21* ✉ *Williams House, 20 Reid St., downstairs, Hamilton* ☎ *441/292–1043, 441/296–6226* ⊙ *No lunch Sun.*

The Cottage Café & Bistro

$ | CAFÉ | FAMILY | Tucked inside the Washington Mall, this café run by a husband-and-wife team is best known for its outstanding breakfasts, changing lunch specials, and friendly service. Try the plate-sized fluffy pancake topped with homemade lemon curd, or give the Azorean eggs Benedict, topped with crispy chorizo and fresh Portuguese cheese, a try. **Known for:** inventive salads and sandwiches; pecan-crusted chicken and biscuit sandwich; easy takeout options. ⑤ *Average main: $16* ⊠ *Washington Mall, 20 Church St., 2nd fl., Hamilton* ☎ *441/292–0880* ⓧ *Closed Sun. No dinner.*

Crown & Anchor

$$ | ECLECTIC | Light and airy, with an upscale hotel feel, the Crown & Anchor offers everything from quiet afternoon tea service to lively happy hour specials. The casual fare for lunch and dinner focuses on island pub favorites such as fish-and-chips and chicken curry, as well as small bites perfect for sharing. **Known for:** good people-watching; breakfast buffet; attentive service. ⑤ *Average main: $23* ⊠ *Hamilton Princess & Beach Club, 76 Pitts Bay Rd., Hamilton* ☎ *441/295–3000* ⓦ *www.thehamiltonprincess.com.*

Devil's Isle Cafe

$$ | EUROPEAN | With an emphasis on fresh, healthy ingredients, Devil's Isle's large menu has plenty of creative options, many available in both small and large plates. The small plates are the perfect way to try a few different options and share at the long communal table that dominates the center of this small, buzzy space. **Known for:** rockfish tacos; customizable harvest bowls; good coffee. ⑤ *Average main: $29* ⊠ *19 Burnaby St., Hamilton* ☎ *441/292–3284* ⓦ *www.devilsislecoffee.bm.*

The Docksider Pub & Restaurant

$ | BRITISH | Whether it's high noon, happy hour, or late Saturday night, locals love to mingle at this sprawling Front Street sports bar. Classic pub fare with a Bermudian twist—think nachos with homemade chili, barbecue chicken leg with peas 'n' rice, and fish-and-chips—pairs perfectly with the impressive variety of beers, ciders, and spirits. Join the English Premier League Football fans that gather en masse to watch their favorite teams or sip your dessert—a Dark 'n' Stormy—out on the porch as you watch Bermuda stroll by. **Known for:** passionate sports fans; crowded nightlife drinking scene; weekend brunch. ⑤ *Average main: $19* ⊠ *121 Front St., Hamilton* ☎ *441/296–3333* ⓦ *www.docksider.bm.*

Flanagan's Irish Pub

$$ | IRISH | Bermuda's only Irish pub is a dining, music, and sports hot spot with a balcony overlooking Hamilton Harbour. Choose from an extensive list of tasty homemade comfort-food classics such as beer-battered fish-and-chips and shepherd's pie, while sipping a handcrafted island cocktail. **Known for:** good list of beers and ciders; local musicians at night; spot for international sports enthusiasts. ⑤ *Average main: $24* ⊠ *Emporium Bldg., 69 Front St., 2nd fl., Hamilton* ☎ *441/295–8299* ⓦ *www.flanagans.bm.*

Harbourfront Restaurant

$$$ | INTERNATIONAL | Whether you dine inside beside the enormous floor-to-ceiling windows or outside on the dock, every seat in this restaurant next to Bermuda Underwater Exploration Institute has beautiful views of Hamilton Harbour. Expertly prepared fresh sushi shines alongside international specialties and locally caught fish on the remarkably eclectic menu, so don't hesitate to ask your attentive, personable server to recommend a dish. **Known for:** sophisticated harborside setting; lower-priced sushi for weeknight happy hour; fish chowder. ⑤ *Average main: $37* ⊠ *40 Crow La., Hamilton* ⚓ *Next to Bermuda Underwater Exploration Institute (BUEI)* ☎ *441/295–4207* ⓦ *www.harbourfront.bm* ⓧ *No lunch Sun.*

Harry's

$$$ | **STEAKHOUSE** | A sleek bar and sophisticated decor provide an elegant backdrop for intimate dinners and classy power lunches. The steak-house classics, which feature flavorful aged beef and a variety of gourmet sides, are highly regarded; there's also plenty of fresh seafood on offer. **Known for:** perfect wine pairings; lively happy hour on the patio; tasty bar snacks. $ *Average main: $39* ⊠ *The Waterfront, 96 Pitts Bay Rd., Hamilton* ☎ *441/292–5533* ⊕ *www.harrys.bm* ⊙ *Closed Sun.*

Hog Penny Pub

$$ | **BRITISH** | Veterans of London pub crawls may feel nostalgic at this dark, wood-filled watering hole off Front Street where you can enjoy old-style British comfort food and the ambience of Hamilton's oldest licensed establishment, opened in 1957. Imported ales as well as local craft beers from Dockyard Brewing Company are on offer to pair with your homemade shepherd's pie, fish-and-chips, or bangers and mash. **Known for:** nostalgic feel; delicious fish chowder; live music. $ *Average main: $25* ⊠ *5 Burnaby St., Hamilton* ☎ *441/292–2534* ⊕ *www.hogpennypub.com.*

★ House of India

$ | **INDIAN** | Slightly off the beaten track, this authentic Indian restaurant is well worth the 10-minute walk or short cab ride from the town center. Outstanding chicken tikka masala, beef curry, and plenty of vegetarian options can be perfectly spiced to your liking. **Known for:** fresh naan; weekday lunch buffet; quick takeout counter. $ *Average main: $18* ⊠ *58 North St., Hamilton* ☎ *441/295–6450* ⊕ *www.houseofindia.biz* ⊙ *No lunch weekends.*

Jamaican Grill

$ | **JAMAICAN** | Journey outside the familiar city center to North East Hamilton and Court Street and you'll find Jamaican food at its best. The Thomas family is proud of their Jamaican heritage and wants everyone to taste Caribbean classics like jerk and curry chicken, fried dumplings, and beans and rice. **Known for:** large portions of authentic Jamaican specialties; convenient takeout; genuinely friendly staff. $ *Average main: $15* ⊠ *32 Court St., Hamilton* ☎ *441/296–6577* ⊙ *Closed Sun.*

★ La Trattoria

$$ | **ITALIAN** | **FAMILY** | Tucked away in a narrow Hamilton alley, this family-favorite Italian restaurant has a warm yellow and brick interior and a crew of friendly Italian waiters. Without a doubt the king of the menu is pizza—La Trattoria's pies are cooked in a brick, wood-burning pizza oven and can be garnished with over 20 inventive toppings. **Known for:** reservations needed for lunch and dinner; Italian waitstaff; family-friendly charm. $ *Average main: $25* ⊠ *23 Washington La., Hamilton* ☎ *441/295–1877* ⊕ *www.latrattoria.bm* ⊙ *No lunch Sun.*

Little Venice

$$$ | **ITALIAN** | It's a little pricey, but Little Venice also sets the bar with its attentive, old-world hospitality, flavorful Italian dishes, and freshly made pasta. Bermuda's business elite gather for drinks and appetizers after work, making their way through a wine list that boasts 1,000 different wines from around the world. **Known for:** top-notch Italian food worthy of the price tag; exceptional service; homemade pasta. $ *Average main: $37* ⊠ *32 Bermudiana Rd., Hamilton* ☎ *441/295–3503* ⊕ *www.littlevenice.bm* ⊙ *No lunch Sat. Closed Sun.*

Lobster Pot & Boat House Bar

$$ | **SEAFOOD** | **FAMILY** | Bermudians swear by this spot, where a maritime-themed dining room is filled with brass nautical gear, lobster traps, and sun-bleached rope. The fresh local lobster, available September through March, is most requested, next to rockfish, snapper, wahoo, and mahimahi with fried bananas and almonds, all local favorites. **Known for:** Cup Match Special fried seafood

dinner; Bermuda fish chowder; laid-back atmosphere. $ *Average main: $27* ✉ *6 Bermudiana Rd., Hamilton* ☎ *441/292–6898* ⊗ *No lunch weekends.*

L'Oriental

$$ | ASIAN | Above its sister restaurant, Little Venice, this Asian hot spot is a favorite among locals for its fresh sushi bar. Take the footbridge—over an indoor stream—to the raised seating at the lively teppanyaki table, where trained chefs stylishly slice, stir, and season your steak and veggies onto your plate. **Known for:** range of regional cuisines, including delicious curries; open kitchen; Asian-themed decor. $ *Average main: $29* ✉ *32 Bermudiana Rd., Hamilton* ☎ *441/296–4477* ⊕ *www.loriental.bm* ⊗ *No lunch weekends.*

Mad Hatters

$$$ | EUROPEAN | Guests can spend their meal trying on all manner of crazy hats at this quirky restaurant, but fortunately, the food here shines, mixing traditional European fare with Asian influences in dishes such as the mussels in a Thai coconut curry. The daily specials are always tempting and worth hearing before making your decision. **Known for:** small space, so revervations needed; tantalizing daily specials; Asian fusion dishes. $ *Average main: $36* ✉ *22 Richmond Rd., Hamilton* ☎ *441/297–6231* ⊕ *www.madhatters.bm* ⊗ *Closed Sun.*

★ Marcus'

$$$ | CARIBBEAN | Bringing Marcus Samuelsson's fried chicken and waffles, made famous at his acclaimed Harlem restaurant Red Rooster, to Bermuda, this trendy, namesake restaurant inside the Hamilton Princess & Beach Club also mixes local flavors into the small but tantalizing menu. The space housed a staid ballroom, yet it now feels airy, allowing the harbor views to take center stage with soaring windows and a large see-through bar. **Known for:** fish chowder bites; inventive cocktails; Sunday champagne brunch. $ *Average main: $36*

✉ *Hamilton Princess & Beach Club, 76 Pitts Bay Rd., Hamilton* ☎ *441/295–3000* ⊕ *thehamiltonprincess.com.*

The Pickled Onion

$$ | CARIBBEAN | FAMILY | A former whiskey warehouse, this is now a lively restaurant serving crowd-pleasing Bermudian cuisine, as well as a handful of Latin- and Asian-flavored dishes. If you get there early enough, grab a table on the veranda overlooking the harbor and be sure to stick around—this is a fabulous spot to hang out and enjoy live music. **Known for:** balcony overlooking Front Street; Sunday brunch; long menu includes rockfish tacos. $ *Average main: $26* ✉ *53 Front St., Hamilton* ☎ *441/295–2263* ⊕ *www.thepickledonion.com.*

★ Port O' Call

$$$ | SEAFOOD | A two-level restaurant and sushi bar (Pearl) with a modern look and elegant atmosphere, Port O' Call is one of the few ground-entry dining spots on Front Street, with an outdoor dining area reminiscent of a chic European sidewalk café. The fresh local fish—such as wahoo, tuna, grouper, and snapper—is cooked perfectly, and the preparations are creative. **Known for:** long wine list and creative drinks; sceney happy hour; delicious cheesecake. $ *Average main: $39* ✉ *87 Front St., Hamilton* ☎ *441/295–5373* ⊕ *www.portocall.bm* ⊗ *No lunch Sat. Closed Sun.*

Portofino

$$ | ITALIAN | FAMILY | Even after a refurbishment and update to the interior of this Italian-owned restaurant, it still has all the charm of an unassuming-but-good eatery in a small Italian village. On balmy evenings, share the calamari or garlic bread—two starters for which the restaurant is renowned—outside on the dining area patio, and then move on to the pastas and pizzas. **Known for:** margherita pizza; good-size portions; speedy takeout. $ *Average main: $21* ✉ *20 Bermudiana Rd., Hamilton* ⊕ *Off Front St.* ☎ *441/292–2375, 441/295–6090*

takeout ⊕ www.portofino.bm ⊗ No lunch weekends.

The Red Carpet

$$$ | EUROPEAN | Old-fashioned charm and consistently attentive service are two reasons why this tried-and-true bar and restaurant is a favorite among local politicians and businesspeople. Located in the old Armoury building, it's a very popular lunch spot, serving plenty of fresh seafood and local favorites like fish chowder. **Known for:** excellent seafood, including the mixed seafood kettle; dinner more relaxed than lunch; casual bar area. ⑤ Average main: $38 ⊠ Armoury Bldg., 37 Reid St., Hamilton ☎ 441/292–6195 ⊕ www.redcarpet.bm ⊗ Closed Sun.

Rosa's

$$ | MEXICAN | FAMILY | Just a three-minute stroll from the ferry terminal to the opposite end of Front Street is Bermuda's own taste of Mexico, complete with easygoing, friendly service, balcony seating, and a comprehensive menu of Tex-Mex favorites. Share a towering plate of loaded nachos to start, followed by sizzling hot fajitas delivered to your table in a cast-iron skillet. **Known for:** award-winning fish sandwich; notable margaritas; Taco Tuesday special. ⑤ Average main: $22 ⊠ 121 Front St., Hamilton ☎ 441/295–1912 ⊕ www.rosas.bm.

Ruby Murrys

$ | INDIAN | Serving authentic, affordable Indian cuisine, this relaxed eatery on a quiet, cobblestoned alley off Front Street is a particularly popular lunchtime destination for its à la carte and buffet-style fare. The quality and variety of dishes will suit any palate—just be sure to sample one of the fresh breads from the tandoor, and don't miss out on the deliciously inventive tandoori chicken flatbread. **Known for:** traditional and modern Indian food; great value; vegetarian options. ⑤ Average main: $19 ⊠ Chancery La., Hamilton ☎ 441/295–5058 ⊕ www.rubymurrys.bm ⊗ No lunch weekends.

Not-So-Fast Food 🍴

If you think something may be missing from the horizon of Bermuda eateries, you are quite right. Apart from a lone KFC (which snuck in sometime during the 1970s), you won't find any fast-food chains on the island. The majority of Bermuda's residents strongly believe that allowing American franchises onto the island would dilute Bermuda's distinctive foreign (and rather upscale) appeal, eventually leading to the island's resembling Anyplace, USA. Adjust your eyes (and belly) to the absence of big golden double arches!

1609 Bar & Restaurant

$$ | CARIBBEAN | Ascend a short flight of stairs at the end of the Hamilton Princess pier and enjoy the chic island vibe at this harbor-view restaurant. Stylish, buzzy, and modern, the 1609 is the perfect spot for a romantic rendezvous, complete with a tasteful assortment of wines, tasty salads, and fish chowder to start, and a flatbread or fresh fish tacos. **Known for:** bird's-eye harbor view great at sunset; seafood-focused menu; specialty cocktails by the pitcher. ⑤ Average main: $29 ⊠ Hamilton Princess & Beach Club, 76 Pitts Bay Rd., Hamilton ☎ 441/295–3000 ⊕ www.thehamiltonprincess.com/dining.

Streetwize

$ | BRITISH | With menu items such as fish-and-chips and battered, deep-fried sausage, Streetwize brings comfort food influenced by British street-food favorites to the streets of Bermuda. Tucked in a small shop on Chancery Lane just off Front Street, it has limited seating inside, but if you can, pull up a seat at the counter by the windows. **Known for:** street

food for takeout; lively atmosphere; good chips and burgers. [$] *Average main: $9* ⊠ *3 Chancery La., Hamilton* ☏ *441/292–9493* ⊘ *Closed Sun.*

The Terrace

$$ | CARIBBEAN | True to its name, the terrace at this casual eatery is the place to be, and during the day it's a great spot to try the mix-and-match tacos or share a flatbread. On Friday night, young professionals flock to the indoor bar for the stylish vibe and vast selection of wines and cocktails, as well as entertainment. **Known for:** harbor-view patio seating; good bar snacks for sharing; Friday happy hour. [$] *Average main: $30* ⊠ *55 Front St., Hamilton* ☏ *441/292–7331* ⊕ *www.theterracebermuda.com* ⊘ *Closed Sun.*

Utopia

$$ | CONTEMPORARY | Across the street from the ferry terminal, this spot with Asian and West Coast culinary influences is a lunchtime favorite among locals. Dine and people-watch from the patio lounge chairs on street level or sip a rum swizzle while enjoying a view of Hamilton Harbour on the rooftop Skybar. **Known for:** healthy menu options; house-made desserts; good vegetarian choices. [$] *Average main: $28* ⊠ *17 Front St., Hamilton* ☏ *441/296–8788* ⊕ *www.utopia.bm* ⊘ *Closed Sun.*

🏨 Hotels

Stay in the heart of the city for added convenience and some sophisticated options. You won't need to worry about paying for a rental bike because everything you could need, such as stores, restaurants, and attractions, is right on your doorstep. This location will prove particularly useful to the business travelers who need to be close to Hamilton's financial sector. It's not the best of locations, however, for families or beach lovers, as the island's noteworthy beaches are on the south side.

Edgehill Manor

$$$ | B&B/INN | Quaint rooms and light continental breakfasts make you feel right at home at this comfortable colonial-style 20th-century guesthouse within walking distance of the restaurants, stores, and attractions of Hamilton. **Pros:** quiet pool; well maintained; private balconies in all rooms. **Cons:** no in-house dining; isolated from beaches; outdated room furnishings. [$] *Rooms from: $350* ⊠ *36 Rosemont Ave., Hamilton* ☏ *441/295–7124* ⊕ *www.edgehill.bm* ⇄ *14 rooms* ❍ *Breakfast.*

★ Hamilton Princess & Beach Club

$$$$ | HOTEL | The only full-service resort in Hamilton and located right on the harbor, just steps away from the liveliness of Front Street, the pastel-pink Princess is the reigning royalty of Bermuda lodging, boasting some of the island's most comfortable rooms and catering to its mainly business guests like no place else. **Pros:** luxurious pools and spa; only full-service resort in Hamilton; beautiful harbor-front locale. **Cons:** mainly corporate guests; ferry or cab necessary to reach beaches; large property may not suit all tastes. [$] *Rooms from: $575* ⊠ *76 Pitts Bay Rd., Hamilton* ☏ *441/295–3000, 800/441–1414* ⊕ *www.thehamiltonprincess.com* ⇄ *458 rooms* ❍ *No meals.*

The Oxford House

$$ | B&B/INN | It's the only true bed-and-breakfast in Hamilton, and one imagines that even if this elegant beige two-story town house, just two blocks from the capital's shops, ferries, and buses had competition, it would still be the best. **Pros:** friendly and attentive service; individually furnished rooms; right in Hamilton. **Cons:** no pool; isolated from beaches; very traditional furnishings may not suit all tastes. [$] *Rooms from: $270* ⊠ *20 Woodbourne Ave., Hamilton* ☏ *441/295–0503* ⊕ *www.oxfordhouse.bm* ⇄ *12 rooms* ❍ *Breakfast.*

The Hamilton Princess & Beach Club is the only full-service resort in the city of Hamilton.

Robin's Nest Guest Apartments

$$ | RENTAL | A tad off the beaten path, this well-maintained valley property is in a quiet residential neighborhood about a mile north of Hamilton and within walking distance to a secluded beach cove. **Pros:** well-kept rooms and grounds; pool and lounge chairs; private and quiet. **Cons:** out-of-the-way location; public transport stops at 6 pm; few food options nearby. ⑤ *Rooms from: $280* ⊠ *10 Vale Close* ☎ *441/292–4347, 800/637–4116 from U.S.* ⤴ *8 apartments* ⦿ *No meals.*

Rosedon Hotel

$$$ | HOTEL | Expect a tranquil, refined environment, good dining, and friendly service from longtime staff at this bright, blue-shuttered, white manor house in the center of Hamilton, a member of the Relais & Chateaux group of luxury hotels. **Pros:** free shuttle to beach; nice gardens and pool; complimentary afternoon tea. **Cons:** no beach; old-fashioned decor; small pool and no fitness center. ⑤ *Rooms from: $390* ⊠ *61 Pitts Bay Rd., Hamilton* ☎ *441/295–1640, 800/742–5008*

in U.S. and Canada ⊕ *www.rosedon.com* ⤴ *39 rooms* ⦿ *No meals.*

★ Royal Palms Hotel

$$$$ | HOTEL | A winner for having high standards, great service, and a welcoming touch with fresh-from-the-garden flowers to celebrate your arrival, this is a hotel that stresses quality, service, and atmosphere, but also has enough humor to leave a rubber ducky on your bath mat. **Pros:** beautiful gardens; wonderful breakfast; top-notch service. **Cons:** no beach; may seem pricey for what you get; small pool. ⑤ *Rooms from: $460* ⊠ *24 Rosemont Ave.* ☎ *441/292–1854, 800/678–0783 in U.S. and Canada* ⊕ *www.royalpalms.bm* ⤴ *32 rooms* ⦿ *Breakfast.*

The WaterFront Residence

$$$$ | RENTAL | Nestled within the gardens of a private community on the water's edge, the WaterFront Residence affords luxurious peace and quiet in a convenient location within easy walking distance of Hamilton. **Pros:** peaceful yet central location; beautiful rooms with king-size beds;

The boutique Royal Palms Hotels is known for its personalized service and excellent restaurant.

harbor-view balconies. **Cons:** no pool or beach; short walk off-site to breakfast; few rooms, so can get booked up. ⑤ *Rooms from: $420* ✉ *11 Waterloo La.* ☎ *441/299–0700* ⊕ *www.thewaterfron-tresidence.bm* ⇰ *6 rooms* ❚◉❙ *Breakfast.*

🍸 Nightlife

Follow the crowd and enjoy a night out in Hamilton. This is where you'll find most of the island's bars and clubs—and plenty of people. You can find a good mix of wine bars, sports bars, dance clubs, and live-music venues to suit your mood. Most of the music is reggae, hip-hop, R&B, and chart hits. Most bars serve light pub fare to keep you going through the night. The busiest night of the week in Hamilton is typically Friday, when everyone heads to the happy hours straight from work. Entrance fees are rare, especially for women, but you can expect to wait in line outside venues for up to 10 minutes. Most late-night parties don't get started until around 11 pm.

BARS AND LOUNGES
Astwood Arms

BARS/PUBS | Take a seat at the massive and detailed Victorian-style bar that wouldn't be out of place in a London pub. You can opt for an expertly mixed cocktail or taste a selection from the extensive beer menu. This is a great spot for late-afternoon drinks, particularly on the Front Street porch perfect for people-watching. ✉ *85 Front St., Hamilton* ☎ *441/292–5818* ⊕ *www.astwoodarms.bm.*

Bermuda Bistro at the Beach

BARS/PUBS | A cross between an outdoor café and a sports bar, this place (generally called just The Beach) is clean and relatively cheap, with large television screens showing live sports during the day. At night it operates somewhere between a bar and a nightclub, attracting a mixed (and often rowdy) collection of tourists and locals. The outdoor seating area gets especially crowded into the wee hours of the morning. There's usually a DJ, and sometimes bands; if you're walking down Front Street and you hear

loud music, it's probably coming from The Beach. ⊠ *103 Front St., Hamilton* ☎ *441/292–0219* ⊕ *www.thebeachbermuda.com.*

Coconut Rock

BARS/PUBS | With a restaurant in front and a sushi bar called Yashi in the back, Coconut Rock has a relaxed and friendly buzz. This is more of a locals' hangout, probably because it's hard to find, tucked away underneath Hamilton's main shopping street. Huge TV screens show music videos and sports. Watch out—the friendly bar staff are more than happy to help you get tipsy or, as Bermudians say, "tapped"! Don't confuse this place with Coconuts, the upscale restaurant at the Reefs resort in Southampton. ⊠ *Williams House, 20 Reid St., downstairs, Hamilton* ☎ *441/292–1043.*

The Docksider Pub & Restaurant

BARS/PUBS | Commonly known as Dockies, this bar attracts a loud and fun-loving crowd that can linger long into the night. Sports fanatics and competitive drinkers gather en masse to support their favorite teams, face off in weekly beer pong tournaments, and play a couple of rounds of darts. The no-frills bar at the entrance always offers a lively party atmosphere and reasonably priced pub food. On weekends, the large back room is opened to make space for hundreds of partiers and a live DJ. There's sometimes a cover charge for theme parties, bands, and tie-ins with local sporting events. ⊠ *121 Front St., Hamilton* ☎ *441/296–3333* ⊕ *www.docksider.bm.*

★ The Dog House

BARS/PUBS | With a wall of doors that open up on to Front Street, one of the widest selections of beers on the island, and multiple large television screens around the room, the Dog House is pretty much "where we all end up," and it's a very happy place. Along with a great beer selection, there are various cocktails on offer, and bar snacks are served until 10 pm. Multiple DJs play mostly R&B, soca, and Top 40 hits; during the summer DJs take over upstairs at the sister event space, Cafe Cairo. On weekends, the place is packed with late-night revelers. ⊠ *93 Front St., Hamilton* ☎ *441/232–3644.*

Flanagan's Irish Pub

BARS/PUBS | With live music or a DJ on weekends and all the expected beverages, as well as a host of fun drinks like frozen mudslides, homey Flanagan's Irish Pub is a firm favorite of folks who like to dance and talk over drinks. Adjoining the Irish pub is its sister bar, Outback Sports Bar, at the same address. Twenty-two giant screens show live sports, and the walls are plastered with photographs of Bermuda's sporting heroes. ⊠ *Emporium Building, 69 Front St., 2nd fl., Hamilton* ☎ *441/295–8299* ⊕ *www.flanagans.bm.*

Hamilton Princess & Beach Club

BARS/PUBS | During the high season from May through October, the hotel's Marina Nights happy hour is the place to be seen on Friday from 5 to 9 pm. Enjoy special drink prices, tasty cocktails, live bands, and a selection of themed food. The views of elegant yachts in the harbor draw a lively crowd of locals and visitors alike to the magnificent lawns of the famous hotel. The vibe is trendy, so don your stylish duds for this night. ⊠ *76 Pitts Bay Rd., Hamilton* ☎ *441/295–3000* ⊕ *www.thehamiltonprincess.com.*

Hog Penny Pub

BARS/PUBS | Small, cozy Hog Penny, aka the *Cheers* bar, was the inspiration for the Bull & Finch Pub in Boston. With dark-wood paneling and hearty, comforting fare like steak-and-kidney pie and bangers and mash, the Hog Penny will likely remind you more of an English country pub than a Boston hangout. Live music plays most nights in the summer, and the floor is cleared for dancing. It can be very busy. ⊠ *5 Burnaby St., Hamilton* ☎ *441/292–2534* ⊕ *www.hogpennypub.com.*

The Pickled Onion

BARS/PUBS | With a cosmopolitan feel and a harbor-view terrace, the Pickled Onion's restaurant and bar cater to a well-heeled crowd of locals and visitors. Live music, usually pop, plays from about 10 pm to 1 am on Tuesday through Saturday in the summer. Open mic nights are extremely popular, as is the dance floor—expect it to be packed. ⊠ *53 Front St., Hamilton* ☎ *441/295–2263* ⊕ *www.thepickledonion.com.*

★ Port O' Call

WINE BARS—NIGHTLIFE | While this restaurant is known for its elegant interior and modern take on European fare, on Friday nights this is where the after-work crowd goes to unwind with a glass of wine before heading along Front Street for a late-night bar crawl. The international wine list has abundant choices. ⊠ *87 Front St., Hamilton* ☎ *441/295–5373* ⊕ *www.portocall.bm.*

Robin Hood

BARS/PUBS | Casual, friendly Robin Hood is popular for inexpensive pub fare, pizza, and beer served on the patio under the stars. There's almost always something sports related on the TV, and a late-night snack menu is served until 11 pm. A quiz competition on Tuesday nights focuses on general knowledge and entertainment themes; the ever-popular beer pong tournaments and live music are also worth the short walk from Front Street. ⊠ *25 Richmond Rd., Hamilton* ☎ *441/295–3314* ⊕ *www.robinhood.bm.*

Yours Truly

BARS/PUBS | For a sophisticated nightlife experience, it's worth seeking out the dimly lit, speakeasy-style Yours Truly. The location of this bar is meant to be a little more difficult to find (there's no sign, and you ring a doorbell to enter), but once inside you'll appreciate the eclectic, expertly handcrafted cocktail offerings prepared using house-made syrups, bitters, and infused liquors. Just

don't expect a bar scene; there is only table service, lending the evening a more upscale vibe. ⊠ *2 Chancery La., Hamilton* ☎ *441/295–0429* ⊕ *www.yourstruly.bm.*

MUSIC AND DANCE CLUBS

Bermuda Folk Club

MUSIC CLUBS | Known for its open mic nights, the Bermuda Folk Club also has other events and venues that change, so it's worth checking the website for specifics and locations before you visit. Note that musicians might perform any number of musical styles besides folk, including blues and acoustic. ⊕ *www.bermudafolkclub.com.*

Cosmopolitan Ultra Lounge & Nightclub

BARS/PUBS | Cosmo is a chic addition to Hamilton's eclectic party scene. Whether it's Mid-Week Madness or Full Moon Saturday, this spot attracts a crowd that likes to dance. Ascend a red-carpeted flight of stairs into a modern lounge and order a drink from the sleek bar. ⊠ *95 Front St., Hamilton* ☎ *441/705–2582.*

🎭 Performing Arts

Bermudians are proud of their cultural offerings and incredibly supportive of the arts. From street festivals to dance and theater performances, this area is where you will find most of the performing arts on the island.

★ Harbour Nights

CULTURAL FESTIVALS | **FAMILY** | Every Wednesday night in summer Front Street in Hamilton hosts a free street festival featuring Bermudian artists, crafts, Gombey dancers, and face painting. Harbour Nights encompasses most of Hamilton: Front Street and Queen Street are closed to traffic, stores stay open later, and throngs of locals and visitors alike sample local art stalls, bouncy castles and rides, food vendors, and live music. It's a great time to try local cuisine like fish cakes, fresh fish, fried chicken, meat pies, and Portuguese deep-fried

doughnuts. ■TIP→ **Make dinner reservations at a restaurant with a balcony overlooking Front Street for a bird's-eye view of the action (the Terrace and the Pickled Onion are very popular).** ⊠ *Front St., Hamilton.*

DANCE
Bermuda Civic Ballet
DANCE | Since 1972, the Bermuda Civic Ballet has fostered dance education on the island through its acclaimed summer dance program. Along with performances, the Civic has brought talented international choreographers and instructors to the island to work with aspiring local dancers over the years. The company's most important performances of the year are during the summer months, when internationally known artists sometimes appear as guests. Showtimes and venues vary, so check the website. ⊕ *www. bermudacivicballet.bm.*

National Dance Foundation of Bermuda
DANCE | The foundation funds workshops and develops local dance talent, attracting both local and international students as well as support from Bermuda's most famous resident, actress Catherine Zeta-Jones. Check local events listings for information on upcoming performances. ☎ *441/278–0709.*

Sabor Dance School
DANCE | Feel the Latin beat with group classes in salsa, cha-cha, Argentine tango, and merengue. Bermuda has a thriving salsa scene with classes open to all levels; no experience is necessary. Dancers also show off their fancy footwork at a series of social dancing events across the island; check the website for more info. ⊠ *Old Berkeley School, 23 Berkeley Rd., Hamilton* ☎ *441/337–2267* ⊕ *www.bermudasalsa.com.*

United Dance Productions
DANCE | Every style of dance is taught to adults and children at this popular dance school. Performances are held at various venues throughout the year, including annual recitals in June. Shows include ballet, modern, hip-hop, and also musical theater. ⊠ *Alexandrina Hall, 75 Court St., Hamilton* ☎ *441/232–9933* ⊕ *www. uniteddanceproductions.com.*

FILM
Speciality Cinema & Grill
FILM | Across the street from City Hall, the Speciality Cinema is Bermuda's most popular two-screen theater. There are usually three showtimes per day per movie. This cinema has a great café out front selling hot food, snacks, and baked goods that you can eat during the movie. Lots of 3-D movies are shown here. ⊠ *11 Church St., Hamilton* ☎ *441/292–2135* ⊕ *www.specialitycinema.bm.*

MUSIC
Bermuda School of Music
CONCERTS | The school hosts a number of popular events including guitar and piano festivals, concerts, and the well-attended annual Some Enchanted Evening fund-raising event. Check the website for upcoming performances. ⊠ *23 Berkeley Rd.* ☎ *441/296–5100* ⊕ *www.music-school.bm.*

READINGS AND TALKS
Bermuda National Gallery
READINGS/LECTURES | The gallery often presents a series of lunchtime lectures on art and film in addition to its revolving exhibits. Stop by or call the gallery for a schedule. ⊠ *City Hall, 17 Church St., Hamilton* ☎ *441/295–9428* ⊕ *www. bermudanationalgallery.com.*

THEATER
Bermuda Musical & Dramatic Society
THEATER | Formed in 1944, this active theater society has some good amateur actors on its roster and stages performances year-round at its Daylesford headquarters, one block north of City Hall. The Christmas pantomime is always a sellout, as are most other performances, especially the annual Famous for Fifteen Minutes. Visit or call the box office at Daylesford, on Dundonald

3

City of Hamilton and Pembroke Parish

Gombey Dancers

The Gombey dancer is one of the island's most enduring and uniquely Bermudian cultural icons. The Gombey (pronounced *gum*-bay) tradition here dates from at least the mid-18th century, when enslaved Africans and Native Americans covertly practiced a unique form of dance incorporating West Indian, British, and biblical influences. Nowadays, Gombeys mainly perform on major holidays. The Gombey name originates from a West African word, which means rustic drum. The masked, exclusively male dancers move to the accompaniment of Congolese-style drums and the shrill, whistle-blown commands of the troupe's captain. The dancers' colorful costumes include tall headdresses decorated with peacock feathers and capes covered with intricate embroidery, ribbons, and tiny mirrors.

The Gombey tradition is passed from father to son (some of the dancers are as young as 10 years old), and many of the same families have been involved in Bermuda's troupes for generations. Bermudians are extremely proud of their musical heritage, and the sight of the colorful Gombey troupe's ducking and twirling to the mesmerizing rhythm of the rapid drumbeat is one of the most enchanting spectacles on the island. The Gombeys appear at all major events on the island and are the central element of the Bermuda Day parade. It's traditional for crowds to toss money at the dancers' feet. Gombeys also perform regularly at the Bermuda Harbour Nights event on Front Street in Hamilton. Consult the Visitor Services Centre for other locations.

Street, for reservations and information. ✉ *Daylesford Theatre, 11 Washington St., Hamilton* ☎ *441/292–0848 box office, 441/295–5584 bar telephone* ⊕ *www. bmds.bm.*

Gilbert & Sullivan Society

THEATER | The "G & S" holds big-name theater shows and musicals once or twice a year at City Hall. Bermuda may be a small island, but the talent is amazing; past productions have included *South Pacific, The Full Monty, Jesus Christ Superstar, Oliver!,* and *Animal Farm.* Visit the website to check what's on the calendar. ⊕ *www.gands.bm.*

Hasty Pudding Theatricals

THEATER | Bermuda is the only place outside the United States where Harvard University's Hasty Pudding Theatricals perform. For more than 50 years this satirical troupe has entertained the island

during March or April. Each of these Bermuda-based shows incorporates political and social issues of the past year and is staged at The Earl Cameron Theatre in Hamilton's City Hall. ✉ *City Hall, 17 Church St., Hamilton* ⊕ *www.hastypudding.org.*

VENUES AND SOCIETIES

★ Chewstick

READINGS/LECTURES | Despite a fire that destroyed its headquarters in 2017, Chewstick is still going strong as a community arts organization attracting a diverse crowd of artists. Open mics are still popular, but check the website for upcoming dates and locations as there is currently no permanent space. Anything goes, whether it's music, spoken word, or dance. Chewstick is a great place to mingle with locals. ✉ *Hamilton* ☎ *441/292–2439* ⊕ *www.chewstick.org.*

The Earl Cameron Theatre
ARTS CENTERS | The major venue for quality cultural events in Bermuda, the Earl Cameron Theatre hosts fashion shows, comedic acts, and live music—all hugely popular with locals. ⊠ *City Hall, 17 Church St., Hamilton* ☎ *441/292–1234.*

Rock Island Coffee
ARTS CENTERS | Not only is Rock Island Coffee the unofficial watering hole for Bermuda's eclectic group of artists, but it also doubles as an informal art space. Stop by to find out where all the hip happenings on the island are. ⊠ *48 Reid St., Hamilton* ☎ *441/296–5241* ⊕ *www.rockisland.bm.*

🛍 Shopping

Whether you are shopping for souvenirs, gifts, new clothes, or jewelry, Hamilton is the place to head for all your shopping needs. Hamilton has Bermuda's largest concentration of stores; however, note that some stores are closed on Sunday. The main shopping streets are Front Street and Reid Street, but don't forget to browse all the side streets and alleyways, where some of the best stores are.

ANTIQUES AND COLLECTIBLES
Bermuda Monetary Authority
ANTIQUES/COLLECTIBLES | The agency issues and redeems Bermuda currency, and also oversees financial institutions operating in and through Bermuda. On weekdays at its offices in Hamilton, it sells collectors' coins, including replicas of the old Bermuda "hogge" money of the early 17th century. Cahow, Hawksville turtle, and gold shipwreck coins are among the many other pieces for sale. ⊠ *BMA House, 43 Victoria St., Hamilton* ☎ *441/295–5278* ⊕ *www.bma.bm.*

ART GALLERIES
Bermuda Society of Arts
ART GALLERIES | The island's oldest arts organization has four galleries, and many highly creative society members sell

their work at the perennial members' shows and during special group exhibits. You can find watercolor, oil, and acrylic paintings; pastel and charcoal drawings; and some photographs, collages, and sculptures. Admission is free. ⊠ *City Hall, 17 Church St., 3rd fl. West Wing, Hamilton* ☎ *441/292–3824* ⊕ *www.bsoa.bm.*

Gallery One Seventeen
ART GALLERIES | Former Windjammer Gallery manager Danjou Anderson has created his own purpose-built commercial gallery space showcasing top Bermudian artists. Over 60 artists are represented, including many well-known names such as Otto Trott, Sharon Wilson, and Christopher Marson. ⊠ *117 Front St., Hamilton* ☎ *441/295–1783* ⊕ *www.gallery117bda.com.*

Picturesque Bermuda
ART GALLERIES | Roland Skinner, one of the island's most loved photographers, captures the island's architecture, landscapes, and flora. The Front Street gallery, in the main A. S. Cooper shop, showcases his portfolio, with photos selling from $100 to $800. ⊠ *A. S. Cooper & Sons, 59 Front St., Hamilton* ☎ *441/295–3961* ⊕ *www.ascooper.bm.*

BOOKS
★ Bermuda Book Store
BOOKS/STATIONERY | Owner Hannah Willmott doesn't believe in wasting space, so she crammed as many books as she could into her small bookstore. The shop is known for its cozy atmosphere and is well stocked with best sellers, children's books, and special Bermuda titles (including some out-of-print books), plus diaries and calendars. ⊠ *3 Queen St., Hamilton* ☎ *441/295–3698* ⊕ *bookstore.bm.*

Bookmart
BOOKS/STATIONERY | The island's largest bookstore carries plenty of contemporary titles and classics, plus a complete selection of books on Bermuda. Paperbacks and children's books are here in abundance, as well as a wide selection

of popular beauty, technology, and travel books. The Hallmark store at the front of the shop offers the expected greeting cards, balloons, party supplies, and little gift items. Its café has a balcony overlooking Front Street, perfect for grabbing a sandwich or a drink after a hard day's shopping. ⊠ *Brown & Company, 3 Reid St., Hamilton* ☎ *441/279–5443* ⊕ *www.bookmart.bm.*

CIGARS
House of Cigars: Chatham House

TOBACCO | In business since 1895, this shop looks like an old-time country store. Thick, gray, lusty cigar smoke fills the air, and a life-size statue of a Native American princess greets you as you walk in. You can find top-quality cigars from the Dominican Republic, Jamaica, and Cuba (Romeo y Julieta, Bolivar, Partagas, Punch); briar pipes; tobacco; and Swiss Army knives. ⊠ *63 Front St., Hamilton* ☎ *441/292–8422.*

CLOTHING
CHILDREN'S CLOTHING
Blukids

CLOTHING | FAMILY | The Italian brand's affordable clothing line for children (newborn up to size 14 for boys and girls) is surprisingly high quality for the prices. Styles are modern and practical and always on trend. Some of the standouts in the line include clothing featuring popular characters such as Spiderman, Hello Kitty, and Mickey Mouse. ⊠ *Washington Mall, 12 Reid St., Hamilton* ☎ *441/292–5065.*

Pirates Port

CLOTHING | FAMILY | The store is small and crowded, but it has bargains on casual clothing for girls and boys from toddlers to teens. There's also a Pirates Port women's wear store on the lower level of the Washington Mall. ⊠ *Washington Mall, upper level, 7 Reid St., Hamilton* ☎ *441/292–1080.*

Time of Your Life 👜

While shopping on Reid Street in Hamilton, glance up and admire a famous city landmark hanging from the Phoenix Centre. The clock was imported from Boston in 1893 by watchmaker Duncan Doe. When you're at the Clocktower Mall in Dockyard, you'll notice the clocks on the two 100-foot towers tell different times. This isn't an error; one was installed to show the actual time and the other the time of the high tide.

MEN'S CLOTHING
A. S. Cooper Man

DEPARTMENT STORES | The menswear division of the classy department store is first-rate, with staff who are reserved and courteous but very helpful when needed. It is full of men's casual and dress clothes, plus accessories such as belts and wallets. The store is the exclusive Bermuda supplier of Polo Ralph Lauren. It also stocks brands such as Lacoste, Tommy Bahama, Perry Ellis, Izod, and Helly Hansen. ⊠ *29 Front St., Hamilton* ☎ *441/295–3961.*

Coral Coast Clothing

CLOTHING | After quitting their jobs in the financial sector, the two locals behind this label knew they wanted to make the perfect button-down men's shirt for the Bermuda lifestyle. It had to fit well and look professional in the boardroom but also easily transition to a more casual beach or dockside dinner. The shirts come in colorful hues and prints; all bear a signature angelfish logo. Also check out the duo's take on Bermuda shorts that pair perfectly with their shirts, as well as the label's hats, belts, socks, and swimwear. ⊠ *15 Front St., Hamilton* ☎ *441/400–5030* ⊕ *www.coralcoastclothing.com.*

Bermuda Shorts in the Office

You may have heard of Bermuda's unique business fashion, and you may have seen pictures of businessmen in shorts and long socks, but nothing can quite prepare you for the first sighting. After all, where else could a businessman walk into a boardroom wearing bright-pink shorts without anyone batting an eyelid? Only in Bermuda. These unique, all-purpose garments, however flamboyantly dyed, are worn with seriousness and pride. Bermudians would go so far as to say it's the rest of the world that is peculiar, and they have a point—particularly in the steaming humidity of the summer months.

What is surprising is how the original khaki cutoffs evolved into formal attire. They were introduced to Bermuda in the early 1900s by the British military, who adopted the belted, baggy, cotton-twill version to survive the sweltering outposts of the empire. By the 1920s Bermudian pragmatism and innovation were at play as locals started chopping off their trousers at the knees to stay cool. Tailors seized on the trend and started manufacturing a smarter pair of shorts, and men were soon discovering the benefits of a breeze around the knees.

But for an island that has a love affair with rules, there was always going to be a right and a wrong way to wear this new uniform. Bermudas had to be worn with knee-high socks, and a jacket and tie were the only acceptable way of dressing them up for business. But it didn't stop there. Obsession with detail prevailed, fueled by gentlemen who were disturbed at the unseemly shortness of other men's shorts. A law was passed to ensure propriety, and the result was patrolling policemen, armed with tape measures and warning tickets, scouring the capital for men showing too much leg. Officially, shorts could be no more than 6 inches above the knee, although 2 to 4 was preferable.

Other rigid but unwritten rules made it unheard-of to wear them in hotel dining rooms after 6 pm or in churches on Sunday morning, and even to this day they are out of bounds in the Supreme Court, although in 2000 legislation was changed to allow them to be worn, even by ministers, in the House of Assembly. Nowadays Bermudians still wear their colorful Bermuda shorts with pride, and while many still opt for the traditional look paired with a tie and knee-high socks, others keep it casual with a polo shirt and a pair of Docksides.

But if Bermuda shorts are practical dress for men, where does that leave the island's women during the sticky summer months? While you will see many women wearing brightly colored dresses and skirts when the heat is on, tailored updates to women's Bermuda shorts styles have made it acceptable for women to wear shorts even in business settings.

Sports Source

CLOTHING | Popular with locals, Sports Source offers men's and youth's urban wear and hip-hop gear. The labels are trendy, but the prices are reasonable. There's also a good selection of sneakers, football jerseys, and shorts. The store has another location at 49 Middle Road, Warwick. ⊠ *Washington Mall, Reid St., Hamilton* ☎ *441/292–9442.*

MEN'S AND WOMEN'S CLOTHING

The Booth

CLOTHING | Named after owner Darren Booth, this shop sells a good selection of luggage as well as trendy brands including DC shoes, G-Shock watches, and jackets by Helly Hansen and North Face. It also stocks skateboards and backpacks. ⊠ *51 Reid St., Hamilton* ☎ *441/296–5353.*

★ Calypso

CLOTHING | Bermuda's fashionable set comes to this boutique to spend on sophisticated designer wear such as Eileen Fisher. Calypso has the island's largest selection of swimwear, including Vilebrequin. Pick up a straw hat and sunglasses to make the perfect beach ensemble. Eclectic novelty items from Europe make great gifts, too. Calypso's sister shop in Butterfield Place, Voila!, carries Longchamp handbags and Johnston & Murphy men's shoes. There are branches at the Fairmont Southampton Resort and at Clocktower Mall at Dockyard. ⊠ *45 Front St., Hamilton* ☎ *441/295–2112* ⊕ *www.calypso.bm.*

English Sports Shop

CLOTHING | This shop specializes in knitwear, but walk through the front door and you can't miss the selection of colorful Bermuda shorts and knee-high socks. Upstairs there's a good supply of men's business and formal wear and children's clothes. Menswear and suits are from Alexandre of London, Hugo Boss, and Michael Kors. Women's clothing and accessories are at the back of the store on the ground level. There are branches

at Fairmont Southampton Resort, in Somerset Village, and on Water Street in St. George's. ⊠ *49 Front St., Hamilton* ☎ *441/295–2672.*

FH Boutique

CLOTHING | In the Hamilton Princess & Beach Club, FH Boutique curates high-end and dressy island wear "For Him" and "For Her." There's a selection of upmarket international labels including perfectly tailored Thomas Pink shirts and clothing and accessories from Elie Tahari, as well as jewelry and clothing from local designers and vendors. In the same retail arcade is sister store Resort Life + Style shop with a focus on casual resort wear and swimwear as well as boat-friendly SWIMS shoes. Between both stores, you will find all you need to put together the perfect island outfit. ⊠ *Hamilton Princess & Beach Club, 76 Pitts Bay Rd., Hamilton* ☎ *441/298–6095* ⊕ *luxury.bm/fh.*

French Connection

CLOTHING | This chic urban-wear shop carries trendy skirts, pants, tops, and accessories for day and night. Women's clothing is on the ground level and men's is on the lower level. Follow the locals to the 50%–75% end-of-season sales. ⊠ *15 Reid St., Hamilton* ☎ *441/295–2112* ⊕ *www.calypso.bm.*

Jeans Express

CLOTHING | If you didn't pack denim for those cool Bermuda evening breezes, then this store—crammed with every style of Levi's—is the place to go. All shapes and sizes are catered to, and—with no sales tax—prices are comparable to the United States (or cheaper). The store also sells Dockers casual clothing. ⊠ *30 Queen St., Hamilton* ☎ *441/295–0084.*

Makin' Waves

CLOTHING | Casual clothing and swimsuits by big-name brands Roxy, Billabong, O'Neill, Reef, and Quicksilver are sold at this beachy shop. There are plenty of shorts, T-shirts, and summer dresses to

choose from, and surf gear is a specialty. You can also take your pick from Oakley sunglasses, beach bags, hats, flip-flops, water shoes, and snorkeling and dive gear. There's another store on Camber Road in Dockyard. ⊠ *11 Church St., Hamilton* ✢ *At the junction of Church St. and Wesley St.* ☎ *441/292–4609* ⊕ *www. makinwaves.bm.*

Stefanel

CLOTHING | With clothes for men and women, this long-running fashion brand brings the very latest in quality Italian-made casual, business, and dress wear, made of primarily natural fibers in neutral colors. The shop also stocks brands from its sister store Mambo, including True Religion. ⊠ *12 Reid St., Hamilton* ☎ *441/295–5698.*

★ TABS

CLOTHING | Designed by Bermudian Rebecca Singleton, TABS (which stands for The Authentic Bermuda Shorts) offers the quintessential Bermuda short for men, women, and children in modern fits and fabrics. The cotton-twill and cotton-linen shorts are lined with fun prints and available in island-inspired colors, such as oleander pink, loquat yellow, and lagoon green. You can have your shorts customized with a word or letters embroidered on the inside fly of the shorts (it takes two weeks, but you can have them shipped to you). Tailored swim shorts, limited-edition collections, and accessories (traditional Bermuda socks) are also available. The Reid Street store also stocks jewelry designed by local Rebecca Little. ⊠ *Walker Arcade, 12 Reid St., Hamilton* ☎ *441/704–8227* ⊕ *www. tabsbermuda.com.*

27th Century Boutique

CLOTHING | Khakis, polo shirts, and dress shirts predominate in this boutique's sizable men's section, and women can find colorful dresses, sparkly tank tops, and great-fitting black pants alongside office-appropriate blouses. Owner Sharon Bartram can help you assemble a perfect outfit—she has an excellent eye for style and detail. ⊠ *92 Reid St., Hamilton* ☎ *441/292–2628.*

Vineyard Vines

CLOTHING | The shop known for its iconic pink whale logo brought its first overseas outpost to Bermuda in 2016. Both men's and women's clothing can be found here, with plenty of the well-known pastels and preppy prints. The exclusive Bermuda-branded items make this store worth a stop, though. It's in department store A. S. Cooper. ⊠ *27 Front St., Hamilton* ☎ *441/278–3445* ⊕ *www.ascooper.bm.*

WOMEN'S CLOTHING
Atelerie

CLOTHING | A boutique that wouldn't feel out of place in a stylish New York City neighborhood, Atelerie carries designer labels such as Diane von Furstenburg, Cynthia Vincent, and Helmut Lang in this beautifully designed space. The selection of jewelry may be the highlight here. Layer up with long chains from GINETTE NY and brightly colored gemstone earrings from Coralia Leets. ⊠ *9 Reid St., Hamilton* ☎ *441/296–0280* ⊕ *www. atelerie.com.*

Benetton

CLOTHING | This branch of the Italian brand has a wide variety of casual-chic women's and children's clothing, in brash, bright colors and more subdued tones. Head upstairs when there's a sale: you can pick up amazing deals on well-made, trendy clothes for kids. ⊠ *24 Reid St., Hamilton* ☎ *441/295–2112* ⊕ *www. calypso.bm.*

Boutique C.C

CLOTHING | Owned by the English Sports Shop, the store sells quality casual and work wear for women of every age, but the highlight is the selection of evening wear. Look for reasonably priced cocktail dresses along with stylish contemporary separates and trendy accessories. ⊠ *1 Front St., Hamilton* ☎ *441/295–3935.*

Eve's Garden Lingerie

CLOTHING | Silk and satin panties, boxers, brassieres, and nightgowns, in sizes small to full figure, are tucked away in this discreet shop at the back of the Emporium Building. You can also find massage oils and an adult section. The store houses the Bra Boutique, which sells a wide range of top-quality lingerie for all shapes and sizes. ⊠ *Emporium Bldg., 69 Front St., Hamilton* ☎ *441/296–2671.*

Jazzy Boutique

CLOTHING | Purses, faux-gem jewelry, Spandex, jeans, and colorful accessories lure shoppers looking for the latest in urban fashion to this affordable store. There are also good selections of shoes and plus-size options. ⊠ *Washington Mall, 7 Reid St., Hamilton* ☎ *441/295–9258.*

Max Mara

CLOTHING | Prices for this Italian designer's clothing average about 20% less in Bermuda than in the United States, although the accessories sell at much the same as U.S. prices. The boutique is much smaller than its counterpart on Madison Avenue, but it still has a good selection of conservative casual wear and evening attire. You'll find the labels Max Mara, SportMax, and Studio. ⊠ *57 Front St., Hamilton* ☎ *441/295–2112* ⊕ *www. calypso.bm.*

Modblu

CLOTHING | Featuring popular names in women's clothing and jewelry and a mix of casual and dressy pieces, this bright, airy addition to the Bermuda shopping scene offers a positive love-yourself vibe with its flattering and stylish selections. Shoppers will find breezier items from Raga, denim and trendier pieces from Blank NYC, and dresses from Cooper & Ella. Local designers here include jewelry label Airy Heights. The shop also stocks a small selection of handbags and sunglasses from designers such as Quay Australia. ⊠ *46 Reid St., Hamilton*

☎ *441/405–3250* ⊕ *www.modblubermuda.com.*

Revelation Boutique

CLOTHING | Cool, contemporary linen and cotton clothing is the focus of Paulette Wedderburn's shop, which also has an impressive collection of formal wear. ⊠ *27 Queen St., Hamilton* ☎ *441/296–4252.*

Sisley

CLOTHING | Follow the trendsetters to this store to get your hands on the latest women's fashions including suits, party dresses, and casual basics. A sister store to Benetton, Sisley is known for its edgy, contemporary designs with feminine flair. ⊠ *Front St., Hamilton* ✛ *Corner of Par-La-Ville Rd.* ☎ *441/295–2112* ⊕ *www. calypso.bm.*

Women'secret

CLOTHING | The Spanish brand offers a good range of fun and feminine underwear, lingerie, nightwear, loungewear, sportswear, and swimwear. ⊠ *14 Reid St., Hamilton* ☎ *441/295–2112* ⊕ *www. calypso.bm.*

COSMETICS AND BEAUTY

M.A.C. Cosmetics

PERFUME/COSMETICS | This chic store of the popular M.A.C. Cosmetics brand has every beauty, makeup, and skin-care product you could ever want. Its trained makeup artists offer walk-in makeovers. ⊠ *53 Front St., Hamilton* ☎ *441/295–8843* ⊕ *www.gibbons.bm.*

The Perfume Shop

PERFUME/COSMETICS | In addition to being the exclusive Bermuda agent for Guerlain's complete line of cosmetics and skin-care products, the Perfume Shop boutique stocks perfume, soap, lotions, and bubble bath. It's also the island's exclusive seller of Chanel and Dior makeup. There's a branch in the Clocktower Mall in Dockyard, and in St. George's this is the Bermuda Island Shop on Water Street. ⊠ *Gibbons Co. Perfume*

Department, 21 Reid St., Hamilton
☎ 441/295–0022 ⊕ www.gibbons.bm.

DEPARTMENT STORES

A. S. Cooper & Sons

DEPARTMENT STORES | Cooper's is best known for its extensive inventory of crystal and china, with pieces and sets by Waterford, Wedgwood, Villeroy & Boch, and Portmeirion, many sold at 15% to 20% less than U.S. prices. The store also carries tasteful Bermudian souvenirs, jewelry, fragrances, and cosmetics on the ground level. Brands on sale include Estée Lauder, Clinique, Clarins, Bobbi Brown, Lancôme, and Elizabeth Arden. The main store also carries its private-label clothing collection for women and a ladies' sportswear department, which carries Calvin Klein, Ralph Lauren, DKNY Jeans, Jones New York, and Nic and Zoe. There are several branches, including one at the Fairmont Southampton Resort and in Dockyard. Cooper's also owns Astwood Dickinson jewelry stores and the Bermuda outpost of Vineyard Vines, which carries specially branded items only found in the Bermuda store. ⊠ 59 Front St., Hamilton ☎ 441/295–3961 ⊕ www.ascooper.bm.

Brown & Co.

DEPARTMENT STORES | Although there are several standout sections in this sprawling store, including a perfume department, home decor, and a fun assortment of upscale Bermuda-inspired gifts and trinkets, it's now also the location of the Body Shop and sells a large range of its natural and ethically produced products. Look for the deliciously scented body butters and the popular gift sets. ⊠ 35 Front St., Hamilton ☎ 441/279–5442.

★ Gibbons Co.

DEPARTMENT STORES | One of Bermuda's oldest retailers (still run by the Gibbons family) has transformed itself into a contemporary department store with a wide range of men's, women's, and children's clothing. Brands include Calvin Klein, Mango, and DKNY, and there's a substantial lingerie selection, as well as Gap clothing and products, active and swimwear, accessories, and fashion jewelry. The perfume and cosmetics department stocks many French, Italian, English, and American lines at duty-free prices. The housewares department is the exclusive supplier of Denby tableware, which sells at a much lower price than in Canada or the United States. The shoe department stocks brands including Nine West, TOMS, and Anne Klein. Gibbons also owns and operates a separate store, in the nearby Washington Mall, that sells bed, bath, and home decor; M.A.C. Cosmetics on Front Street; and the perfume stores in Dockyard and St. George's. ⊠ 21 Reid St., Hamilton ☎ 441/295–0022 ⊕ www.gibbons.bm.

Marks & Spencer

DEPARTMENT STORES | A franchise of the large British chain, Marks and Sparks (as it's called by everyone in Bermuda and England) is usually filled with locals attracted by its moderate prices for men's, women's, and children's clothing. Summer wear, including swimsuits, cotton jerseys, and polo shirts, is a good buy, as is underwear—but don't forget everything is in U.K. sizes rather than U.S. The chain's signature line of food and treats, plus wine from all over the world, is tucked away at the back of the store. ⊠ 18 Reid St., Hamilton ☎ 441/295–0031.

ELECTRONICS

iClick

CAMERAS/ELECTRONICS | The latest Apple gadgets and accessories are crammed into this large store. A full-service center is also available with technicians on hand to help if you get pink sand in your phone. ⊠ 20 Reid St., Hamilton ☎ 441/278–1330 ⊕ www.ptech.bm/iclick.

FOOD

ABC Natural Foods

FOOD/CANDY | ABC is filled with mostly vegan and lacto-ovo food options, but you can also find natural beauty and body products as well as a vegan café

inside the shop where you can grab a refreshing smoothie. It's housed beside the Seventh Day Adventist Church in the City of Hamilton. ⊠ *41 King St., Hamilton* ☎ *441/292–4111.*

Arnold's Family Market

FOOD/CANDY | Close to several centrally located guesthouses, this grocery store in Pembroke Parish is always open, even on public holidays. The Arnold's Express store in Hamilton—on Front Street—is open until midnight. ⊠ *113 St. John's Rd.* ☎ *441/292–3310.*

Down to Earth Health Food

FOOD/CANDY | This natural-food and health shop sells everything from tea and supplements to organic body products and home cleaners. Don't leave without grabbing a fruit smoothie or a vegetable juice from the bar in the corner. There's seating on the porch. ⊠ *56 Reid St., Hamilton* ☎ *441/292–5639.*

Esso City Tiger Market

FOOD/CANDY | Day or night, this gas station sells a good range of fast food and sandwiches, as well as cigarettes, hot drinks, chips, soda, and aspirin. This is the only true 24-hour place on the island. ⊠ *37 Richmond Rd., Hamilton* ☎ *441/295–3776.*

MarketPlace

FOOD/CANDY | The island's largest grocery store and the chain's headquarters, MarketPlace offers homemade hot soups, stir-fries, salads, dinners, and desserts for about $8 a pound. It's the place locals go for a quick takeout lunch; many are drawn by the healthy-eating and organic sections. ⊠ *Church St., Hamilton* ✛ *Near Parliament St.* ☎ *441/295–6006* ⊕ *www. marketplace.bm.*

Miles Market

FOOD/CANDY | Think of Miles as the Balducci's of Bermuda, with a large selection of upscale or hard-to-find specialty food items. The deli encompasses the finest imported and local meats and fish. There's also a mouthwatering range

of pastries, cakes, and Godiva chocolates. Many items are on the expensive side, but the quality and selection are without rival. The supermarket delivers anywhere on the island. ⊠ *96 Pitts Bay Rd., Hamilton* ✛ *Near Hamilton Princess & Beach Club* ☎ *441/295–1234* ⊕ *www. miles.bm.*

Rock On–The Health Store

FOOD/CANDY | Nutritional supplements, sports supplements, diet books, natural teas and remedies, and environmentally friendly toiletries are among the goods offered. The biggest sellers, though, are probably its protein shakes and bars. The staff is knowledgeable and friendly. ⊠ *Butterfield Place, 67 Front St., Hamilton* ☎ *441/295–3468.*

The Supermart

FOOD/CANDY | English products, including the Waitrose brand, are the specialties of this grocery store. You can pick up a picnic lunch at the well-stocked salad-and-hot-food bar. A smaller branch, Somers Supermart, is in St. George's. ⊠ *125 Front St., Hamilton* ✛ *Between Court and King Sts.* ☎ *441/292–2064* ⊕ *www. supermart.bm.*

JEWELRY AND ACCESSORIES

★ Alexandra Mosher Studio Jewellery

JEWELRY/ACCESSORIES | After her line of elegant pink-sand-inspired jewelry took off at craft markets and Harbour Nights, artist Alexandra Mosher opened up a light and airy store to showcase her beautiful designs. The shop is as much a work of art as her jewelry, with a pink-sand-beach-inspired mosaic at the entrance of the store designed by local artist Nikki Murray-Mason. Mosher's designs grace the necks, wrists, and fingers of locals and visitors alike; look no further for the perfect souvenir of time spent in Bermuda. There's a smaller, equally beautifully designed outpost in the Washington Mall. ⊠ *5 Front St., Hamilton* ✛ *Corner of Par-La-Ville Rd.* ☎ *441/236–9009* ⊕ *www.alexandramosher.com.*

Astwood Dickinson

JEWELRY/ACCESSORIES | Established in 1904, this store has built a reputation for its exquisite unmounted stones; upscale jewelry, including designs by Cartier and Hearts on Fire; and a wide range of Swiss watches. Baume & Mercier, Omega, and Tag Heuer watches, among other famous names, are sold at U.S. prices with the benefit of no sales tax. The shop's Bermuda Collection, designed and created in the workshop, ranges from 18-karat gold charms to bejeweled pendants representing the island's flora and fauna. There's also a location in the retail arcade at the Hamilton Princess & Beach Club. ⊠ *Orbis House, 25 Front St., Hamilton* ☎ *441/292–5805* ⊕ *www. ascooper.bm.*

Atlantic Jewellery Studio

JEWELRY/ACCESSORIES | Stocked to the brim with brightly colored baubles, Atlantic Jewellery has many handcrafted statement pieces. Find necklaces, bracelets, earrings, and chunky rings featuring every variation of colorful gemstones. ⊠ *Washington Mall, 7 Reid St., lower level, Hamilton* ☎ *441/542–1554* ⊕ *www. atlanticjewellery.com.*

Crisson Jewellers

JEWELRY/ACCESSORIES | The only store in Bermuda carrying Rolex, Crisson's attracts well-heeled customers who come here to buy merchandise at U.S. prices with no sales tax. The shop also carries an extensive selection of David Yurman, and there is an in-store Pandora store selling a large selection of charms and jewelry. Earrings are a specialty, and there's a large selection, as well as a handful of gold bangles and beads. There are smaller branches at the Fairmont Southampton Resort and Dockyard's Clocktower Mall. ⊠ *55 Front St., Hamilton* ☎ *441/295–2351* ⊕ *www.crisson. com.*

E. R. Aubrey

JEWELRY/ACCESSORIES | Gold, sapphires, colored pearls, and tanzanite (a rare gemstone) are the specialties of this Hamilton jeweler. The store also carries a large selection of certified diamonds and promises to match prices as long as they can be verified. There are additional locations on Queen Street and in Dockyard's Clocktower Mall. ⊠ *101 Front St., Hamilton* ☎ *441/296–3171.*

Everrich Jewelry

JEWELRY/ACCESSORIES | This bargain jewelry store stocks countless styles of basic gold and silver chains, earrings, bangles, and rings. ⊠ *28 Queen St., Hamilton* ☎ *441/295–2110.*

Gem Cellar

JEWELRY/ACCESSORIES | Jewelers here make Bermuda-themed charms selling for $65 and up, including charms with the longtail national bird, the hog penny coin, and a Gombey dancer. They can also produce custom-designed gold and silver jewelry in two to three days. ⊠ *Walker Arcade, 47 Front St., Hamilton* ☎ *441/292–3042.*

1609 Design

JEWELRY/ACCESSORIES | The store is known for its Bermuda-made and Bermuda-inspired designs including delicate necklaces—perfect for layering—with gems in soothing tropical palettes, gemstone bracelets, and a selection of pretty earrings from artist Joanna Stapff. It's also a great resource for handmade cards and canvas bags or coasters printed with Bermuda scenes. ⊠ *Old Cellar La., 47 Front St., Hamilton* ☎ *441/336–1326.*

Sunglass & Watch Shop

JEWELRY/ACCESSORIES | Come here for trendy watches from G-Shock and Dolce & Gabbana, as well as many other brands. The shop expanded to create room for one of the island's best selections of sunglasses—Prada, Gucci, Marc Jacobs, and Ray-Ban, to name a few. It's

also a good place for watch repairs and battery or strap replacements. ⊠ *13 Reid St., Hamilton* ☎ *441/292–7933* ⊕ *www.sunglassandwatchshop.bm.*

Swiss Timing

JEWELRY/ACCESSORIES | Head here for watches, clocks, and jewelry from across Europe, including items from Germany, England, and Italy. The store has a great range of engagement rings, earrings, necklaces, and bracelets, and you can have items custom designed. ⊠ *95 Front St., Hamilton* ☎ *441/295–1376.*

Walker Christopher

JEWELRY/ACCESSORIES | Here you can work with a jeweler to design your own exclusive piece or choose from classic diamond bands, strands of South Sea pearls, and the more contemporary hand-hammered chokers. The workshop also produces a line of Bermuda-inspired gold jewelry and sterling silver Christmas ornaments. ⊠ *9 Front St., Hamilton* ☎ *441/295–1466* ⊕ *www.walkerchristopher.com.*

MUSIC

The Music Box

MUSIC STORES | This independent shop is crammed full of all sorts of musical items from guitars to stereos and other electronics. Inside is a diverse collection of new CDs and DVDs, as well as CD/DVD players and accessories. A handful of music books are for sale. ⊠ *58 Reid St., Hamilton* ☎ *441/295–4839.*

Sound Stage

MUSIC STORES | Small but fairly comprehensive, Sound Stage stocks new-release, mainstream CDs and DVDs. All genres of music are covered. ⊠ *Washington Mall, 20 Church St., upper level, Hamilton* ☎ *441/292–0811.*

NOVELTIES AND GIFTS

&Partners

GIFTS/SOUVENIRS | Scandinavian and Scandinavian-inspired gifts are the highlight of this boutique focused on contemporary style. Along with sleek home accessories

---

In a Former Life 🛍

It may be hard to believe, but the shops at Old Cellar Lane, such as 1609 Design, used to be stables, sheltering horses and carriages for patrons of local businesses in a sort of municipal "parking lot."

---

from HAY and Skultana and jewelry from MoMA Design Store, the shop also champions local artists. Look for Catherine White's Bermuda-inspired prints and ropework doormats and Chris Cabral's key fobs, as well as jewelry from local designer Rebecca Little. ⊠ *46 Par-La-Ville Rd., Hamilton* ☎ *441/296–5250* ⊕ *www.andpartnersbermuda.com.*

Flying Colours

GIFTS/SOUVENIRS | The family-owned and -operated shop, established in 1937, has the island's largest selection of T-shirts, with creatively designed logos in hundreds of styles. It also carries everything for the beach—hats, towels, sarongs, flip-flops, sunglasses, toys for playing in the sand—plus high-quality souvenirs and gifts, like shell jewelry. ⊠ *5 Queen St., Hamilton* ☎ *441/295–0890* ⊕ *www.flyingcolours.bm.*

Hodge Podge

GIFTS/SOUVENIRS | Cluttered and small, this little shop just around the corner from the Ferry Terminal and Visitor Services Centre offers pretty much what its name implies: postcards, sunblock, sunglasses, and T-shirts. ⊠ *3 Point Pleasant Rd., Hamilton* ☎ *441/295–0647.*

The Irish Linen Shop

HOUSEHOLD ITEMS/FURNITURE | With stock from all over the world, this home decor shop carries fine table and bed linens. There is also a small selection of furniture along with an exclusive range of gifts from Michael Aram, Mariposa,

and Cire Trudon. ✉ *31 Front St., Hamilton* ☎ *441/295–4089.*

★ The Island Shop
CRAFTS | Brightly colored island-theme artwork for ceramics, linens, and pillows is designed by owner Barbara Finsness. A number of her original watercolors are available for purchase. She also stocks the store with cedar-handle handbags embroidered with Bermuda buildings, shell napkin rings, plates, monogrammed guest towels, rugs, chunky jewelry, and elegant gifts, as well as candles and bath products. There are also branches at Somers Wharf, St. George's, and at the Fairmont Southampton resort. ✉ *3 Queen St., Hamilton* ☎ *441/292–5292* ⊕ *www.islandexports.com.*

Pulp & Circumstance
GIFTS/SOUVENIRS | If it's an original, quality gift you're after, look no further. There are modern picture frames in all shapes and sizes, photo albums, ceramics, candles, bath products, and gifts for babies. The store also carries a great selection of greeting cards and other stationery items. ✉ *4 Washington La., Hamilton* ☎ *441/542–9586.*

Treats
GIFTS/SOUVENIRS | **FAMILY** | You can find bulk candy in just about every flavor here, but the greatest draws to this tiny store are the fun, seasonal gifts and cute baby toys. Look out for the educational and science toys. There's also a selection of wooden toys, board games, and LEGO products. ✉ *Washington Mall, 7 Reid St., lower level, Hamilton* ☎ *441/296–1123.*

Urban Cottage
GIFTS/SOUVENIRS | What started out as a warehouse of Bermuda and world treasures collected by store owner Nicole Golden has turned into a Front Street boutique with a wide selection of housewares, jewelry, gifts, and clothing. The shop still has the distressed patina of a warehouse and continues to show-case Bermuda treasures such as old

road signs. Keep an eye out for pillows and cards by local company NettleInk, and take home a selection of teas from Bermuda-based NovelTea. ✉ *11 Front St., Hamilton* ☎ *441/599–0038.*

PHOTO EQUIPMENT
P-Tech
CAMERAS/ELECTRONICS | Point-and-shoot digital cameras, SLR cameras, digital photo frames, camcorders, and other small electronics such as iPod docking stations and tech accessories are all here. Brands to look for are Nikon, Canon, and Olympus. There's also a small photo department on the corner of Church and Queen streets with self-service photo booths as well as a full-service photo lab. ✉ *2 Reid St., Hamilton* ☎ *441/295–5496* ⊕ *www.ptech.bm.*

SHOES AND HANDBAGS
Boyle, W. J. & Son Ltd.
SHOES/LUGGAGE/LEATHER GOODS | Bermuda's leading footwear chain sells a wide range of men's, women's, and children's shoes. The Trends location at 22 Reid Street in Hamilton has the most up-to-the-minute foot fashions, although the Sports Locker location on Queen Street in Hamilton has a good stock of running shoes and a wide range of fashion sneakers such as Converse and Keds. The store at 70 Church Street specializes in children's shoes. There are also locations on Water Street in St. George's and in Somerset Village. ✉ *Boyle's Bldg., 31 Queen St., Hamilton* ☎ *441/295–1887.*

Connections Shoes
SHOES/LUGGAGE/LEATHER GOODS | Bright neon hues and funky styles dominate the selection of shoes at this store. Look for on-trend, reasonably priced sandals and sneakers, as well as a wall of brightly colored accessories. ✉ *5 Burnaby St., Hamilton* ☎ *441/296–4883.*

The Harbourmaster
SHOES/LUGGAGE/LEATHER GOODS | Kipling luggage and bags, among other brands, are sold at this store, which prides

itself on having "everything pertaining to travel." Wallets, handbags, and gifts round out the stock. ✉ *Washington Mall, 7 Reid St., lower level, Hamilton* ☎ *441/295–5333.*

Heel Quik

SHOES/LUGGAGE/LEATHER GOODS | Local shoes-in-distress swear by the friendly expert same-day service at Heel Quik. The store also cuts keys and carries shoe-care products and umbrellas. ✉ *Washington Mall, 7 Reid St., upper level, Hamilton* ☎ *441/295–1559.*

Island Sole

SHOES/LUGGAGE/LEATHER GOODS | Opened in 2012 by two podiatrists, Island Sole believes that fashion and comfort can meet in a shoe. The shop is stocked with all manner of shoes from flip-flops by Telic to comfortable high heels. Casual and dress shoes are available for both men and women. ✉ *26 Church St., Hamilton* ☎ *441/292–4523.*

★ Lusso

SHOES/LUGGAGE/LEATHER GOODS | The ultimate island boutique for designer footwear for men and women stocks shoes from Ferragamo, Jimmy Choo, and Fendi. The shop merged with sister shop Cecile, and the ready-to-wear collections include Emilio Pucci, Missoni, and Marchesa. The real standout is the selection of Lily Pulitzer as well as swim collections from Gottex and Manual Canovas. ✉ *51 Front St., Hamilton* ☎ *441/295–6734.*

The Shoe Centre

SHOES/LUGGAGE/LEATHER GOODS | The store is a short distance from the shops of Front and Reid streets, but well worth the walk if you want a bargain. There's a good selection of men's, women's and children's shoes, with prices starting from about $20. Don't miss the bargain basement on the lower level. ✉ *42 Dundonald St., Hamilton* ☎ *441/292–5078.*

Voilà!

SHOES/LUGGAGE/LEATHER GOODS | Women looking for quirky, snazzy footwear should stop here. The shoe and bag section is small but with choice, supertrendy, sometimes weird styles and colors. Items may cost a little more than you want to spend but you'll want them anyway. Serious bargains can be had during sales. ✉ *67 Front St., Hamilton* ☎ *441/295–2112* ⊕ *www.calypso.bm.*

SPAS

Exhale at Hamilton Princess & Beach Club

SPA/BEAUTY | If you're in need of a quick pick-me-up, the city location of the Exhale Day Spa offers a full array of body treatments and massages, as well as its butt-busting barre classes. It has an outdoor spa pool and a gym, and you can also check out the well-being boutique and the Zen lounge. ✉ *Hamilton Princess & Beach Club, 76 Pitts Bay Rd., Hamilton* ☎ *441/298–6046* ⊕ *www.exhalespa.com.*

SPORTING GOODS

The Pro Shop

SPORTING GOODS | Tucked away beneath the ground level, this shop sells men's and women's running and tennis clothes, football jerseys, and sneakers from brands such as Adidas at reasonable prices. ✉ *Kenwood Bldg., 17 Reid St., Hamilton* ☎ *441/292–7487.*

Sports Locker

SPORTING GOODS | While the shop stocks sports sneakers, it's the vast array of fashionable and trendy styles that are the particular draw at this shop. Athleisure styles from brands such as Adidas, Gazelle, Keds, and Converse are the most popular. ✉ *Windsor Place, 18 Queen St., Hamilton* ☎ *441/292–3300.*

Sports 'R' Us

SPORTING GOODS | This store has Bermuda's largest selection of running shoes, plus gear and equipment for most sports. ✉ *Shoppers Fair Bldg., 61 Church St., Hamilton* ☎ *441/292–1891.*

Hamilton has Bermuda's highest concentrations of stores in its downtown area.

SportSeller

SPORTING GOODS | Big-name exercise gear, knapsacks, and running shoes are available at this shop, which also sells Speedo swimwear, sunglasses, and water bottles of every shape and size. Come here to get the best fit in running shoes from a very knowledgeable staff. ⊠ *Washington Mall, 7 Reid St., lower level, Hamilton* ☎ *441/295–2692.*

Winners Edge

SPORTING GOODS | The store sells everything to do with cycling including exercise wear, water bottles, and helmets, and it's the only store in Bermuda to sell Trek equipment. The owners and staff are some of Bermuda's top cyclists; they'll be able to answer just about any biking question you throw at them. ⊠ *73 Front St., Hamilton* ☎ *441/295–6012* ⊕ *www.winnersedge.bm.*

STATIONERY AND ART SUPPLIES

DNA Creative

CRAFTS | Run by artists Lexy and Dion Correia, this store caters to artists of all ages with crafting supplies, tools, and paints of every color and type. ⊠ *129 Front St., Hamilton* ☎ *441/747–5399* ⊕ *www.dnashoppe.biz.*

Stationery Store

BOOKS/STATIONERY | Pens, pencils, envelopes, writing paper, copy paper, file boxes, and note pads are plentiful at this well-stocked stationery store. It's also home to Artcetera, where you can buy paint, charcoal, pastels, sketching pads, canvases, and almost anything else an aspiring artist might need to capture Bermuda in color or black-and-white. The store is also an authorized FedEx shipping center. ⊠ *32 Reid St., Hamilton* ✛ *Corner of Burnaby St.* ☎ *441/295–6311.*

TOYS

The Annex Toys

TOYS | Upstairs at the Phoenix Pharmacy, this large toy department has an up-to-date selection of toys and games for all ages. There's a good supply of kites and beach toys, as well as shelves full of board games and puzzles. Phoenix Kidz, in the same space, stocks baby

equipment and essentials. There's also a small selection of children's clothes and accessories. ✉ *Phoenix Centre, 3 Reid St., Hamilton* ☎ *441/279–5450.*

Nest

TOYS | All the gear you need for baby and toddler is stocked in this well-edited shop. Toys include the Plan line of wooden toys as well as a great selection of Chewbeads. The shop also carries a large selection of natural products and plenty of items to help organize your child's room into a stylish retreat. There is a small selection of kids' clothing and shoes as well as gorgeous maternity wear. ✉ *44 Reid St., Hamilton* ☎ *441/296–6378* ⊕ *www.nestbermuda. com.*

People's Pharmacy

TOYS | FAMILY | Head to the back of this large pharmacy to find Little People's, with one of the island's biggest selections of toys and games—from cuddly toys and rattles for babies to computer games and board games for teens. The shop also stocks a large selection of organic and natural baby products. ✉ *62 Victoria St., Hamilton* ☎ *441/292–7527* ⊕ *www.peoplespharmacy.bm.*

WINES AND SPIRITS

Burrows Lightbourn

WINE/SPIRITS | This wine and spirits merchant has a great selection in stores all over the island. Visitors who want to take duty-free alcohol back home make significant savings on the retail price. The two other locations are on York Street in St. George's and on Harbour Road in Paget. ✉ *127 Front St., Hamilton* ☎ *441/295–1554.*

Front Street Wine & Spirits

WINE/SPIRITS | Here's your one-stop shop for wines, beer, candy, souvenirs, and assorted snacks. ✉ *57 Front St., Hamilton* ☎ *441/292–6620.*

Gosling's Ltd.

WINE/SPIRITS | The maker of Bermuda's Black Seal Rum also stocks wines and other liquors at its stores, where the helpful and knowledgeable staff provide excellent advice. The store also sells T-shirts, ties, and hats with Gosling's logo, a black seal. There's another branch on Dundonald Street in North Hamilton. ✉ *33 Front St., at Queen St., Hamilton* ☎ *441/298–7337* ⊕ *www.goslingsrum. com.*

⚡ Activities

Hamilton Harbour fronts the city, making this a popular spot to charter a sailing or fishing boat, and the government-run tennis stadium, which is open to the public, is walking distance from the center of Hamilton.

BIKING

BIKING RENTALS

Smatt's Cycle Livery

BICYCLING | Smatt's offers standard moped rentals with helmets. Besides the daily rate, you pay the $30 damage-waiver fee. Before a moped is rented, you'll be asked to take a riding test for your safety. There are two additional locations, one in the west end at the Fairmont Southampton resort, and one at the Rosewood Bermuda. A limited number of bicycles are available for rent from the Hamilton and Southampton locations. ✉ *Hamilton Princess & Beach Club, 74 Pitts Bay Rd., Hamilton* ☎ *441/295–1180* ⊕ *www.smattscyclelivery.com* 🔁 *From $55 per day for single seater.*

BIKE TOURS

Island Tour Centre

TOUR—SPORTS | This comprehensive recreational company based in Hamilton offers a wide assortment of memorable excursions on land and water around the island. For example, the bike tour along the Railway Trail begins in Dockyard with a short boat cruise to the trail, where you will pick up your 21-speed mountain bike.

Yo, Ho, Ho and a Bottle of Rum

One of the distinct pleasures of a visit to Bermuda is getting to sample a bit of island rum and rum-based products. Gosling's Black Seal Rum is perhaps the best-loved by locals. It's darker and thicker than the usual stuff, with a hint of caramel flavor—especially when mixed with carbonated ginger beer to make a Dark 'n' Stormy, a famous Bermuda drink (treat it with respect and caution).

Gosling's is one of Bermuda's oldest companies, and its Hamilton liquor shop was established in 1806. Gosling's Black Seal Rum was sold in barrels until just after World War I, and inherited its name from the black sealing wax that sealed the barrel corks. In its 151-proof variety, Black Seal will test

the strongest drinker. Many prefer to buy it in the standard 80 proof.

Bermuda's rum swizzle, another popular drink, uses the ubiquitous Black Seal Rum. Many people hold their recipes close to the chest, but standard swizzles have a mix of fruit juices, grenadine, and Angostura bitters. Gosling's also produces three liqueurs that are big favorites—Bermuda Gold, Bermuda Banana Liqueur, and Bermuda Coconut Rum. These liqueurs can be ordered everywhere, from poolside bars to late-night jazz clubs. They're even found in cakes, as you soon discover in gift shops and on restaurant menus. Classic Bermuda rum cakes are another delicious way to taste the island's famous export.

After the leisurely 1½-hour guided ride and commentary, finish with a cool-off swim and a drink at a beach in the Somerset area. The trip is about 3½ hours, including the cruise and biking. There is a $5 administration fee per reservation. ☎ 441/236–1300 ⊕ www.islandtourcentre.com ⊠ $80 per person for bike tour.

BOATING
Wind Sail Charters
BOATING | You can rent a 41-, 51-, or 60-foot Morgan yacht, including snorkeling equipment, from Wind Sail. Captain Mike or his daughter, Captain Melissa, will sail to your location, including the City of Hamilton, and take you for a spin. The rates for six people are the most affordable ride on the island. You can also join a group (daytime and sunset) for a bargain price, when available. Lunch catering is available for an extra charge. ☎ 441/334–8547 ⊕ www.bermudawindsailcharters.com ⊠ Group sail $50; from $550 for 3-hour charter for 6 people.

FISHING
Hakuna Matata Charters
FISHING | You'll have no worries in the hands of the expert Barnes family on their 51-foot Custom Carolina sportfishing boat. They have a proven record of catching fish on their charter and in local tournaments, and the well-equipped boat includes a fully air-conditioned cabin for when you need a break in between catches. The team is happy to arrange for pickup at a preferred location on the island, including the City of Hamilton. ⊠ Hamilton ☎ 441/505–1611 ⊕ www.hmcharters.com ⊠ From $1,800 for full-day charters for up to 9 people.

Mako Charters
FISHING | Allen DeSilva, one of Bermuda's most knowledgeable skippers, guarantees a fun day of fishing whether you're a complete beginner or a serious angler. His spacious 56-foot fully air-conditioned boat, Mako, based out of Mill's Creek near Hamilton, is one of the best for a safe, comfortable, and exciting cruise. A

full, nine-hour charter costs $3,000 for up to four people, with an additional charge per head, up to eight people. Overnight fishing packages, complete with breakfast and lunch, are also available. Allen's website is a great source of information on local fishing competitions and includes lots of photos of past guests and their record-breaking catches. ⊠ *11 Abri La., Spanish Point* ☎ *441/295–0835 office, 441/505–8626 cell* ⊕ *www.fishbermuda.com.*

SAILING

Royal Hamilton Amateur Dinghy Club

SAILING | If you're a sailor, it's worth checking out this club, which is the main center for sailors in Hamilton (though it is technically in Paget Parish) and offers lessons both for beginners and those looking to up their skills. It's also the only "Royal" Dinghy Club in the world. If you know what you're doing and fancy taking part in some amateur racing, this is the place to be on a Wednesday evening between late April and mid-September. Just turn up at the dock from about 5:30 pm—skippers are always looking for willing crew members. There's also a club barbecue afterward and everyone is welcome. ⊠ *25 Pomander Rd.* ☎ *441/236–2250* ⊕ *www.rhadc.bm* ⊠ *$200 for private 2-hour lesson.*

TENNIS

W. E. R. Joell Tennis Stadium

TENNIS | This government-run facility is the busiest of Bermuda's tennis courts, the inland location ideal for combating strong winds and hosting year-round tournaments. It's only about a 10-minute walk from Front Street. Of the eight all-weather courts available, five are Plexi-Cushion and three are Har-Tru; three courts in the main stadium have floodlights. Small discounts are available for seniors and young adults. Tennis attire is required, and lessons are available from on-site pros on request. ⊠ *2 Marsh Folly Rd.* ☎ *441/292–0105* ⊠ *$12 per hour.*

Chapter 4

CENTRAL
PARISHES

Updated by
Melissa Fox

⊙ Sights	🍴 Restaurants	🛏 Hotels	🛍 Shopping	🍸 Nightlife
★★★★★	★★★★☆	★★★★★	★★★☆☆	★★☆☆☆

ISLAND SNAPSHOT

TOP EXPERIENCES

■ **Beaches:** The central parishes have the island's most popular beaches, including stunning Horseshoe Bay, along a sweeping stretch of the south shore.

■ **Flora:** The lush Bermuda Botanical Gardens features endemic and introduced species on 36 acres of parkland.

■ **Golf:** The area's world-class golf courses include Ocean View in Devonshire, which overlooks the north shore, and Belmont Hills in Warwick.

■ **Snorkeling:** See Bermuda's colorful fish up close at spots such as Church Bay Beach and Warwick Long Bay Beach.

■ **Gibbs Hill Lighthouse:** At one of the world's oldest cast-iron lighthouses, you can climb 185 steps and enjoy a 360-degree view of the island's western shores. Climb down and have a traditional English tea at the Dining Room.

■ **Masterworks Museum of Bermuda Art.** Explore the creations of Bermudian artists as well as those of international artists inspired by the island, from Winslow Homer to Andrew Wyeth.

GETTING HERE

The central parishes see the heaviest traffic on the island, and visitors traveling via moped should use extra caution, particularly during rush hour, the early morning and late afternoon times when locals are going to and from work. If you are relying on public transportation, you'll have no trouble if you wait by a pink or blue pole for buses. Many lines depart the main terminal in the city of Hamilton at regular intervals, heading east or west to points in the central parishes and beyond.

PLANNING YOUR TIME

Bermuda's natural wonders are abundant here. Among the attractions and activities that will hold you for two or three days are pink-sand beaches, bird-watching, water sports, and walks through nearly undisturbed tracts of local foliage.

QUICK BITES

■ **Seaside Bar & Grill.** The fish sandwich has taken on legendary status in Bermuda, and one of the island's best versions is in North Shore Village. Or try fish dishes like grilled shrimp or fish nuggets, with locally sourced fish (like wahoo) when available. ⌂ *81 North Shore Rd., Devonshire* ☎ *441/292–1241* ⊕ *seaside-grill.bm* Ⓜ *Bus 10 or 11 from Hamilton.*

■ **Paraquet Restaurant.** A true island favorite, Paraquet offers a mix of traditional greasy spoon and local fare, as well as home-baked goods and an award-winning codfish and potato breakfast platter. ⌂ *68 South Rd., Paget* ☎ *441/236–9742* ⊕ *www. paraquetrestaurant.com* Ⓜ *Bus 7 from Hamilton.*

■ **Ice Queen.** Open until 5 am daily, this takeout-only spot in the plaza across from Paget Marsh is Bermuda's premier fast-food joint, with a comprehensive menu of burgers and more. ⌂ *130 South Rd., Paget* ☎ *441/236–3136* ⊕ *icequeen.bm.*

The central parishes cover the large area of Southampton, Warwick, Paget, and Devonshire parishes. These parishes are much sleepier than Hamilton and provide great nature and beach respites when you tire of city life. Convenient buses and ferries connect the parishes, so trips outside Hamilton are easy and a fun way to get off the tourist track.

From activities at accommodations to beaches and other attractions, there's much to do in the central parishes, and often the most interesting, scenic spots are within walking distance of each other. There are few shoulders or sidewalks here, so take care when walking along the island's winding streets. Be sure to make some time to explore spots like the Bermuda Botanical Gardens in Devonshire, or the jungle-like paths that wind through magical Southlands Park on South Road. Wet your whistle at Swizzle Inn's sister location in Warwick, or just put your feet up and enjoy the ocean breezes that sweep up over the cliffs at Astwood Park in Warwick.

◉ Sights

Bermuda Arboretum

GARDEN | FAMILY | Established with specimens delivered to the island from the Royal Botanic Gardens in Kew, sent by Queen Elizabeth II, the 22-acre parkland features Bermudian cedar trees, flowing golden acacias, rare rubber trees, and black ebony and avocado trees. Its winding trails and grassy meadows are popular for walking, hiking, and picnicking. The area is also an established bird-watching sanctuary, where you can hope to catch a glimpse of feathered species like cardinals, rare bluebirds, white-eyed vireos, and kiskadees. ⊠ *Montpellier Rd.* 🖼 *Free* Ⓜ *Bus 3 from Hamilton.*

★ Bermuda Botanical Gardens

GARDEN | Established in 1898, the Botanical Gardens are filled with exotic subtropical plants, flowers, and trees. The 36-acre property features a miniature forest, an aviary, a hibiscus garden with more than 150 species, and collections of orchids, cacti, fruits, and ferns. In addition to these must-see sights is an intriguing must-smell one: the Garden for the Sightless. Designed primarily for the visually impaired, it has fragrant plants like geraniums, lemons, lavender, and spices, plus Braille signage. Weather permitting, free 60- to 90-minute guided tours of the gardens begin from the Visitors Information Centre at 10:30 Tuesday, Wednesday, and Friday; call to confirm. ⊠ *169 South Rd.* ☎ *441/236–4201* 🖼 *Free.*

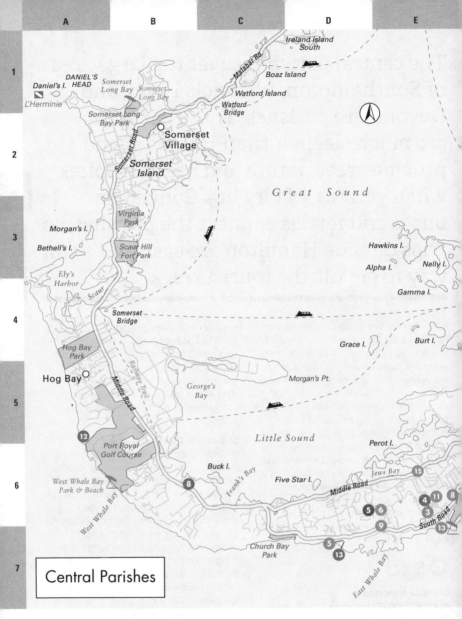

	A	B	C	D	E
1					
2			Great Sound		
3					
4					
5			Little Sound		
6					
7					

Daniel's I.

DANIEL'S HEAD

Somerset Long Bay

Somerset Long Bay

L'Herminie

Somerset Long Bay Park

Somerset Village

Somerset Island

Somerset Road

Virginia Park

Morgan's I.

Scaur Hill Fort Park

Bethell's I.

Ely's Harbor

Scaur

Somerset Bridge

Hog Bay Park

Railway Trail

Hog Bay

Middle Road

Port Royal Golf Course

West Whale Bay Park & Beach

West Whale Bay

George's Bay

Buck I.

Frank's Bay

Five Star I.

Church Bay Park

East Whale Bay

Ireland Island South

Boaz Island

Watford Island

Watford Bridge

Malabar Rd.

Hawkins I.

Alpha I.

Nelly I.

Gamma I.

Grace I.

Burt I.

Morgan's Pt.

Perot I.

Jews Bay

Middle Road

South Road

Central Parishes

Sights ▼

1 Bermuda Arboretum ... **J2**
2 Bermuda Botanical Gardens.................. **J2**
3 Bermuda Farmers' Market.......... **J2**
4 Camden House.......... **J2**
5 Gibbs Hill Lighthouse... **D6**

6 Masterworks Museum of Bermuda Art.......... **J2**
7 Paget Marsh Nature Reserve **I3**
8 Southlands Park **G5**
9 Waterville.................. **I3**

Restaurants ▼

1 Beau Rivage............. **H3**
2 Blu Bar & Grill........... **G4**
3 The Burger Bar at Wickets **E6**
4 Café Coco................. **I4**
5 Coconuts................. **D7**
6 The Dining Room........ **E6**

7 Fourways Restaurant & Inn........ **H4**
8 Gulfstream................ **E6**
9 Henry VIII Restaurant, Sushi Bar & Pub **E6**
10 Lido Restaurant.......... **I4**
11 Mediterra................ **E6**
12 Mickey's Beach Bistro **I4**

SPANISH POINT

Cobbler I.

Spanish Pt. Park

Admiralty House Park

North Shore Road

St. John's Rd.

Marsh Folly Rd.

National Sports Centre

North St.

Agar's I.

Pitts Bay Road

HAMILTON

Front St.

Hamilton Harbour

South Road

Saltus I.

Bluck's I.

Long I.

Ports I.

Marshall Island

Hinson Island

Harbour Road

Hungry Bay

Main Island

Railway Trail

Middle Road

Darrell I.

Southlands Park

South Road

Audubon Bird Sanctuary

Marley Beach

Elbow Beach

Coral Beach

Hermes

Astwood Cove & Park

ATLANTIC OCEAN

Warwick Long Bay

Chaplin & Stonehole Bays

South Shore Park

Horseshoe Bay & Horseshoe Baby Beach

Horseshoe Bay

KEY

Ferry Lines

KEY

1 Exploring Sights

1 Restaurants

1 Hotels

0 — 1 mi
0 — 1 km

Slavery in Bermuda

Within a few years of the colony's founding, slavery had become a fact of life in Bermuda. As early as 1616, slaves—most of whom were "imported" as household servants and tradespeople rather than field workers—began arriving, first from Africa and then from the Caribbean. In the mid-1600s they were joined by Native American captives (among them, the wife of a Pequod chief). The practice flourished to such an extent that by the time British legislation finally abolished it in 1834, slaves made up more than half of the island's population.

The date the abolition decree was issued, August 1, continues to be marked island-wide. Known as Emancipation Day, it's a time for cricket matches, concerts, and, of course, Gombey dancing. This colorful form of self-expression, rooted in African tradition, was banned by slave owners. If you can't time your trip to coincide with the festivities, you can still bone up on the backstory by following the African Diaspora Heritage Trail. Affiliated with UNESCO's international Slave Route Project, it highlights sites related to the Bermudian slave trade.

Some of the trail's 11 stops are already tourist staples. For instance, in St. George's the slave graveyard at St. Peter's Church is a designated site, as is Tucker House, where Joseph Rainey (the first black man to be elected to the U.S. House of Representatives) sat out the Civil War. Also on the list is the Commissioner's House at the Royal Naval Dockyard, which has an exhibit that vividly evokes the age of slavery through artifacts like iron shackles and glass trade beads.

Other sites are obscure, but nonetheless illuminating. Take Cobb's Hill Methodist Church in Warwick Parish. Dedicated in 1827, seven years before Emancipation, it was the first sanctuary in Bermuda built by and for blacks. Because they struggled to complete it in their rare off-hours (often working by candlelight), the church is both a religious monument and a symbol of human resilience. For further details on the African Diaspora Heritage Trail, pick up a brochure at any Visitor Services Centre.

Bermuda Farmers' Market

MARKET | One of the best places to mingle with Onions and, yes, buy a few edible ones is the seasonal Bermuda Farmers' Market, held every Saturday from 8 am to 1 pm, featuring up to 30 vendors who sell only Bermuda-grown, -caught, or-made products. Along with organic produce and assorted home-baked items, goodies like handcrafted soaps and honey derived from the pollen of island wildflowers are for sale. ⊠ *Botanical Gardens, 169 South Rd.* ✛ *Inside the JJ Outerbridge Bldg.* ☎ *441/333–6198* ⏱ *Closed Sun.–Fri. July–mid-Nov.*

Camden House

HOUSE | This gracious white 18th-century house on the grounds of the Bermuda Botanical Gardens is the official residence of Bermuda's premier and contains art and lovely furniture. Tours of the interior are given Tuesday and Friday noon to 2, except when official functions are scheduled. ⊠ *169 South Rd.* ☎ *441/236–5732* ⏱ *Closed Sat.–Mon., Wed., and Thurs.*

Gibbs Hill Lighthouse

LIGHTHOUSE | **FAMILY** | Designed in London and opened in 1846, this cast-iron

lighthouse soars above Southampton Parish, stands 117 feet high and 362 feet above the sea, and offers a 185-step climb to the top for panoramic island views. The light was originally produced by a concentrated burner of four large, circular wicks. Today the beam from the 1,000-watt bulb can be seen by ships 40 miles out to sea and by planes 120 miles away at 10,000 feet. The haul up the spiral stairs is an arduous one—particularly if you dislike heights or tight spaces. But en route to the top you can stop to catch your breath on eight landings, where photographs and drawings of the lighthouse help divert attention from your aching appendages. Once you take in the views up top and return to solid ground, stop in at the Dining Room for refreshments. ⊠ *68 St. Anne's Rd.* ☎ *441/238–8069* ⊕ *www.bermudalighthouse.com* 🎟 *$2.50* ⊘ *Closed Feb.*

★ **Masterworks Museum of Bermuda Art**

MUSEUM | The theme of the island's first purpose-built state-of-the-art museum (2008), like that of its former incarnation (the Masterworks Foundation), is "Bermuda through the Eyes of Artists," and the soaring main gallery is devoted to island-inspired works by internationally renowned figures such as Georgia O'Keeffe, Andrew Wyeth, and Winslow Homer. Two other galleries display (and sell) paintings by native-born artists. The museum is on the grounds of the Bermuda Botanical Gardens. ⊠ *Bermuda Botanical Gardens, 183 South Rd.* ☎ *441/299–4000* ⊕ *www.bermudamasterworks.org* 🎟 *$10* ⊘ *Closed Sun. but call to check.*

Paget Marsh Nature Reserve

NATURE PRESERVE | Along with some of the last remaining stands of native Bermuda palmetto and cedar, this 25-acre reserve—virtually untouched since presettlement times and jointly owned and preserved by the Bermuda National Trust and the Bermuda Audubon Society—contains a mangrove forest and grassy savanna. These unspoiled habitats can be explored via a boardwalk with interpretive signs describing the endemic flora and fauna. When lost in the cries of the native and migratory birds that frequent this natural wetland, you can quickly forget that bustling Hamilton is just minutes away. ⊠ *Lovers La., off South Rd.* ☎ *441/236–6483* ⊕ *www.bnt. bm* 🎟 *Free* Ⓜ *Bus 2, 7, or 8.*

Southlands Park

NATIONAL/STATE PARK | Statuesque banyan trees line the road beyond the gates of Southlands Estate in this sprawling, 37-acre park with rambling gardens and crumbling limestone buildings. Ownership of the estate has changed hands many times since the 1700s, when it was maintained by the ministers of Warwick Parish's Christ Church. Open to the public as a park since 2013, it's an ideal place to explore Bermuda's natural beauty. The winding paths eventually lead you to quiet, secluded Marley Beach along the south shore. ⊠ *Southlands Rd.* 🎟 *Free* Ⓜ *Bus 7 from Hamilton.*

Waterville

HOUSE | Bermuda's National Trust (the nonprofit organization that oversees the restoration and preservation of many of the island's gardens, open spaces, and historic buildings) has its offices in Waterville, a rambling estate overlooking Hamilton Harbour. Waterville was home to the Trimingham family for seven generations. In fact, their much-loved (and still dearly missed) department store started out here in 1842. The drawing and dining rooms, both laden with art and antiques donated by the family, are open to the public during business hours. Also worth seeing is a superb showcase garden planted by the Bermuda Rose Society. ⊠ *National Trust, 2 Pomander Rd.* ☎ *441/236–6483* ⊕ *www.bnt.bm* 🎟 *Free* ⊘ *Closed weekends.*

If the weather permits, you can take a free guided tour of the Bermuda Botanical Gardens at 10:30 am on Tuesday, Wednesday, and Friday.

🏖 Beaches

Of the many places on the island to dip your toes into the ocean, the beaches that stretch along the central parishes of Bermuda's south shore are easily the most popular. With wide swaths of famously pink sand and gentle, rolling waves, hot spots like Horseshoe Bay and Elbow Beach are accessible and spacious enough to accommodate every kind of beachgoer, from families with small kids to adventure-seeking water sport enthusiasts. During the summer months, nightlife spills over from the bars to the beach, with beach parties and concerts happening regularly.

Astwood Cove and Park

BEACH—SIGHT | On weekends you can often find lots of children and families at this small yet popular beach. The Astwood Park area is shady and grassy, with a great view of the ocean, making it popular among locals for birthday parties, picnics, and weddings. Though accessible via one of Bermuda's main roads,

it's quite secluded; the few benches scattered around the area are a great vantage point to share a romantic evening. If you're bringing kids, watch out for the steep climb from the park down to the beach area. **Amenities:** parking (free). **Best for:** solitude; swimming. ⊠ *49 South Shore Rd.* 🚍 *Free* Ⓜ *Bus 7 from Hamilton.*

Chaplin and Stonehole Bays

BEACH—SIGHT | In a secluded area east along the dunes from Horseshoe Bay, these tiny adjacent beaches almost disappear at high tide. Like Horseshoe Bay, the beach fronts South Shore Park; it often experiences a strong wind and surf, so the waters may be too cloudy to snorkel. Wander farther along the dunes and you can find several other tiny, peaceful beaches before you eventually reach Warwick Long Bay. **Amenities:** parking (free). **Best for:** solitude; swimming; walking. ⊠ *Off South Shore Rd.* ✛ *Enter the park across from Warwick Camp and follow the narrow road through a parkland of trees* 🚍 *Free* Ⓜ *Bus 7 from Hamilton.*

Elbow Beach

BEACH—SIGHT | FAMILY | Swimming and bodysurfing are great at this beach, which is bordered by the prime strand of sand reserved for guests of the Elbow Beach hotel on the left, and the ultraexclusive Coral Beach Club beach area on the right. It's a pleasant setting for a late-evening stroll, with the lights from nearby hotels dancing on the water. If you're planning a daytime visit during summer months, arrive early to claim your spot as this popular beach is often crowded. In addition to sunbathers and joggers, groups of locals gather here to play football and volleyball. Protective coral reefs make the waters some of the safest on the island and a good choice for families. It's possible to rent chairs, umbrellas, and other gear from the hotel-owned beach facility, but it can be quite expensive. A lunch wagon sometimes sells fast food and cold drinks during the day, and Mickey's Beach Bar (part of the Elbow Beach hotel) is open for lunch and dinner, though reservations are useful. **Amenities:** parking (free); water sports. **Best for:** snorkeling; swimming; walking. ⊠ *Elbow Beach, Off South Shore Rd.* 🚌 *Free* Ⓜ *Bus 2 or 7 from Hamilton.*

★ Horseshoe Bay

BEACH—SIGHT | FAMILY | When locals say they're going to "the beach," they're generally referring to Horseshoe Bay, the island's most popular. With clear water, a 0.3-mile (0.5-km) crescent of pink sand, a vibrant social scene, and the uncluttered backdrop of South Shore Park, Horseshoe Bay has everything you could ask of a Bermudian beach. An on-site bar and restaurant, changing rooms, beach-rental facilities, and lifeguards add to its appeal. The Annual Bermuda Sand Castle Competition also takes place here.

The undertow can be strong, especially on the main beach. A better place for children is **Horseshoe Baby Beach,** at the western end of Horseshoe Bay. Sheltered from the ocean by a ring of rocks,

Go for Gold 👁

To sightsee like a VIP, sign up for a National Trust guided tour. The outing begins at Waterville with a "special access" stroll through the historic house and surrounding gardens. After being served refreshments, groups continue on by taxi to Paget Marsh for an exclusive tour of the reserve. Contact the Bermuda National Trust, as reservations are required in advance, at ☎ 441/236–6483. You must have at least four people in your group.

this cove is shallow and almost perfectly calm. In summer, toddlers can find lots of playmates. **Amenities:** food and drink; lifeguards; parking (free); showers; toilets. **Best for:** partiers; swimming; walking. ⊠ *Off South Shore Rd.* 🚌 *Free* Ⓜ *Bus 7 from Hamilton.*

Warwick Long Bay

BEACH—SIGHT | Different from the covelike bay beaches, Warwick Long Bay has about a ½-mile (1-km) stretch of sand—the longest of any beach here. Its backdrop is a combination of steep cliffs and low grass- and brush-covered hills. The beach is exposed to some strong southerly winds, but the waves are usually moderate because the inner reef is close to shore. A 20-foot coral outcrop less than 200 feet offshore looks like a sculpted boulder balancing on the water's surface. South Shore Park, which surrounds the bay, is often empty, a fact that only heightens the beach's appealing isolation and serenity. A summertime concession stand offers snacks for purchase. Note that the beach does not have changing rooms. **Amenities:** parking (free); toilets. **Best for:** solitude; snorkeling; swimming; walking. 🚌 *Free* Ⓜ *Bus 7 from Hamilton*

4

Central Parishes

Did You Know?

It's possible to climb to the top of the iconic Gibb's Hill Lighthouse, assuming you are willing to do all 185 steps.

Bermuda's Blushing Beaches

In only a few regions where tropical coral reefs flourish offshore do pink-sand beaches form. What makes Bermuda's sand pink is an amalgam of calcium-rich shells and fragments of invertebrate sea creatures, from minute, single-cell protozoa to spiny sea urchins. Chiefly responsible are *foraminifera* ("foram" for short), a type of protozoan that lives in great profusion in reef environments. The microscopic red *Homotrema rubrum* (red foram) variety is numerous both on the reefs and in the ocean sediments that surround Bermuda, and their persistent red pigment remains even in the microscopic "skeletons" these animals leave behind when they die. The red gets mixed in with other (predominantly white) reef debris—broken clam and snail shells, fragments of coral—and, when washed ashore, forms the island's signature pink sand.

The most visited pink-sand beaches are Warwick Long Bay Beach and Horseshoe Bay in Southampton. But just about any beach you visit on the south shore will have the famous sand in abundance. ■ TIP→ **Think twice before pocketing pink sand for the trip home. Bermuda has placed a premium on this national treasure, and it is illegal to take sand from a Bermudian beach. You can bring souvenir sand home, however, as most tourist shops carry small, labeled bottles at a reasonable price.**

West Whale Bay

BEACH—SIGHT | This beach can be a secluded oasis if you go at the right time: sunset. To get to the beach, you need to cross a large grassy field and walk down a natural rock formation path. If you're looking to avoid the crowds and experience a breathtaking view, this is your spot. West Whale Bay is one of the best spots in Bermuda to view humpback whales as they pass through the waters near the island on the way to their northern feeding grounds in late winter and early spring. The park also features several picnic tables and public bathroom facilities. **Amenities:** parking (free); toilets. **Best for:** solitude; snorkeling; sunset; swimming. ⊠ *Whale Bay Rd., off Middle Rd.* ⊠ *Free* Ⓜ *Bus 7 or 8 from Hamilton.*

🍴 Restaurants

Right in the middle of the island, you'll find some of the finest dining opportunities in Bermuda. The central parishes cover the large area of Southampton, Paget, Warwick, and Devonshire, and many of the best restaurants here are in luxury hotels and resorts. The only downside is that if you're not staying in one of these resorts, the area is not easily reachable by public transport. Taking a cab is your best option.

Beau Rivage

$$$ | **FRENCH** | This upscale, waterfront French eatery with an alfresco patio, a vast selection of wines, and an extensive menu adds a little ooh-la-la to Bermuda's restaurant scene. Specialties include leg of lamb, lobster risotto, and beef Wellington, but save room for desserts such as soufflés, chocolate fondant, and crème brûlée. **Known for:** panoramic views of Hamilton Harbour; private table in kitchen; Sunday brunch. Ⓢ *Average main: $39* ⊠ *Newstead Belmont Hills Resort, 27 Harbour Rd.* ☎ *441/232–8686* ⊕ *www.beaurivagebda.com.*

Did You Know?

Warwick Long Bay has Bermuda's longest beach, which is about a half-mile long and isn't usually too crowded.

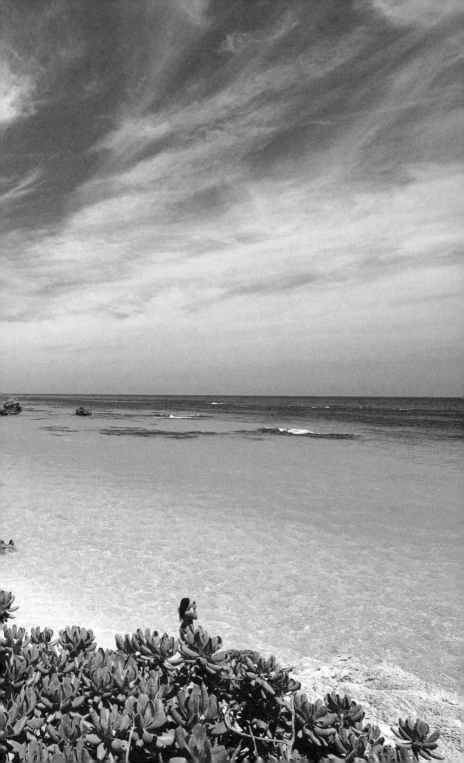

Best Bets for Kids

Harbour Nights. The popular festival in Hamilton (Wednesday evening, May through September) lets kids eat on their feet. Choose fish sandwiches, patties, wraps, sweets, and more from booths and kiosks along Front, Reid, and Queen streets.

Paraquet. This American-style diner's low counter with stools is ideal for little ones to watch what's going on in the kitchen (and to have a friendly chat with the taxi drivers who frequent the lunch counter). The large selection of kids' food, milkshakes, and the well-priced menu make this a great spot for families. ✉ *68 South Shore Rd., Paget Parish*

Pizza House. Youngsters love being creative and eating with their hands, so let them have the best of both worlds by creating their own pizza. Head here to see who can come up with the tastiest combination of toppings. Especially hungry kids will love the double cheeseburger or jumbo hot dog. Choose from three convenient locations: on Southside Road in St. David's, Shelly Bay in Hamilton Parish, and Heron Bay Plaza in Southampton. ⊕ *pizzahouse.bm*

Shelly Bay Beach Park. Bermuda has the ideal picnic venue to keep the younger set entertained all day long. Shelly Bay in Hamilton Parish has a huge children's play area right next to its sandy beach, so little ones won't have time to be bored. Bring a picnic or sample from the food truck that often stops in the parking lot, and prepare for a fun—and probably tiring—day by the ocean. ✉ *North Rd.*

Warwick Lanes. Let the kids knock 'em down with a family bowling challenge at Warwick Lanes in the late afternoon or evening. Between games, pick off the menu at the on-site Last Pin restaurant. Kids' meals include all the favorites: pizza, hamburgers, chicken nuggets, and french fries. ✉ *47 Middle Rd., Warwick Parish.*

Blu Bar & Grill

$$$ | **ECLECTIC** | An expansive vista of aquamarine waters, white roofs, and green palm trees—not to mention the view across the manicured golf course—makes Blu Bar & Grill one of the island's prettiest spots for dinner, especially at sunset. The cuisine, which is loosely American but eclectic, with bold flavors and lots of exotic herbs and spices, encompasses not only steaks and ribs but also fish and tempuras. **Known for:** sunset views from the patio; good, fresh seafood and sushi; eclectic menu. ⑤ *Average main: $40* ✉ *Newstead Belmont Hills Golf Course, 25 Belmont Dr.* ☎ *441/232–2323* ⊕ *www.blu.bm* ⊙ *No lunch.*

The Burger Bar at Wickets

$ | **AMERICAN** | **FAMILY** | Simple yet satisfying American fare and prompt service make this social restaurant a great spot for families. Swim up an appetite in the pool, then build your own beef, chicken, wahoo, or veggie burger and retire to the shade with a Dark 'n' Stormy milkshake. **Known for:** sandwiches, salads, and burgers; outdoor dining by the pool; on-site coffee bar. ⑤ *Average main: $19* ✉ *Fairmont Southampton Resort, 101 South Shore Rd.* ☎ *441/238–8000* ⊕ *www.fairmont.com/southampton-bermuda* ⊙ *No dinner. Closed Nov.–May.*

Café Coco

$$$ | CARIBBEAN | At this warm, ocean-side restaurant with a real European vibe, you can enjoy a candlelit dinner in the dining room, which looks like a white Mediterranean villa, with archways and art depicting typical street scenes, or enjoy your meal on the outside terrace overlooking the swimming pool and coastline. Start with the roasted beets and goat cheese salad, then sample the braised lamb shanks or crispy-skinned salmon. **Known for:** spectacular water views; intimate dining room; summer barbecue buffets. $ *Average main: $33* ✉ *Coco Reef Resort, 3 Stonington Circle* ⊕ *Off South Shore Rd.* ☎ *441/236–5416* ⊕ *www.cocoreefbermuda.com.*

Coconuts

$$$ | CARIBBEAN | Nestled between high cliff rocks and a pristine private beach on the southern coast, this outdoor restaurant is one of the best, most romantic places to nab that table overlooking the ocean. The menu changes often, but you can always be sure of an eclectic selection of items—from mussels to rockfish to braised oxtail—prepared with customary Bermudian flair. **Known for:** romantic but expensive fixed-price dining on the beach; varied menu including good local fish; cheaper lunch menu offers weekly specials. $ *Average main: $34* ✉ *The Reefs, 56 South Shore Rd.* ☎ *441/238–0222* ⊕ *www.thereefs.com* ⊗ *Closed Nov.–Apr.*

The Dining Room

$$ | EUROPEAN | At the base of Gibbs Hill Lighthouse, in the old Lighthouse Tea Room, this adorable little restaurant is the perfect place to rest after the climb up and down the tower's 185 spiraling steps. Eclectic lunch and dinner menus include everything from traditional fish and chicken dishes to salads and homemade lasagna. **Known for:** bird's-eye views of the island; delicious fresh seafood; intimate dining, perfect at sunset. $ *Average main: $27* ✉ *68 St.*

Anne's Rd. ☎ *441/238–8679* ⊕ *www.bermuda-dining.com* ⊗ *Closed Mon.; no lunch Tues.–Thurs.*

★ Fourways Restaurant & Inn

$$$$ | EUROPEAN | Fourways has risen to preeminence as much for its lovely 17th-century surroundings as for its award-winning European cuisine and famous Sunday brunch. The elegant yet charming interior, with mahogany banisters, burgundy carpeting, impressionist prints, and silver-and-crystal table settings, evokes the image of a fine French manor and provides a gracious setting for beautifully presented traditional dishes such as veal tenderloin, rack of lamb, and Bermuda-style fresh fish. **Known for:** popular Sunday brunch; live piano music; decadent dessert soufflés. $ *Average main: $42* ✉ *1 Middle Rd.* ☎ *441/236–6517* ⊕ *www.fourways.bm* ⊗ *No lunch. No dinner Sun.*

Gulfstream

$$ | SEAFOOD | Opposite the entrance to one of Bermuda's most popular beaches, Horseshoe Bay, this restaurant offers a selection of surf-and-turf dishes (including oysters, clams, and lobsters) plus plenty of options for vegetarians and picky eaters. Guests rave about the thin-crust pizzas and the fish, but sandwiches, tacos, and wraps are also available for a satisfying meal after a day at the beach. **Known for:** market-fresh local fish; good wine list; friendly staff. $ *Average main: $26* ✉ *117 South Rd.* ☎ *441/238–1897* ⊕ *www.bermuda-dining.com.*

Henry VIII Restaurant, Sushi Bar & Pub

$$$ | BRITISH | FAMILY | As popular with locals as it is with vacationers from near-by Southampton resorts, the lively Henry VIII exudes an Old English charm that stops just short of "wench" waitresses and Tudor styling. It's a bit pricey for what you get, but you can find a mix of English and Bermudian menu favorites, including steak-and-mushroom pie, rack of lamb, and fish chowder. **Known for:** Sunday

brunch; sushi adds variety; live jazz music. $ *Average main: $33* ⊠ *69 South Shore Rd.* ☎ *441/238–1977* ⊕ *www. henrys.bm.*

Lido Restaurant

$$$ | **MEDITERRANEAN** | The beachfront dining room at the Elbow Beach Resort, with waves breaking just below, is regarded as one of the island's most romantic settings. Reserve a table near the window—or even more romantic, a table on the beach—and choose from an excellent seafood selection, including a delicious octopus salad and stuffed Bermuda lobster, for a truly memorable dining experience. **Known for:** expansive beach views; gluten-free and vegan menu options; lively nightlife scene on the terrace. $ *Average main: $37* ⊠ *El-bow Beach Resort, 60 South Shore Rd.* ☎ *441/236–9884* ⊕ *www.lido.bm* ⊗ *No lunch.*

Mediterra

$$ | **MEDITERRANEAN** | **FAMILY** | Amid the sea of sushi bars and Italian restaurants that make up the majority of cuisines at Bermuda's higher-end establishments is Mediterra, a laid-back and family-friendly restaurant at the Fairmont Southampton that is inspired by the Mediterranean. The menu focuses on tapas and shared dishes, though other specialties include seafood paella and a Moroccan vegetable tagine. **Known for:** nautical interior design; homemade pastas; casual atmosphere. $ *Average main: $30* ⊠ *Fairmont Southampton, 101 South Shore Rd.* ☎ *441/238–8000* ⊕ *www.fairmont.com/ southampton-bermuda* ⊗ *Closed Tues. in winter.*

Mickey's Beach Bistro

$$$ | **SEAFOOD** | At Mickey's—hands-down the place for an unforgettable alfresco meal on the beach—you can enjoy the view while you savor a tropical cocktail and peruse an extensive list of Continental and local specialties. One of the friendly waiters will happily recommend a favorite dish, but you can't go wrong

with the daily fish special, the chicken mango salad, or flavorful pastas featuring herbs from the garden on-site. **Known for:** on-the-beach dining with relaxed island vibe; portions on the small side; family-friendly lunch. $ *Average main: $35* ⊠ *Elbow Beach Resort, 60 South Shore Rd.* ☎ *441/236–9107* ⊕ *www.lido. bm* ⊗ *Closed Nov.–Apr.*

★ Ocean Club

$$$$ | **SEAFOOD** | This seasonal spot at the Fairmont Southampton has earned its reputation as one of the top restaurants on the island for fresh, local fish dishes, but the lively terrace location, which overlooks the beach, also hosts regular events with live entertainment. Catch an island sunset while you sip a colorful cocktail and sample signature dishes like the traditional Bermudian fish chowder or a seafood tower that is perfect for sharing. **Known for:** varied, expensive fish and seafood dishes; relaxed atmosphere; incredible sunsets. $ *Average main: $42* ⊠ *Fairmont Southampton, 101 South Shore Rd.* ☎ *441/238–8000* ⊕ *www. fairmont.com/southampton-bermuda* ⊗ *Closed Oct.–Mar.*

Seaside Grill

$ | **CARIBBEAN** | When it comes to iconic food on the island, the battered fish sandwich is king. Even though Seaside Grill is just a take-out counter overlooking the North Shore, it has the towering sandwich down to an art form. **Known for:** Instagram-worthy fish sandwiches; quick take-out options; locally caught fish. $ *Average main: $13* ⊠ *81 N. Shore Rd.* ☎ *441/292–1241* ⊕ *www.seasidegrill.bm.*

★ Waterlot Inn

$$$$ | **STEAKHOUSE** | This graceful, two-story manor house, which dates from 1670 and once functioned as a bed-and-breakfast, now holds one of Bermuda's most elegant and elaborate steak restaurants, owned by the Fairmont Southampton. Arrive early to enjoy cocktails, live music, and spectacular sunsets from the chic outdoor lounge, the Dock. **Known for:**

Picnic Perfect

Ditch your proper place settings for a little sea breeze with that sandwich.

With verdant open spaces sprinkled with shady poinciana trees, the **Bermuda Botanical Gardens**, on Middle Road in Paget, make a peaceful inland setting for a picnic. The gardens have a few picnic tables and plenty of benches, plus spacious lawns where you can spread a blanket. Bring your own supplies, or pick up lunch at Homer's Café, located just inside the Masterworks Museum of Bermuda Art, also on the premises.

Clearwater Beach in St. David's is one of Bermuda's nicest picnic spots, with tables near to and on the beach. You can pick up picnic supplies on your way or order lunch to go from one of St. David's casual eateries.

Just west of popular Warwick Long Bay, tiny, tranquil **Jobson Cove** beach is backed by the dramatic cliffs and greenery of South Shore Park. There are no tables and no snack bars, and often no people—perfect for a private picnic on the sand.

If you want a tried-and-tested picnic spot, head to **John Smith's Bay** in Smith's Parish. The wooden picnic tables beneath the trees make it a popular spot for locals. Get there early if you want a good spot overlooking the beach.

Adjacent to a Bermuda Audubon Society nature reserve and also terrific for birding, **Somerset Long Bay Park** in Sandys has a semicircular beach, fluffy spruce trees, and shallow water. You can find tables under the trees near the beach and a grocery store less than ½ mile (1 km) away.

first-class steaks and seafood; excellent service; sticky toffee pudding. $ *Average main: $51 ⊠ Jew's Bay, Middle Rd. ☎ 441/238–8000 ⊕ www.waterlotinn. com ⊗ No lunch. Closed Mon. in winter.*

🛏 Hotels

If you can't decide whether to opt for the city or the beach, your best bet is to position yourself between the two. In the central parishes you are close enough to enjoy the south shore beaches by day and Hamilton by night. Southampton, Warwick, Paget, and Devonshire parishes have plenty of hotels to choose from, as this is one of the most picturesque areas of the island.

Clairfont Guest Apartments

$ | **RENTAL** | It's probably the island's best buy if you're on a budget; although the Clairfont is not exactly fancy, it's spotlessly clean and the beach is just a five-minute stroll away. **Pros:** kitchens make it even more affordable; very well maintained; spacious units. **Cons:** basic furnishings; not beachfront, though there is a pool; popular with families, so can fill up early. $ *Rooms from: $185 ⊠ 6 Warwickshire Rd. ☎ 441/238–3577 ⊕ www. clairfontapartments.bm ⊅ 8 apartments ⍑ No meals.*

Coco Reef Resort

$$$$ | **HOTEL** | In a prime location on the highly desirable Elbow Beach, this hotel may have dated, but you'll probably be too busy admiring the gorgeous views to let it bother you. **Pros:** close to the beach; impressive pool; steps from restaurants at Elbow Beach Resort. **Cons:** outdated furnishings in rooms and public areas; prices steep for what you get; limited attractions within walking distance. $ *Rooms from: $500 ⊠ 3 Stonington*

124

Circle ⚓ *Off South Shore Rd.* ☎ *441/236–5416* ⊕ *www.cocoreefbermuda.com* ⇔ *64 rooms* ⦿ *No meals.*

Elbow Beach Resort

$$$$ | **RESORT** | **FAMILY** | It may be pricey, but this intimate hideaway at Elbow Beach, with simple and elegant rooms tucked away in cottages dotted through 50 acres of lush gardens and tennis courts, is well worth a stay. **Pros:** great beach; luxurious spa with ocean views; many restaurants to entertain you. **Cons:** some room amenities need renovation; huge property requires a lot of walking; meal portions small for the price. ⑤ *Rooms from: $750* ⊠ *60 South Shore Rd.* ☎ *441/236–3535, 855/463–5269 in U.S. and Canada* ⊕ *www.elbowbeachbermuda.com* ⇔ *98 rooms* ⦿ *No meals.*

Fairmont Southampton

$$$$ | **RESORT** | **FAMILY** | With everything you could need on-site and many of the island's bests—the best restaurants, the best private beach, the best kids' club, the biggest spa, the best hotel golf course, lobby, shops, and so on—it is easy to overlook the fact that the Fairmont Southampton is also a clunky, high-rise chain hotel often overrun with families. **Pros:** all-year kids' camp with arcade; full-service resort with golf course; all-inclusive option for an extra fee. **Cons:** not much to do outside the hotel; bit of a walk to beach; very busy with families in high season. ⑤ *Rooms from: $600* ⊠ *101 South Shore Rd.* ☎ *441/238–8000, 866/540–4497* ⊕ *www.fairmont.com/southampton-bermuda* ⇔ *630 rooms* ⦿ *No meals.*

★ Fourways Restaurant & Inn

$$ | **B&B/INN** | With a top-notch restaurant on-site, this pleasant cottage colony comes to life at mealtimes; for the rest of the day, lose yourself in Fourways' quiet solitude and bountiful hospitality. **Pros:** great dining in atmospheric historical buildng; excellent, old-fashioned service; breakfast delivered daily. **Cons:** little to do in the immediate area; no activities for

kids; away from the beaches. ⑤ *Rooms from: $287* ⊠ *1 Middle Rd.* ☎ *441/236–6517, 800/962–7654 in U.S.* ⊕ *www.fourways.bm* ⇔ *11 rooms* ⦿ *Breakfast.*

★ Granaway Guest House

$$ | **B&B/INN** | A 1734 manor house with villa-like lawn and gardens, Granaway is an affordable accommodation option for those who do not need to be on the beach. **Pros:** individually decorated rooms; relaxing terrace, lawn, and pool area; near a ferry terminal. **Cons:** not waterfront or easy walk to beaches; no on-site restaurant; too small for some people's taste. ⑤ *Rooms from: $225* ⊠ *1 Longford Rd.* ⚓ *Off Harbour Rd.* ☎ *441/236–3747* ⊕ *www.granaway.com* ⇔ *5 rooms* ⦿ *Breakfast.*

Greenbank Guest House & Cottages

$$ | **B&B/INN** | The north shore guesthouse has been family run since the 1950s, and this is what Bermuda vacations were like back then: by way of entertainment you had a due-west pier with chairs to watch the sunset and a private dock for deepwater swimming. **Pros:** close to ferry; secluded, relaxed area; cottages have harbor views. **Cons:** no pool or beach; may be too quiet for some people; units could use updating. ⑤ *Rooms from: $250*

✉ 17 Salt Kettle Rd. ☎ 441/236–3615 ⊕ www.greenbankbermuda.com ⇨ 11 rooms ⎮○⎮ Breakfast.

Greene's Guest House

$ | **B&B/INN** | Avoid the crowds and head west to this spacious home where you'll be treated to beautiful views of the Great Sound from the huge front and backyards. **Pros:** on Bermuda Railway Trail; affordable option 10-minute walk from beach; use of kitchen for lunch and dinner. **Cons:** aging rooms, amenities, and decor; away from island action; not a beachside property. $ Rooms from: $185 ✉ 71 Middle Rd., Jennings Bay ☎ 441/238–0834 ▭ No credit cards ⇨ 6 rooms ⎮○⎮ Breakfast.

Inverurie Executive Suites

$$$ | **HOTEL** | Ovehauled in 2017, this harbor-front hotel was designed with the corporate client in mind, outfitted with sleek, modern amenities including galley kitchens and offering private balconies overlooking Hamilton Harbour. **Pros:** balconies over the harbor; next to ferry service; near restaurants. **Cons:** no leisure activities; feels a little impersonal; limited front desk hours. $ Rooms from: $359 ✉ 1 Harbour Rd. ☎ 441/232–5700 ⊕ www.inverurie.bm ⇨ 15 rooms ⎮○⎮ No meals.

Newstead Belmont Hills Golf Resort & Spa

$$$ | **HOTEL** | Linked to a private golf course, the hotel has perhaps the ritziest and most contemporary design aesthetic in Bermuda, with some of the sleekest rooms and a gorgeous infinity pool right on the edge of the harbor. **Pros:** harbor views; amazing pool; stylish spa and contemporary amenities. **Cons:** golf course not on premises; beach is 10-minute drive away; can be rowdy on weekends. $ Rooms from: $369 ✉ 27 Harbour Rd. ☎ 441/236–6060 ⊕ www.newsteadbelmonthills.com ⇨ 45 rooms ⎮○⎮ No meals.

Paraquet Tourist Apartments

$ | **HOTEL** | For those not picky about room furnishings, Paraquet (pronounced "parakeet") provides a centrally located, motel-like, no-frills stay with simple, clean, and unadorned accommodations. **Pros:** convenient on-site diner; some rooms with kitchenettes; close to lovely Elbow Beach. **Cons:** no views; no pool; no amenities. $ Rooms from: $180 ✉ 72 South Shore Rd. ☎ 441/236–5842 ⊕ www.paraquetapartments.com ⇨ 18 rooms ⎮○⎮ No meals.

Pompano Beach Club

$$$$ | **RESORT** | **FAMILY** | Pompano, which is passionately run by an American family, understands its customers—and those customers return year after year for the casual atmosphere and beach-front location. **Pros:** private and intimate resort; cliff-side hot tubs; magnificent views. **Cons:** rooms and amenities are dated; menu in need of an overhaul; hilly grounds. $ Rooms from: $520 ✉ 36 Pompano Beach Rd. ☎ 441/234–0222, 800/343–4155 in U.S. and Canada ⊕ www.pompanobeachclub.com ⇨ 75 rooms ⎮○⎮ Breakfast.

The Reefs Resort & Club

$$ | **RESORT** | An upscale cliffside property that remains a popular wedding, honeymoon, and luxurious vacation getaway, the Reefs offers serenity and old-world charm as well as a private beach, excellent dining options, and top-notch service. **Pros:** romantic feel; small but beautiful beach; highly rated spa. **Cons:** too serious for families seeking fun; rooms and decor in need of refurbishment; beach is downhill from suites. $ Rooms from: $295 ✉ 56 South Shore Rd. ☎ 441/238–0222, 800/742–2008 in U.S. and Canada ⊕ www.thereefs.com ⇨ 81 rooms ⎮○⎮ Breakfast.

Salt Kettle House

$ | **B&B/INN** | Although longtime innkeeper Hazel Lowe has sadly passed, Salt Kettle House, which rests directly on a secluded bay adjoining Hamilton Harbour (as well as being a stone's throw from the ferry), remains a family-run guesthouse with an intimate, inviting atmosphere and

friendly, welcoming hosts. **Pros:** steps from ferry; wonderful private setting and gardens; rooms include some cottages with kitchens. **Cons:** no beach; no pool; rooms are on small side. ⑤ *Rooms from: $160* ✉ *10 Salt Kettle Rd.* ☎ *441/236–0407* ⊕ *www.saltkettlehousebermuda.com* ⌁ *7 rooms* ¶◎¶ *Breakfast* ☞ *Rate based on double occupancy; no additional taxes or gratuities.*

Serendipity Guest Apartments

$ | **RENTAL** | The family of the owner of these two budget-friendly studio apartments in residential Paget has been on the island since 1612, and return guests are welcomed as part of that extended family. **Pros:** clean and well maintained; private setting; near Railway Trail and Paget Nature Reserve. **Cons:** have to walk to beach; no hotel-style services; credit cards not accepted. ⑤ *Rooms from: $160* ✉ *6 Rural Dr.* ☎ *441/236–1192* ▭ *No credit cards* ⌁ *2 apartments* ¶◎¶ *No meals.*

⊙ Nightlife

Though islanders and vacationers tend to congregate around the bars and clubs in Hamilton for an evening of fun, the central parishes are not without nighttime entertainment options. Be sure to sort out transportation in advance, however: difficult during the day, Bermuda's curvaceous roads can be downright despicable once the sun goes down, and it's not recommended that you walk to or from these happening locations.

BARS AND LOUNGES

★ The Dock

BARS/PUBS | If you prefer to while away your evening in a leisurely fashion, the Dock at Waterlot Inn restaurant offers a more sophisticated alternative to happy hour. In summer, relax in comfortable loungers under the stars and take in an uninterrupted view of Jew's Bay while you sip a locally sourced cocktail and have some elegant bar bites. Local musicians liven up the evening in style.

Suggested dress is resort casual. ✉ *Waterlot Inn, Middle Rd.* ☎ *441/238–8000* ⊕ *www.waterlotinn.com.*

Henry VIII Restaurant, Sushi Bar & Pub

BARS/PUBS | The popular restaurant and bar, decorated with rich oak paneling and polished brass, has reliably decent live entertainment, especially on weekends. There's a grand piano in the bar, and local entertainers often perform sing-along sessions. A chill, Sunday-night jazz session is a great way to recharge your batteries; afterward, follow the locals as the crowds head from Henry VIII to the nearby Fairmont Southampton. ✉ *69 South Shore Rd.* ☎ *441/238–1977* ⊕ *www.henrys.bm.*

Jasmine Cocktail Bar & Lounge

BARS/PUBS | At night, Jasmine draws the smartly dressed to its lounge and dance floor. Definitely check out the live entertainment, jazz in particular. A variety of craft cocktails like the exotic coconut froth martini and the classic Bermuda old-fashioned will quickly take the edge off. ✉ *Fairmont Southampton Resort, 101 South Shore Rd.* ☎ *441/238–8000* ⊕ *www.fairmont.com/southampton-bermuda.*

Ocean Club

BARS/PUBS | With its terrace overlooking the south shore, the seasonal Ocean Club is a romantic spot to watch a pretty pink sunset or dance the night away to live local entertainment. This restaurant-cum-bar regularly hosts special events and parties that are well attended by revelers with more sophisticated tastes. Visit the website for a schedule of upcoming events. Suggested dress is resort casual. ✉ *Fairmont Southampton, 101 South Rd.* ☎ *441/238–8000* ⊕ *www.fairmont.com/southampton-bermuda.*

Seabreeze

BARS/PUBS | With intimate dining areas and expansive bars, both Seabreeze and downstairs (right on the sand) Mickey's Beach Bar overlook the cool blue waters

just beyond the south shore's Elbow Beach. On weeknights, this complex is simply perfect for a quiet evening for two; on Friday and Saturday things heat up with tapas, cocktails, and live music. ✉ *Elbow Beach Resort, 60 South Shore Rd.* ☎ *441/236–9884* ⊕ *www.lido.bm.*

🛍 Shopping

The best shopping on the island is in the city of Hamilton, but you can find a few worthwile shops to peruse once you get past the city limits, particularly galleries carrying oils, watercolors, and limited-edition lithographs by island-renowned artists.

ART GALLERIES

Art House Gallery

ART GALLERIES | Watercolors, oils, and limited-edition color lithographs by Bermudian artist Joan Forbes are displayed in this gallery. The gallery isn't open every day, so check the website or call for hours or to make an appointment. ✉ *80 South Shore Rd.* ☎ *441/236–6746* ⊕ *www. arthousebermuda.com.*

Birdsey Studio

ART GALLERIES | Renowned artist Alfred Birdsey, who painted Bermuda scenes for more than 60 years, died in 1996, but thanks to his daughter, Jo Birdsey Linberg, the studio remains open and the tradition continues. Watercolors cost from $100 and oils from $350 to $1,000. Prints of Birdsey's paintings are also available on note cards. The studio is usually open weekday mornings, but call before you visit, as appointments are preferred. ✉ *Rosecote, 5 Stowe Hill* ✛ *Bus 8 from Hamilton* ☎ *441/236–6658.*

FOOD

A1 Paget

FOOD/CANDY | This grocery store is near several Paget accommodations, and it's an easy enough walk to do with bags of shopping. You could also stop here to grab snacks and drinks before hitting nearby Elbow Beach. Organic items are

Superstar Grocer 🛍

Dai James, a manager at Lindo's in Warwick, has become something of a cult hero as the star of a series of wacky TV adverts. Don't be surprised to hear locals asking Mr. Jones, "Can you wrap?" In one advert he mistakenly starts to rap when a customer asks him to wrap her tomatoes.

4

available, and there's a 5% discount on Wednesday. ✉ *1 Valley Rd., junction of Middle Rd.* ☎ *441/236–0351* ⊕ *www. marketplace.bm.*

Heron Bay MarketPlace

FOOD/CANDY | Part of the island-wide MarketPlace chain, this location has a large selection of fresh vegetables, as well as meats and seafood. It's a convenient drive to Marley Beach from here. ✉ *Heron Bay Plaza, 227 Middle Rd.* ☎ *441/238–1993* ⊕ *www.marketplace. bm.*

Lindo's Family Foods, Ltd.

FOOD/CANDY | Lindo's is a medium-size store with a good selection of groceries, plus organic foods, fresh seafood, and fine imported French and Italian cheese and pâtés. It's within walking distance of several Warwick accommodations. There's also a Devonshire location, Lindo's Family Foods on Watlington Road. Both stores have a pharmacy. ✉ *128 Middle Rd.* ☎ *441/236–1344* ⊕ *www. lindos.bm.*

Modern Mart

FOOD/CANDY | Part of the MarketPlace chain but smaller than its flagship Hamilton store, this location has all the essentials and organic foods. You get a 5% discount on Wednesday. The store is easily accessible from Paraquet Apartments and other south shore hotels.

It's also the nearest food stop to Elbow Beach. ⊠ *104 South Rd.* ☏ *441/236–6161* ⊕ *www.marketplace.bm.*

SPAS

Gillian's

SPA/BEAUTY | Located in an unassuming pink cottage on the south shore in Devonshire, the locally popular Gillian's offers more than 30 treatments that will relax you from head to toe. Luxurious Pamper Packages provide a variety of treatments. ⊠ *14 South Shore Rd.* ✛ *Beside Demco Florists* ☏ *441/232–0496* ⊕ *www.gilliansbermuda.com.*

The Spa at Elbow Beach

SPA/BEAUTY | For the most pampering treatments in Bermuda, the Spa at Elbow Beach includes personal and couples spa suites overlooking the Atlantic. The suites include personal showers, a vanity area, a granite bath, and daybeds on private balconies outside the suite. Treatments, which include everything from aromatherapy to facials to scrubs, blend island and Asian influences and use ESPA products. Although not the largest, this is the most lavish, personal, private, and relaxing spa on the island. There is also a gym. ⊠ *Elbow Beach Resort, 60 South Shore Rd.* ☏ *441/239–8900* ⊕ *www. elbowbeachbermuda.com/spa.*

Three Graces Day Spa at Pompano Beach Club

SPA/BEAUTY | With two of its three treatment rooms overlooking the calming waters of the south shore, Three Graces Day Spa at Pompano Beach Club offers a full range of individual and couples' treatments, including baths, scrubs, and massages. There's another location, with a full salon, at the Newstead Belmont Hills in Paget. ⊠ *Pompano Beach Club, 36 Pompano Beach Rd.* ☏ *441/234–0333* ⊕ *www.threegracesdayspa.com.*

★ Willow Stream Spa

SPA/BEAUTY | The Fairmont Southampton's Willow Stream Spa is the island's largest facility. Besides a complete health club,

including personal trainers, there are a garden-enclosed indoor pool, a sundeck overlooking the ocean, two Jacuzzis, three lounges, steam rooms, inhalation rooms, and 15 treatment rooms. Lengthy, specially designed treatments combine baths, wraps, and massage; all are conducted with the utmost skill. Yoga is another option. ⊠ *Fairmont Southampton, 101 South Shore Rd.* ☏ *441/239–6924* ⊕ *www.fairmont.com/ southampton-bermuda.*

🏃 Activities

From Devonshire to Southampton, there's lots to do and see, particularly for nature lovers. Some of the best spots to spy local and visiting birds are in the central parishes, including secluded Seymour's Pond Nature Reserve. A pedal bike will take you from one landmark to the next if you follow the Bermuda Railway Trail, which curves along the island's northern shore through these parishes. On this island obsessed with sports, there are ample opportunities to get moving, from a world-class round of golf to a rousing set of tennis.

BIKING

Biking in Bermuda can pose a challenge due to the consistently high humidity. Don't let that stop you from enjoying the scenic views of the **Bermuda Railway Trail,** particularly from parts of the path that lace the stretch along the north shore before the trail follows Middle Road on its winding way to the West End. Take advantage of pedal power to access amenities like public beaches and parks too.

Oleander Cycles

BICYCLING | The agency is known primarily for its selection of motorbikes and scooters for rent and sale, although bicycles, as well as electric powered two-seaters, are also available to rent. Single and double bikes are available, and a damage waiver is charged. Oleander

Cycles's main store is in Paget, but its Southampton location is convenient for the Reefs Resort & Club guests since it's right across the street. ✉ *6 Valley Rd.* ✛ *Off Middle Rd.* ☎ *441/236–5235* ⊕ *www.oleandercycles.bm* 🚲 *From $41 for 2 hours.*

South Shore Road

BICYCLING | This main island road covers almost the full length of the island and passes absolutely gorgeous ocean views. South Shore Road—also known as South Road—is well paved and, for the most part, wider than Middle Road, North Shore Road, and Harbour Road, with relatively few hills. However, it's one of Bermuda's windiest and most heavily traveled thoroughfares. Highlights are through Warwick and Southampton, looking down on the popular south shore beaches.

Tribe Road 3

BICYCLING | Tribe roads are small, often unpaved side roads, some of which date to the earliest settlement of Bermuda in the 17th century. They make for good exploring, though many are quite short and lead to dead ends. Beginning at Oleander Cycles in Southampton, Tribe Road 3 steeply climbs the hillside just below Gibbs Hill Lighthouse, with views of the south shore below. It eventually leads to a point from where you can see both the north and south shores.

BIRD-WATCHING

Casual and more serious birders are guaranteed to catch sight of an interesting feathered friend here, depending on the time of year. In the central parishes, places like the **Bermuda Arboretum** have been designated as bird sanctuaries and offer a variety of environments for birds.

Seymour's Pond Nature Reserve

BIRD WATCHING | Managed by the Bermuda Audubon Society, Seymour's Pond is smaller and less exciting than Warwick (central parishes) and Spittal (eastern parishes) ponds, but it has the advantage of being a bit farther inland, and therefore both better protected and better suited to serious birders. Twenty-eight species of ducks are recorded in Bermuda, and you're quite likely to see many of them here. Keep an eye out for moorhens, American coots, and pied-billed grebes, three species known to breed around this location. ✉ *Middle Rd.* ✛ *near Barnes Corner Park* ⊕ *audubon.bm.*

Sherwin Nature Reserve

BIRD WATCHING | Also referred to as Warwick Pond, this is Bermuda's second-largest freshwater pond and prime bird-viewing territory. Shorebirds and herons gather en masse in the surrounding allspice woodland and cattail marsh during the fall and winter seasons. Note: in the heat of summer, the stagnant water lets off a rather putrid smell. ✉ *Middle Rd.* ✛ *Near Ettrick Animal Hospital.*

BOATING

Pompano Beach Club

WATER SPORTS | For a relaxed aquatic experience, check out Pompano Beach Club. Several low-speed vessels are available including motorized Fun Cat cruisers, Hobie Cat sailboats, two-person glass-bottom kayaks, and paddleboards. Discounted rates are offered to Pompano Beach Club hotel guests. The watersports center is open from May to October. Snorkeling equipment is available to rent; the club also offers snorkeling trips, harbor cruises, and fishing trips. ✉ *36 Pompano Beach Rd.* ☎ *441/234–0222* ⊕ *www.pompanobeachclub.com* 🚤 *From $6 per hour for snorkel gear rental, $40 per hour for kayaks and paddleboards, $80 per hour for vessels.*

Tam-Marina

BOATING | Founded in 1967, Tam-Marina has a reputation for lively group charter–only dinner and cocktail cruises on a fleet of elegant white motor yachts. *Lady Charlotte* and *Lady Tamara* often accommodate large private parties on the Great Sound, whereas *Boss Lady* is smaller and more intimate, tailored for groups

From Tee Time to Bed Time

If you stay in a hotel with its own golf course or one that has agreements with some of the golf clubs, it cuts out much of the planning you'll have to do on your own. For instance, the **Fairmont Southampton** has its own 18-hole executive course. Hotels block tee times for guests and provide a shuttle to and from the course.

At the **Tucker's Point Golf Club,** which opened its hotel and spa in 2009, you can contrast the old and the new in golf course designs without straying very far from the resort. On-site is Roger Rulewich's fabulous design, laid down atop the old Castle Harbour Golf Club, designed by his mentor, Robert Trent Jones Sr. Literally next door is the classic **Mid Ocean Club,** a Charles Blair Macdonald track redesigned by

Jones in 1953. Mid Ocean has hosted PGA Grand Slams.

Guests staying at the **Newstead Belmont Hills Golf Resort & Spa** on Hamilton Harbor can enjoy 18 rounds on the greens of **Belmont Hills Golf Club,** a course designed in 2002 by Algie M. Pulley Jr. It's worth noting that while the hotel is in Paget, the course itself is in Warwick Parish. Your hotel staff should be able to arrange a cab for the 5- to 10-minute ride if you have golf gear in tow.

When you make your lodging arrangements, check to see what golf packages and perks are available. Many hoteliers are also members at the clubs and are happy to facilitate arrangements.

of 10 guests or fewer. Join the ranks of celebrities that have cruised aboard these luxurious charter boats—a plush interior, fully stocked bar, and impeccable service awaits. ✉ *Jonathan's Landing, 61 Harbour Rd.* ☎ *441/236–0127* ⊕ *www. ladyboats.com* ✆ *Boss Lady, $850 for up to 10 people for 3 hrs; Lady Tamara and Lady Charlotte, from $2,850 for 70 people (and more) for 3 hrs.*

BOWLING
Warwick Lanes

BOWLING | Bowling shoes are included at this popular recreational spot that opens later in the afternoon. Take advantage of the small restaurant inside, as well as vending machines, for a midgame snack. Though there are 24 lanes, this place can fill up, so it's best to call to make a reservation and confirm the hours. ✉ *47 Middle Rd.* ✛ *Near Warwick Esso* ☎ *441/236–5290* ✆ *$15.50 for 2 games.*

GOLF
Belmont Hills Golf Club

GOLF | Belmont Hills, opened in 2003, was designed by California architect Algie Pulley Jr. and built on the site of the former Belmont Manor and Golf Club, a haven for celebrities in the early 1900s. This course is now a real shot-making test, heavily contoured and with more water than most other Bermuda courses. The sand in the bunkers is the same used at Augusta National, site of the Masters. A waterfall connects two man-made lakes that can come into play on several holes. The final four holes are challenging because of their tight landing areas bordered by out-of-bounds stakes. The pressure continues until the ball is in the hole, because the greens are heavily bunkered and multitiered. The course has the island's only double green, a 14,000-square-foot putting surface on holes 1 and 10. ■**TIP**➔ **The 7th hole, a 178-yard par 3, is bordered by a waterfall.**

✉ *25 Belmont Hills Dr.* ☎ *441/236–6060*
🌐 *www.newsteadbelmonthills.com*
🎫 *$100 daily (including cart), $50 sunset*
⛳ *18 holes, 6017 yards, par 70.*

Bermuda Golf Academy

GOLF | **FAMILY** | When you just want to practice or have some fun teaching the kids how to play golf in a relaxed environment, head for the Bermuda Golf Academy. The 320-yard driving range is floodlit at night until 10 pm, and there are 40 practice bays. If you get a rainy day, fine-tune your game in one of the 25 covered bays. You can also work on sand shots in the practice bunker or sharpen your putting on a practice green. Especially attractive for families is the 18-hole miniature golf course, which features pagodas, a waterfall, waterways—and even a drawbridge to hit over on the 16th hole. The minicourse is lighted at night and takes 45 to 60 minutes to complete. Afterward, have a tasty bite to eat at the food truck parked nearby. ✉ *12 Industrial Park Rd.* ✛ *Off Middle Rd.* ☎ *441/238–8800* 🎫 *Driving range $6 (40 balls); club rentals $2; miniature golf $12; lessons $85/hr.*

Ocean View Golf Course

GOLF | If you want to play with locals or just mingle to talk golf, Ocean View is the place to be after the workday ends. Only 10 minutes from Hamilton, it's very popular. Switch tees on your second loop of the 9 holes for an 18-hole round playing 5658 yards to par 70. The first hole is a tough par 5 with a long, tight fairway flanked by a coral wall and a drop-off to the shore. The course is aptly named; there are panoramas from many holes as well as from the clubhouse. The club has a 260-yard driving range where the wind is often at your back, so your drives seem longer than they really are. ■ **TIP→ The green on the 192-yard, par-3 9th hole is cut into a coral hillside landscaped with colorful plants. It's a demanding shot when the wind is gusting from the north or west.** ✉ *2 Barker's Hill* ✛ *Off North Shore Rd.*

☎ *441/295–9092* 🌐 *www.oceanviewgolf-club.com* 🎫 *$50 with cart, $50 sunset* ⛳ *9 holes (9 holes are played "out" followed by the same 9 holes played "in" to total 18), 2940 yards, par 35.*

Port Royal Golf Course

GOLF | One of two government-owned courses (Ocean View is the other), Port Royal is a perennial local and visitor favorite. A 2009 added irrigation, rebuilt tees, rebuilt and returfed greens, and redesigned bunkers. It hosted the PGA Grand Slam in October from 2009 to 2014. The 16th, arguably Bermuda's best-known golf hole, has a green that occupies a treeless promontory with a backdrop of the blue waters and pink sands of Whale Bay. When the wind is blowing hard onshore, as it frequently does, this can be a tough green to reach. The holes leading up to the 16th are the icing on the cake, with ocean views on 7, 8, 9, and 15. The 1970 Robert Trent Jones Sr. layout has many elevated tees and greens and some clever doglegs. There are plenty of hills. ✉ *5 Port Royal Golf Course Rd.* ✛ *Off Middle Rd.* ☎ *441/234–0974 for automated tee-time reservations* 🌐 *www.portroyalgolfcourse.com* 🎫 *$180; sunset $110* ⛳ *18 holes, 6842 yards, par 71.*

Turtle Hill Golf Club

GOLF | Spreading across the hillside below the high-rise Fairmont Southampton, this executive golf course is known for its steep terrain, giving players who opt to walk (for sunset tee times only) an excellent workout. The Ted Robinson design is a good warm-up for Bermuda's full-length courses, offering a legitimate test of wind and bunker play. The front nine has almost constant views of the ocean and is more difficult than the back nine, with tight holes calling for careful club selection. Club rentals and lessons are also available. Because the hotel and its restaurants are so close, there's no golf clubhouse per se, just a 10th-hole Golf Hut for snacks and drinks. ✉ *Fairmont*

Southampton, 101 South Shore Rd.
☎ *441/239–6952* ⊕ *www.fairmont.com/*
southampton-bermuda ✉ *$99 before*
noon (with cart), $69 after 12 pm (with
cart), $45 sunset (walking) ⅃. *18 holes,*
2684 yards, par 54.

HORSEBACK RIDING
EQUESTRIAN EVENTS
Events are held at the National Equestrian Centre in Devonshire most weekends
from October to May. One highlight is
the FEI Competition in dressage and
show jumping in March and April, an
intense event for young riders. These
events are free to attend, though you
may need a few dollars to purchase a
drink or snack if there is a concessions
stand. Harness pony racing is held on
weekends between October and March,
with an atmosphere more friendly than
competitive. Ponies are harnessed to
sulkies (small, two-wheeled frames with
an unsprung seat) and race against each
other around the 0.2-mile track.

Bermuda Equestrian Federation
HORSE RACING/SHOW | The federation
organizes a number of international dressage and show jumping competitions;
the busy season features evening and
Sunday afternoon shows from September through May. Year-round action takes
place at the National Equestrian Centre
on Vesey Street in Devonshire. Don't
miss the very popular Harness Pony
Races beginning the first weekend of
October. Contact BEF or visit their website for information on shows and races.
✉ *National Equestrian Centre, 48 Vesey*
St. ☎ *441/234–0485* ⊕ *www.bef.bm.*

Driving Horse & Pony Club
HORSE RACING/SHOW | The club, affiliated
with the Bermuda Equestrian Federation,
organizes a variety of events for horse
enthusiasts and aspiring competitors.
Stay up to date with recent performances and upcoming events on its website.
✉ *National Equestrian Centre, Vesey St.*
☎ *441/291–7223* ⊕ *www.dhpc.yolasite.*
com ✉ *From $6.*

SCUBA DIVING
★ **Dive Bermuda** (*Blue Water Divers*)
SCUBA DIVING | The company operates
several locations across the island, one
of which is at the Southampton Fairmont,
where you can rent equipment for both
scuba diving and snorkeling, as well as
book excursions out on (or under) the
water. Beginner and advanced certification classes for diving are available.
✉ *Southampton Fairmont, 101 South*
Shore Rd. ☎ *441/238–332* ⊕ *www.*
divebermuda.com ✉ *From $95 for 1-tank*
dive, $150 for 2-tank dive.

Dive Bermuda
SCUBA DIVING | At this environmentally
friendly dive shop, instructors go out of
their way to protect Bermuda's reefs and
fish. Dive Bermuda has been awarded
National Geographic Dive Centre status
and is the only center on the island to
offer courses sanctioned by the world-re-
nowned environmental organization.
It has also received an environmental
excellence award from PADI (Professional Association of Diving Instructors). A
Discover Scuba Diving course includes
a lesson, dive, and equipment. For
experienced divers, there are single-tank
and double-tank dives. Group rates and
multiple dives cost less. Dive Bermuda
has a second location at Grotto Bay
Beach Resort in Hamilton Parish. ✉ *Fair-*
mont Southampton, 101 South Shore Rd.
☎ *441/238–2332* ⊕ *www.bermudascuba.*
com ✉ *$195 for Discover Scuba course;*
$95 for single-tank dive, $150 for two-
tank dive.

SNORKELING
Bermuda's clear water is perfect for
snorkeling, whether you seek out spots
yourself or take a snorkel cruise. Snorkeling equipment and, sometimes, underwater cameras are available for rent at
most major hotels and at several marinas
here, and sometimes right on the beach.
A deposit or credit-card number is usually required when renting equipment.

Equipment may be a bit costly, but the experience is well worth it.

★ Church Bay Beach

SNORKELING | Fairly secluded and a little off the beaten path, Church Bay Beach in Southampton Parish may offer little to families, but it is an ideal spot to get up close and personal with Bermuda's sea life. The reef is quite close to shore and is home to various colorful local fish and other sea creatures. The beach can be quite rocky, and when the wind picks up, the ocean can be quite rough. There's no lifeguard, so swimmers and snorkelers are urged to exercise caution at all times. ✉ *Church Bay Park ✛ Off South Rd.* ✆ *Free* Ⓜ *Bus 7 from Hamilton.*

Elbow Beach Resort

SNORKELING | **FAMILY** | The gentle curve of Elbow Beach is an excellent spot for families to enjoy snorkeling in the south shore surf. Part of the beach is owned by the Elbow Beach Resort; equipment is complimentary for hotel guests, but beachgoers can rent masks, snorkels, and other gear by the hour. ✉ *Elbow Beach Resort, 60 South Shore Rd.* ☎ *441/236–3535* ⊕ *www.elbowbeachbermuda.com* ✆ *Rentals from $20 per hour for nonguests.*

Rum Bum Beach Bar

SNORKELING | Snorkel gear, umbrellas, and sun loungers are available to rent at this beachside bar and restaurant at the entrance to Horseshoe Bay Beach. Rentals must be returned by 5 pm. ✉ *Horseshoe Bay Beach Park, 94 South Shore Rd.* ☎ *441/238–0088* ⊕ *www.rumbumbeachbar.com* ✆ *$20–$25 for 1-day snorkel and mask rental; $20–$25 deposit.*

SQUASH

Bermuda Squash & Fitness Club

SQUASH/RACQUETBALL/PADDLEBALL | The club makes its four courts available to nonmembers between 10 am and 10 pm by reservation, and a staff member may be able to hook you up with a suitable partner. A nominal fee buys a good chunk of play time, and you can borrow rackets and balls. Temporary one-month memberships are available, if you plan to play a lot. Bermuda made squash headlines in 2005 when the island hosted the world's top 30 players at the Bermuda Masters, and squash seems poised to become a big part of Bermuda's sports scene; 40-minute private lessons are available from former pros. ✉ *111 Middle Rd.* ☎ *441/292–6881* ⊕ *www.bermudasquash.com* ✆ *From $8 for court time, private lessons from $55; guest fees $20 for nonmember.*

TENNIS

Coral Beach & Tennis Club

TENNIS | Introduction by a member is required to play at this exclusive club, which was once the site of the USTA-sanctioned XL Capital Bermuda Open tournament. Coral Beach has eight clay courts, three of which are floodlighted. Resident pros are on hand to arrange private lessons. The club also hosts several well-attended senior and junior tournaments throughout the year. Tennis whites are required. ✉ *34 South Shore Rd.* ☎ *441/236–2233* ⊕ *www.coralbeachclub.com* ✆ *Introduced guests $50 per person per day; private lessons from $100 per hour.*

Elbow Beach Tennis Facility

TENNIS | The facility is fortunate to have as its director of tennis David Lambert, a former president of the Bermuda Lawn Tennis Association. There are five Plexipave courts, three with lights, and daily play. Lessons and match play can be arranged for hotel guests or other visitors. Dedicated tennis fans may consider Elbow's tennis package, which includes time on the court, equipment, continental breakfast, and a luxury room. This facility also rents and repairs rackets. ✉ *Elbow Beach Resort, 60 South Shore Rd.* ☎ *441/236–8737* ✆ *Courts $12 per hour for Elbow Beach guests, $15 per hour for public; lessons from $50 for 30 min.*

Fairmont Southampton Tennis Club

TENNIS | Despite their position at the water's edge, the Plexipave hard courts at the Fairmont are reasonably shielded from the wind, although the breeze can be swirling and difficult. Six courts are at hand, open daily. Racket rentals and balls are available, and you can book time with a pro. You can also book a complete tennis package, which includes luxury Fairmont accommodations, breakfast, and lessons. ✉ *Fairmont Southampton, 101 South Shore Rd.* ☎ *441/236–6950* ⊕ *www.fairmont.com/southampton-bermuda* 💰 *$19 per nonguest per day; lesson $115 per hour for up to 2 players.*

Pomander Gate Tennis Club

TENNIS | There are five hard courts available (four with lighting) at this scenic club located off Hamilton Harbour. Temporary membership is available on a weekly basis, or you can can rent a court for a session (one hour of play time during the day or 45 minutes at night). ✉ *21 Pomander Rd.* ☎ *441/236–5400* ⊕ *www.pgtc. bm* 💰 *$6 per 1-hour session; $7 charge to run lights for night play.*

Chapter 5

ST. GEORGE'S

Updated by
Robyn Bardgett

👁 Sights
★★★★★

🍴 Restaurants
★★★★★

🛏 Hotels
★★☆☆☆

🛍 Shopping
★★★★★

🍸 Nightlife
★☆☆☆☆

ISLAND SNAPSHOT

TOP EXPERIENCES

■ **St. George's:** A UNESCO World Heritage site, the Town of St. George is the oldest inhabited town on Bermuda.

■ **Naval stronghold:** Many of Bermuda's historic forts are dotted across the east end of the island, including Fort St. Catherine and Alexandra Battery.

■ **Cup Match:** Every other year, St. George's hosts this spirited summer cricket match and festive gatherings surrounding it.

■ **St. Peter's:** The oldest continuously operating Anglican church in the Western hemisphere dates to 1620 and is both stunningly simple and rich in island history.

■ **Bermuda Perfumery:** Visit this historic perfumery to learn how the island's iconic smells are bottled.

■ **Cooper's Island Nature Reserve.** Discover the natural wonders of Cooper's Island in St. David's.

GETTING HERE

The Town of St. George is accessible by public transport from Hamilton; catch Bus 1, 3, 10, or 11. St. David's is accessible by taking Bus 6, which also passes Clearwater Beach. A ferry from Dockyard runs from April to November and docks near Penno's Wharf in St. George's. All tickets and passes are sold at the main bus terminal in Hamilton. Parking is available, along with charging stations for electric vehicles, and there are spaces for rented bikes, too.

PLANNING YOUR TIME

St. George's has a disproportionately large number of historic buildings, plus pleasant gardens and enticing shops. It's the perfect place to spend a day exploring museums, picking up a gift bag of locally made soap, and enjoying a glass of something cold at one of the harborfront restaurants. They say you can't get lost here—but you can certainly lose track of time. It's also worth it to spend a day exploring the rest of the parish as well as Cooper's Island Nature Reserve in St. David's.

QUICK BITES

■ **Sweet SAAK.** Come to this unassuming bakery for the ultimate cinnamon bun experience or sample any of their delicious homemade baked selections. ⊠ *16 York St., St. George* ☏ *441/297-0663.*

■ **Temptations Cafe.** Grab a freshly made sandwich and take a seat in one of the window booths to people-watch, or pack your goodies for a beach or waterside picnic. ⊠ *31 York St., St. George* ☏ *441/297-1368.*

■ **GoJo's Coffee Shop.** This is the perfect spot in the center of town to grab a coffee or a quick bite to eat. ⊠ *7 King's Sq., St. George* ☏ *441/297-0614.*

St. George's and Hamilton are about 10 miles and 200 years apart. The latter wasn't even incorporated as a town until 1792, and by the time Hamilton became the capital in 1815, St. George's had already celebrated its bicentennial.

The settlement of Bermuda began in what is now the Town of St. George (or St. George's, which is also the name of the parish) when the *Sea Venture*—flagship of an English fleet carrying supplies to Jamestown, Virginia—was wrecked on Bermuda's treacherous reefs in 1609. Four hundred years later, no visit to the island would be complete without a stop in this picturesque and remarkably preserved example of an early New World outpost.

Although St. George's is a living community—not a living-history museum—it retains the patina of authenticity. In fact, in 2000 it was named a UNESCO World Heritage site. That designation puts it on par with spots like the Great Wall of China and the Taj Mahal in India. But don't expect awe-inspiring edifices here. On the contrary, St. George's chief charm lies in tiny walled cottages, simple colonial churches, and labyrinthine alleys that beg to be explored.

Across St. George's Harbour is more bucolic St. David's. While much of this area of the parish seems to be taken up by the L. F. Wade International Airport's runways, explore further and you will come across some natural and historical wonders, including Cooper's Island Nature Reserve.

◉ Sights

A stroll through the alleys barely one-car wide will reveal well-preserved examples of Bermuda's unique and practical architecture. St. George's has the largest collection of historical buildings on the island, but because of the town's size, most of the sights are relatively close and easily reached. If you have limited time, stick to the sights on York and Water streets and nearby King's Square.

Bermuda National Trust Museum at the Globe Hotel

MUSEUM | Erected as a governor's mansion around 1700, this building became a hotbed of activity during the American Civil War and is now a museum focusing on the island's history. From here, Confederate Major Norman Walker coordinated the surreptitious flow of guns, ammunition, and war supplies from England, through Union blockades, into American ports. It saw service as the Globe Hotel during the mid-19th century and became a National Trust property in 1951. A short video, *Bermuda, Centre of the Atlantic*, recounts the history of Bermuda, and a memorabilia-filled exhibit entitled "Rogues & Runners: Bermuda and the American Civil War" describes St. George's when it was a port for Confederate blockade runners. This is also the location of the Trustworthy Gift Shop. ⊠ *32 Duke of York St., St. George's* ☏ *441/297–1423* ⊕ *www.bnt.bm* ⊠ *$5; $10 combination ticket includes*

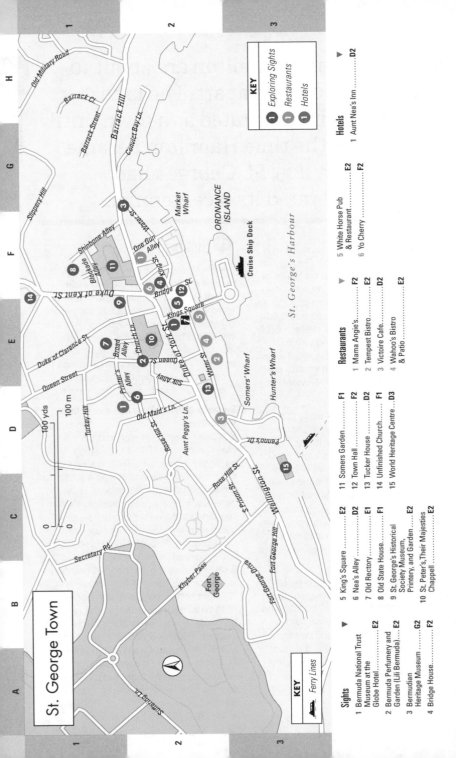

St. George Town

KEY
⛴ Ferry Lines

KEY
① Exploring Sights
① Restaurants
① Hotels

St. George's Harbour

ORDNANCE ISLAND

Cruise Ship Dock

Sights ▶

1 Bermuda National Trust Museum at the Globe Hotel	**E2**
2 Bermuda Perfumery and Garden (Lili Bermuda)	**E2**
3 Bermudian Heritage Museum	**G2**
4 Bridge House	**F2**
5 King's Square	**E2**
6 Nea's Alley	**D2**
7 Old Rectory	**E1**
8 Old State House	**F1**
9 St. George's Historical Society Museum, Printery, and Garden	**D3**
10 St. Peter's, Their Majesties Chappell	**E2**
11 Somers Garden	**F1**
12 Town Hall	**F2**
13 Tucker House	**D2**
14 Unfinished Church	**F1**
15 World Heritage Centre	**D3**

Restaurants ▶

1 Mama Angie's	**F2**
2 Tempest Bistro	**E2**
3 Victoire Cafe	**D2**
4 Wahoo's Bistro & Patio	**E2**
5 White Horse Pub & Restaurant	**E2**
6 Yo Cherry	**F2**

Hotels ▶

1 Aunt Nea's Inn	**D2**

admission to Tucker House and Verdmont (Smith's Parish) ♡ Closed Sun.

★ Bermuda Perfumery and Garden (Lili Bermuda)

MUSEUM | Originally in Hamilton Parish but in historic Stewart Hall since 2005, this perfumery founded in 1928 allows you to visit to learn about the process of making the scents. Although the location changed, the techniques did not: the perfumery still manufactures and bottles all its island-inspired scents on-site using more than 3,000 essential oils extracted from frangipani, jasmine, oleander, and passionflower. Guides are available to explain the entire process, and there's a small museum that outlines the company's history. You can also wander around the gardens and stock up on your favorite fragrances in the showroom. ⊠ Stewart Hall, 5 Queen St., St. George's ☎ 441/293–0627 ⊕ www.lilibermuda.com ⊠ Free ♡ Closed Sun.

Bermudian Heritage Museum

MUSEUM | The history, trials, and accomplishments of black Bermudians are highlighted in this museum in a converted 1840s warehouse. Photographs of early black residents including slaves, freedom fighters, and professionals line the walls, and the works of black artisans are proudly exhibited. Look, in particular, for the display about the Enterprise, a slave ship that was blown off course to Bermuda while sailing from Virginia to South Carolina in 1835. Since slavery had already been abolished on the island, the 78 slaves on board were technically free—and the Local Friendly Societies (grassroots organizations devoted to liberating and supporting slaves) worked to keep it that way. Society members obtained an injunction to bring the slaves' case into court and escorted the "human cargo" to their hearing in Hamilton, where many spoke in their own defense. All except one woman and her four children accepted the offer of freedom. Today countless Bermudians trace their ancestry back to those who arrived on

the Enterprise. Appropriately enough, the museum building was once home to one of the Friendly Societies. ⊠ 29 Water St., at Duke of York St., St. George's ☎ 441/297–4126 ⊕ bermudianheritagemuseum.com ⊠ $3 ♡ Closed Mon.

Bridge House

BUILDING | Today Bridge House serves as a gallery featuring local artists and Bermuda-centric artwork, but this 17th-century building, owned by the National Trust, was previously home to several of Bermuda's governors—and at least one ghost. Mistress Christian Stevenson, who was condemned as a witch in 1653, proclaimed her innocence at this spot, and now seems reluctant to leave it. Other National Trust properties also qualify as "favorite haunts." For instance, the Old Rectory on Broad Alley is said to have a spirit who plays the spinet in the wee hours of the morning. ⊠ 1 Bridge St., St. George's ⊕ www.bnt.bm ⊠ Free.

Fort St. Catherine

MILITARY SITE | FAMILY | Surrounded by a dry moat and accessed by a drawbridge, this restored and formidable hilltop fort has enough tunnels, towers, redoubts, and ramparts to satisfy even the most avid military historian—or adrenaline-fueled child. The original fort was built around 1614 by Bermuda's first governor, Richard Moore, but it was remodeled and enlarged at least five times. In fact, work continued on it until late in the 19th century. On-site an intriguing collection of antique weapons complements the impressive architecture. Standing out among the pistols and muskets is an 18-ton muzzle-loading cannon, which was capable of firing 400-pound shells a full half mile. ⊠ 15 Coot Pond Rd., St. George's ☎ 441/297–1920 ⊠ $7 ♡ Closed weekends.

King's Square

PLAZA | Today it looks rather inauspicious, more a patch of pavement than a leafy common, yet this square is St. George's undisputed center. In a town where age

A Good Walk in St. George's

Start your tour in **King's Square**, then stroll out onto **Ordnance Island** to see a replica of *Deliverance*: the ship built as a replacement for the *Sea Venture*. Behind you, just up the street, is the **Bermuda National Trust Museum at the Globe Hotel**, and across the square is the **Town Hall**. Venturing up King Street, notice the fine Bermudian architecture of **Bridge House**. At the top of King Street is the **Old State House**, the earliest stone building in Bermuda.

Walk up Princess Street to Duke of York Street and turn right, following the sidewalk to the **Bermudian Heritage Museum**. Across Duke of York Street, you can find **Somers Garden**, where Sir George Somers's heart is reportedly buried. After walking through the garden, climb the steps to Blockade Alley for a view of the **Unfinished Church** on a hill ahead. To your left are Duke of Kent Street, Featherbed Alley, and the **St. George's Historical Society Museum, Printery, and Garden**. Next, cross Clarence Street to Church Lane and turn right on Broad Alley to reach the **Old Rectory**. Straight ahead (or as

straight as you can go among these twisted streets) is Printer's Alley, which in turn links to **Nea's Alley**, where a whiff of 19th-century scandal still lingers.

Return to Church Lane and enter the yard of **St. Peter's Church**, a centuries-old sanctuary that, until the building of the Old State House, did double duty as the colony's only public meeting place. (The main entrance is on Duke of York Street.) From the church, continue down Duke of York Street until you reach Queen Street on your right. A short walk up it brings you to the **Bermuda Perfumery and Garden** at Stewart Hall, which will be on the left. You can learn about perfume making here. Turn around and walk back to Duke of York Street and go right until you get to Barber's Alley, turning left to reach **Tucker House**, which has been transformed from a prominent merchant's home into a museum. From there continue along Water Street, veering left again on Penno's Drive to visit the new **World Heritage Centre** at Penno's Wharf.

is relative, King's Square is comparatively new, created in the 19th century after a marshy part of the harbor was filled in. Locals frequently congregate here for civic celebrations. Visitors, meanwhile, come to see the replica stocks and pillory. Formerly used to punish petty crimes, these grisly gizmos—together with a replica ducking stool—are now popular props for photo ops. Reenactments of historical incidents, overseen by a town crier in full colonial costume, are staged in the square April through November, Monday to Thursday and Saturday at 12:30, and December through March

on Wednesday and Saturday at 12:30. ⊠ *Water St., St. George's* ⊕ *www.corpst-george.bm*.

Nea's Alley

NEIGHBORHOOD | While roaming the back streets, look for Nea's Alley. Nineteenth-century Irish poet Thomas Moore, who lived in St. George's during his tenure as registrar of the admiralty court, waxed poetic about both this "lime-covered alley" and a lovely woman he first encountered here: his boss's teenaged bride, Nea Tucker. Though arguably the most amorous, Moore wasn't the only writer to be inspired by Bermuda. Mark

Twain wrote about it in *The Innocents Abroad,* and his exclamation "you go to heaven if you want to; I'd druther stay in Bermuda" remains something of a motto in these parts. Two 20th-century playwrights, Eugene O'Neill and Noel Coward, also wintered—and worked—on the island. More recently, Bermuda resident Peter Benchley took the idea for his novel *The Deep* from the ships lost offshore. ⊠ *St. George's* ⊹ *Between Printer's Alley and Old Maid's La.*

Old Rectory

HOUSE | Built around 1699 by part-time privateer George Dew, this charming limestone cottage is mainly associated with a later resident, Alexander Richardson (the rector of St. Peter's Church), who lived here between 1763 and 1805. In addition to handsome gardens, the house with its cedar beams, multiple chimneys, and "welcoming arms" entrance is a lovely example of traditional Bermudian architecture. It is currently a private residence, but you can see many features of the Old Rectory from the road. ⊠ *1 Broad Alley, St. George's* ⊹ *Behind St. Peter's Church* ☎ *441/236–6483* ⊕ *www.bnt.bm.*

Old State House

GOVERNMENT BUILDING | A paltry peppercorn is the rent paid annually for the Old State House by the Masonic Lodge St. George No. 200 of the Grand Lodge of Scotland, the fraternal organization that has occupied the building since Bermuda's Parliament—the third oldest in the world after Iceland's and England's—vacated it in 1815 when the capital moved to Hamilton. A curious ritual takes place every April in King's Square as one peppercorn, placed upon a velvet pillow, is presented to the mayor of St. George's amid much pomp and circumstance. The Old State House was erected in 1620 in what Governor Nathaniel Butler believed was the Italian style, so it's one of the few structures in Bermuda to feature a flat roof. Builders used a mixture of turtle oil and lime as mortar, setting the style for future Bermudian buildings. The building is visible only from the street, as the interior is currently not accessible to the public. ⊠ *4 Princess St., St. George's* ☎ *441/297–8043.*

Ordnance Island

ISLAND | The island, directly across from King's Square, is dominated by a splendid bronze statue of Sir George Somers, commander of the *Sea Venture.* Somers looks surprised that he made it safely to shore—and you may be surprised that he ever chose to set sail again when you spy the nearby *Deliverance.* It's a full-scale replica of one of two ships—the other was the *Patience*—built under Somers's supervision to carry survivors from the 1609 wreck onward to Jamestown. But considering the ship's size (just 57 feet from bow to stern), *Deliverance* hardly seems seaworthy by modern standards. In complete contrast, Ordnance Island is often host to some of the world's most spectacular motor and sailing yachts, who use Bermuda as a mid-Atlantic stopover. ⊠ *Across from King's Sq., St. George's.*

St. David's Island

ISLAND | In a place famous for manicured lawns and well-tended gardens, St. David's Island feels comparatively wild; nevertheless, the real highlight is—quite literally—St. David's Lighthouse. Built in 1879 of Bermuda stone and occupying the tallest point on the East End, this red-and-white-striped lighthouse rises 208 feet above the sea, providing jaw-dropping views of St. George's, Castle Harbour, and the reef-rimmed south shore. Although the lighthouse itself isn't accessible to the public, this is also a great place to spot humpback whales passing through Bermuda's waters in April and May. St. David's is also the site of L. F. Wade International Airport, the main gateway to Bermuda. ⊠ *Lighthouse Hill, St. David's Island* ☎ *441/236–5902* ⊠ *Free.*

Bermuda's parliament once met in the former Government House, but when the capital moved to Hamilton in 1815 it became a Masonic lodge.

St. George's Historical Society Museum, Printery, and Garden

MUSEUM | Furnished to resemble its former incarnation as a private home, this typical Bermudian building reveals what life was like in the early 1700s. Along with period furnishings, such as a 1620 statehouse table, it has assorted documents and artifacts pertaining to the colonial days. But it's the re-created kitchen—complete with palmetto baskets and calabash dipping gourds—that really takes the cake. Downstairs the printery features a working replica of a Gutenberg-style press, as well as early editions of island newspapers. The beautiful cottage gardens behind the museum are also worth a visit. ⊠ *3 Featherbed Alley, St. George's* ⊹ *Near Duke of Kent St.* ☎ *441/297–8013* ✉ *$5* ⊘ *Closed Sun.; also Mon., Tues., Thurs., and Fri. Jan.–Mar.*

⭐ St. Peter's, Their Majesties Chappell

RELIGIOUS SITE | Because parts of this whitewashed stone church date back to 1620, it holds the distinction of being the oldest continuously operating Anglican church in the Western Hemisphere. Befitting its age, St. Peter's has many treasures. The red cedar altar, carved in 1615 under the supervision of Richard Moore (a shipwright and the colony's first governor) is the oldest piece of woodwork in Bermuda. The late 18th-century bishop's throne is believed to have been salvaged from a shipwreck, and the baptismal font, brought to the island by early settlers, is an estimated 900 years old. There's also a fine collection of Communion silver from the 1600s in the vestry. Nevertheless, it's the building itself that leaves the most lasting impression. With rough-hewn pillars, exposed cedar beams, and candlelit chandeliers, the church is stunning in its simplicity.

After viewing the interior, walk into the churchyard to see where prominent Bermudians, including Governor Sir Richard Sharples who was assassinated in 1973, are buried. A separate graveyard for slaves and free blacks (to the west of the church, behind the wall) is a reminder of Bermuda's segregated past. ⊠ *33 Duke of York St., St. George's* ☎ *441/297–2459*

www.stpeters.bm ✉ *$2 donation*
🕙 *Closed Sun., except for worship.*

Somers Garden

GARDEN | The history of the park goes back centuries: after sailing to Jamestown and back in 1610, Sir George Somers—the British admiral charged with developing the Bermudian colony—fell ill and died. According to local lore, he instructed his nephew Matthew Somers to bury his heart in Bermuda, where it belonged. Matthew sailed for England soon afterward, sneaking the body aboard in a cedar chest, and eventually buried it near Somers's birthplace in Dorset. Although it can't be proven that Matthew actually carried out his uncle's wishes, it's generally believed that Admiral Somers's heart was indeed left behind in a modest tomb at the southwest corner of the park. When the tomb was opened many years later, only a few bones, a pebble, and some bottle fragments were found. Nonetheless, ceremonies were held at the empty grave in 1920, when the Prince of Wales christened this pleasant, tree-shrouded park Somers Garden. ✉ *Bordered by Shinbone and Blockade Alleys, Duke of Kent and Duke of York Sts., St. George's* ✉ *Free.*

Town Hall

GOVERNMENT BUILDING | St. George's administrative offices are housed in a putty-color two-story structure that dates back to 1808. Inside the cedar-paneled hall—where the civic government still meets—you can see portraits of past mayors. ✉ *5 King's Sq., St. George's* ☎ *441/297–1532* ✉ *Free.*

Tucker House

MUSEUM | Owned and lovingly maintained as a museum by the Bermuda National Trust, Tucker House was built in the 1750s for a merchant who stored his wares in the cellar (a space that now holds an archaeological exhibit). But it's been associated with the Tucker family ever since Henry Tucker purchased it in

All Fired Up 👁

In 1775 America's Continental Congress imposed a ban on exports to colonies not supporting their trade embargo against England. A delegation of Bermudians traveled to Philadelphia offering salt in exchange for the resumption of grain shipments. Congress rejected the salt but agreed to lift the ban if Bermuda sent gunpowder instead. A group of Bermudians, including two members of the esteemed Tucker family, then broke into the island's arsenal, stole the gunpowder, and shipped it to Boston. The ban was soon lifted.

1775. The house is essentially a tribute to this well-connected clan whose members included a Bermudian governor, a U.S. treasurer, a Confederate navy captain, and an Episcopal bishop.

The kitchen, however, is dedicated to another notable—Joseph Hayne Rainey—who is thought to have operated a barber's shop in it during the Civil War. (Barber's Alley, around the corner, is also named in his honor.) As a freed slave from South Carolina, Rainey fled to Bermuda at the outbreak of the war. Afterward he returned to the United States and, in 1870, became the first black man to be elected to the House of Representatives. A short flight of stairs leads down to the kitchen, originally a separate building, and to an enclosed kitchen garden. ✉ *5 Water St., St. George's* ☎ *441/297–0545* ⊕ *www. bnt.bm* ✉ *$5; $10 combination ticket includes admission to Bermuda National Trust Museum at the Globe Hotel and Verdmont (in Smith's Parish)* 🕙 *Closed Sun.–Tues.*

Unfinished Church

RELIGIOUS SITE | Work began on this intended replacement for St. Peter's Church in 1874, but just as it neared completion, construction was halted by storm damage and disagreements within the church community. Hence the massive Gothic Revival pile sat—unfinished and crumbling—until the Bermuda National Trust stepped in to stabilize the structure in 1992. With soaring stone walls, a grassy floor, and only the sky for a roof, it's the sort of atmospheric ruin that poets and painters so admire. The inside of the building isn't currently accessible to the public, but part of the church is still opened for weddings. ⊠ Duke of Kent St., St. George's ☎ 441/297–2459 ⊕ www.stpeters.bm/UnfinishedChurch ⊠ Free.

World Heritage Centre

MUSEUM | FAMILY | Housed in an 1860 customs warehouse next to the Penno's Wharf Cruise Ship Terminal, the World Heritage Centre was developed under the auspices of the St. George's Foundation and includes an exhibits gallery; an education center; retail galleries; and regular talks, tours, and historical reenactments. You can view an introductory film (A Stroll Through St. George's) and visit the ground-floor Orientation Exhibits Gallery, which showcases several hundred years of civic history. A recent addition includes an exhibit highlighting pilot "Jemmy" Darrell, a former slave who became one of Bermuda's first King's boat pilots in 1795. In an effort to make the past palatable—even to very young guests—this gallery has engaging models, ranging from a miniaturized version of St. George's (circa 1620) to a full-scale mock-up of the deck of the Sea Venture. It also contains a costume corner where kids can dress up in period outfits. ⊠ 19 Penno's Wharf, St. George's ☎ 441/297–5791 ⊕ www.sgf.bm ⊠ $5.

Good to Know 🏃

If you rent a motorboat, be sure to ask for directions to Castle Island Nature Reserve in Castle Harbour, one of the most secluded and beautiful spots on the island's East End. Tread lightly here: The nature reserve and surrounding islands are home to many of the island's critically endangered, endemic species, such as the Bermuda skink and the cahow.

🏖 Beaches

While the beaches at the eastern end of the island are smaller, they are often less busy than those on the south shore at the western end of the island. They're also a bit more family-friendly because the water is shallower and tends to be calmer.

Clearwater Beach

BEACH—SIGHT | FAMILY | On the eastern tip of the island in St. David's, Clearwater is a long sandy strip of beach that's popular with serious swimmers and triathletes who use it as a training ground. But don't be intimidated: the young and old also flock here to wade in the shallow water, and there are buoy markers that identify where the beach becomes deeper. Keep your eyes peeled for turtles!

Clearwater is one of the few beaches in Bermuda that has a restaurant on the premises. Gombey's serves kids' picnic favorites such as burgers and fries as well as island classics like Bermudian fish chowder and Jamaican jerk chicken. There's also an in-house bar when the five-o'clock-somewhere mood strikes. Beach bathrooms, lifeguards during the tourist season (April through September), and a playground make this a great choice for families. **Amenities:** food and drink; lifeguards; parking (free); toilets.

Bermuda's famous "Unfinished Church" was begun in 1874 as a replacement for St. Peter's Church, but it was abandoned after being damaged in a storm.

Best for: partiers; sunrise; swimming; walking. ✉ *Off Cooper's Island Rd., St. David's Island* 🎫 *Free* Ⓜ *Bus 6 from St. George's.*

★ Cooper's Island Nature Reserve

BEACH—SIGHT | Past Clearwater Beach on St. David's Island and inaccessible to vehicles, Cooper's Island Nature Reserve is a blissfully secluded spot. While it is about a quarter-mile walk to get to the beach from the nearest parking area, and there are no amenities, it is worth the effort for the unspoiled views and virtually empty beaches. Walking trails around the nature reserve make this a good option for the adventurous beachgoer. **Best for:** snorkeling; swimming; walking. ✉ *Off Cooper's Island Rd., St. David's Island* 🎫 *Free.*

Fort St. Catherine Beach

BEACH—SIGHT | One of the larger north-shore beaches has water deep enough for a serious swim. If and when you get beach-bummed out, head over to the military fort next door, for which this beach is named. A quick tour of the structure will be a welcome break from the strong sun, as there is little shade along the beach. For a romantic evening, enjoy a beautiful alfresco meal at Black-beard's Hideout overlooking Achilles Bay just across the street. **Amenities:** food and drink; parking (free). **Best for:** solitude; snorkeling; sunset; swimming. ✉ *Coot Pond Rd., off Retreat Hill Rd., St. George's* 🎫 *Free* Ⓜ *Bus 10 or 11 from Hamilton.*

Gates Fort Park and Builder's Bay Beach

BEACH—SIGHT | **FAMILY** | Named after its neighboring military fort, Gates has a very small beach that is popular with local families. The park is off Barry Road, not far from Alexandra Battery, a favorite diving spot of St. George's children. It's also near Builder's Bay Beach, a good spot for snorkeling. From the Gates Fort you can enjoy an unobstructed view of cruise ships as they navigate the reefs through the Town Cut. **Amenities:** parking (free). **Best for:** solitude; sunrise. ✉ *Barry Rd., St. George's* 🎫 *Free* Ⓜ *Bus 1, 3, 10, or 11 from Hamilton.*

Tobacco Bay

BEACH—SIGHT | The most popular beach near St. George's, this small north-shore strand with ample parking is huddled in a coral cove surrounded by rock formations. Its beach house serves burgers and salads as well as specialty cocktails. Equipment rentals including umbrellas, chairs, floaties, and snorkel sets. It's a 10-minute hike from the bus stop in the town of St. George's, or you can flag down a taxi. In high season the beach is busy, especially midweek, when the cruise ships are docked; check the website for information on Friday-night events, bonfires, and live music. **Amenities:** food and drink; parking (free); toilets; water sports. **Best for:** snorkeling; swimming. ⊠ *9 Coot's Pond Rd., St. George's* ✛ *Off Barry Rd.* ☎ *441/297–2756 main* ⊕ *www.tobaccobay.bm* 🏷 *Free* Ⓜ *Bus 10 or 11 from Hamilton.*

Turtle Bay Beach

BEACH—SIGHT | FAMILY | Down a stretch from Clearwater Beach, adjacent to Cooper's Island Nature Reserve on St. David's Island, Turtle Bay Beach offers the same tranquility but with a bit less traffic. The water's also a deeper turquoise color here and very calm. If you're lucky, you might even spot a turtle. There's also a lifeguard on duty from April to September. When your tummy grumbles, it's a short walk to Gombey's Restaurant. **Amenities:** food and drink lifeguards. **Best for:** solitude; snorkeling; swimming. ⊠ *Cooper's Island Rd., St. David's Island* 🏷 *Free* Ⓜ *Bus 6 from St. George's.*

🍴 Restaurants

St. George's is a lovely dining spot, with many restaurants right by the water's edge. You can sit back and relax as you watch life at sea and even dip your toes to cool down. It's the perfect place to stop for dinner after you've built up an appetite walking around the Old Town's museums and historic buildings. The restaurants here are less crowded and

Atten-SHUN! 👁

The evolution of British military architecture between 1612 and 1956 can be traced through fortifications that dot the coast near St. George's. To get a sense of how diverse they are, follow your visit to **Fort St. Catherine** with a trip to **Alexandra Battery** (about a mile away along Barry Road) and nearby **Gates Fort**. The former, built in the mid-1800s, features Victorian innovations like cast-iron facings and concrete emplacements. The latter is a reconstruction of a small militia fort from the 1620s that was named for Sir Thomas Gates, the first survivor of the *Sea Venture* to reach dry land.

more relaxed than those in Hamilton and Dockyard. You'll probably find yourself dining with some of the country's politicians without even realizing it.

Blackbeard's Hideout

$$ | CARIBBEAN | Well off the beaten path, overlooking Achilles Bay next to the historic Fort St. Catherine, Blackbeard's Hideout offers a dining experience unlike that of anywhere else on the island. Some of the best views are up for grabs from the balcony seating; enjoy the vibrant sunset with a chilled glass of wine to set the scene for a memorable evening. **Known for:** tranquil beachfront location; plenty of burgers and bar snacks; seafood selection. Ⓢ *Average main: $28* ⊠ *St. George's Club, 6 Rose Hill, St. George's* ☎ *441/297–1400* ⊕ *www.stgeorgesclub.bm* ⊙ *Closed Nov.–Apr.*

Mama Angie's

$ | CAFÉ | For an authentic Bermudian fish sandwich, stop into this small roadside café, which is popular with locals. There's nothing fancy about the cash-only spot, but what it lacks in decor, it makes up in delicious tastes. **Known for:** egg

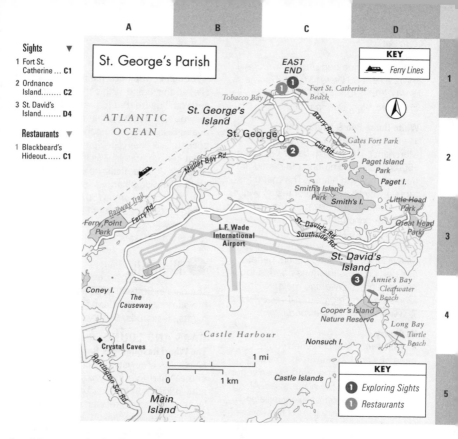

St. George's Parish

EAST
END

KEY

⛴ Ferry Lines

Fort St. Catherine
Beach

Tobacco Bay

St. George's
Island

ATLANTIC
OCEAN

St. George

Barry Rd.

Gates Fort Park

Mullet Bay Rd.

Cut Rd.

Paget Island
Park

Paget I.

Smith's Island
Park

Smith's I.

Little Head
Park

Railway Trail

Ferry Rd.

Ferry Point
Park

L.F. Wade
International
Airport

St. David's Rd.

Southside Rd.

Great Head
Park

St. David's
Island

Coney I.

The
Causeway

Annie's Bay

Clearwater
Beach

Cooper's Island
Nature Reserve

Long Bay
Turtle
Beach

Crystal Caves

Harrington Sd. Rd.

Castle Harbour

Nonsuch I.

0   1 mi

0   1 km

Castle Islands

KEY

1 Exploring Sights

1 Restaurants

Main
Island

---

breakfasts; good-value fare; authentic Bermudian atmosphere. $ *Average main: $15* ⊠ *48 York St., St. George's* ☎ *441/297–0959* ⊘ *Closed Sun. No dinner* ▭ *No credit cards.*

★ Tempest Bistro

$$ | BISTRO | Located a short stroll from King's Square, the inspired Tempest Bistro has a secluded entrance and a stunning view of the harbor, along with a rustic brick-and-tile interior that adds to the restaurant's laid-back, old-fashioned allure. In true bistro style, count on nightly specials to be creative and tasty; entrées rotate daily so you never know what to expect. **Known for:** banana bread pudding; curated wine list; quiet, romantic dining. $ *Average main: $26* ⊠ *22 Water St., St. George's* ☎ *441/297–0861* ⊘ *No dinner Sun. Closed Tues.*

Victoire Cafe

$ | CAFÉ | If you're in need of a high-quality cup of coffee, look no further than this tiny coffee shop. The interior is Swedish minimalist, and the bar seating at the window is the perfect place to people-watch as tourists pour off of the ferries berthed nearby. **Known for:** tasty vegan baked goods; creative coffee art; popular with cyclists. $ *Average main: $5* ⊠ *1 Water St., St. George's* ☎ *441/704–8200* ⊕ *victoirecafe.cc* ⊘ *No lunch or dinner.*

★ Wahoo's Bistro & Patio

$$ | SEAFOOD | FAMILY | With a name like Wahoo's, it's no surprise that this restaurant's menu features a wide variety of fresh, local seafood. Though often crowded, the patio offers an unbeatable view of the water; kids will love throwing scraps to schools of fish near the dock. **Known for:** catch-of-the-day specials; fish

chowder; wahoo nuggets. ⑤ *Average main: $29* ✉ *36 Water St., St. George's* ☎ *441/297–1307* ⊕ *www.wahoos.bm* ☉ *Closed Mon. during winter.*

White Horse Pub & Restaurant
$$ | CARIBBEAN | Located in the former Merchant's Hall, which dates back to the 1600s, this rustic harborside restaurant is overflowing with history. The menu features a variety of pub favorites as well as fresh seafood and pizza: try the sizzling shrimp or conch fritters for an appetizer, then the White Horse Signature Burger or fish-and-chips for your main course. **Known for:** breezy patio dining; generous portions; reservations needed for popular spot. ⑤ *Average main: $28* ✉ *8 King's Sq., St. George's* ☎ *441/297–1838* ⊕ *www.whitehorsebermuda.com.*

Yo Cherry
$ | FAST FOOD | FAMILY | When you're in need of a cool, sweet treat, this self-serve, soft-serve spot with frozen yogurt, ice, and gelato is the place to go. Along with standard favorites like vanilla and chocolate, Yo Cherry carries fun flavors like birthday cake and tiger's blood (blood orange gelato). **Known for:** creative toppings; tasty baked goods; rotating hard ice cream options. ⑤ *Average main: $5* ✉ *38 York St., St. George's* ☎ *441/292–2022* ⊕ *www.yocherry.com.*

🛏 Hotels

Staying in the heart of this UNESCO World Heritage site is a great opportunity to get to know Bermuda's rich history. You'll be surrounded by some of the prettiest streets on the island, with colorful cottages and scores of little alleyways. St. George's is also right on the water's edge with a handful of beaches within walking distance. There's a warm and welcoming feel to St. George's, so stay a couple of days and you will make friends with the locals. Rentals are popular here.

Aunt Nea's Inn
$ | B&B/INN | Stroll down a narrow winding alley to this grand 18th-century home and you'll be treated to the best of St. George's, in a setting that combines quaintness with home comforts. **Pros:** peaceful, pleasant St. George's setting; great service; within walking distance of King's Square. **Cons:** no pool; far from other island destinations; small property. ⑤ *Rooms from: $150* ✉ *1 Nea's Alley, St. George's* ⊹ *Off Old Maid's La.* ☎ *441/296–2868* ⊕ *auntneasinn.com* ⤢ *9 rooms* ⑩ *Breakfast.*

🍸 Nightlife

The bars in St. George's can get lively in the summer, with offerings such as quiz nights, live bands, and themed nights.

BARS AND LOUNGES
The Wharf Restaurant & Bar
BARS/PUBS | The yachting crowd gathers at the Wharf for rum swizzles, moderately priced pub fare, and nautical talk. Waterfront tables, relaxed atmosphere, and quick service make this spot worth the journey to the far northeastern tip of the island. ✉ *14 Water St., St. George's* ☎ *441/297–3305* ⊕ *www.wharf.bm.*

White Horse Pub & Restaurant
BARS/PUBS | This spot is great for an afternoon pint on the wooden terrace overlooking the water, where swarms of fish fight for scraps thrown from the tables. There are large-screen TVs for sports fans; sometimes there's night-time entertainment for everyone else. Finger-licking appetizers, colorful blended drinks, and a view of the water—what more do you need? ✉ *8 King's Sq., St. George's* ☎ *441/297–1838* ⊕ *www.whitehorsebermuda.com.*

🛍 Shopping

If you want to combine shopping with a leisurely stroll, Water Street and Duke of York Street in St. George's have a variety of stores that you can browse at your

ease. History-laden, scenic St. George's is the perfect day trip, as you can pick up some bargains, stop for lunch, and go sightseeing in the same location.

ART GALLERIES
Bridge House Gallery
ART GALLERIES | At this gallery inside one of St. George's well-preserved historical buildings, you can find artwork from watercolors to ceramics to photography, as well as jewelry, all inspired by the island. Look for Bermuda-influenced prints featuring St. David's Lighthouse by gallery owner Peter Matcham. ⊠ *1 Bridge St., St. George's* ☎ *441/261–6000* ⊕ *www.bridgehousegallery.com.*

BOOKS
★ Long Story Short
BOOKS/STATIONERY | The former Book Cellar has been transformed into a unique book and gift shop with an emphasis on books by women of color. Find quirky gifts such as locally handmade cedar jewelry and book-inspired candles and mugs. The shop's owner, Kristin White, also offers unique tours of St. George's, including the spooky Haunted History Tour. ⊠ *5 Water St., St. George's* ☎ *441/297–0448* ⊙ *Closed Sun.–Tues.*

CERAMICS AND GLASSWARE
Vera P. Card
CERAMICS/GLASSWARE | Lladró porcelain and Swarovski silver crystal figurines are available at almost identical prices elsewhere, but this store has the largest selection, including pieces specifically made for the shop, such as the Bermuda Moongate by Lladró. The shop's collection of more than 250 Hummel figurines is one of the world's largest. Limited-edition porcelain plates and vases depicting Bermuda scenes cost $69 to $300. There are also brightly painted chiming cuckoo clocks. Fine and costume jewelry are sold too. ⊠ *22 Water St., St. George's* ⊹ *Above Carriage House restaurant* ☎ *441/295–1729* ⊙ *Closed Sun.*

CLOTHING
Davison's of Bermuda
CLOTHING | Upping the souvenir T-shirt game, Davison's offers a great selection of shirts with stylish logos in great fits and designs. It also offers brightly printed dresses and separates for women and light, comfortable clothes for men, and a large selection of children's clothes from infant to about nine years. The store carries plenty of gift ideas and accessories as well as the perfect beach hat and bags. There are branches on Front Street in Hamilton, in the Fairmont Southampton, and in the Clocktower Mall in Dockyard. ⊠ *16 Water St., St. George's* ☎ *441/296–9552* ⊙ *Closed Sun.*

Frangipani
CLOTHING | This little store sells colorful women's fashions with a Southeast Asian island–resort look. Cotton, silk, and rayon leisure wear are the backbone of the stock. Don't miss the hand-strung, brightly colored, beaded necklaces, bracelets, and earrings, as well as eye-catching bags. There's also a location in the Washington Mall in Hamilton. ⊠ *13 Water St., St. George's* ☎ *441/297–1357* ⊙ *Closed Sun.*

COSMETICS AND BEAUTY
★ Lili Bermuda (Bermuda Perfumery)
PERFUME/COSMETICS | In business since 1928, the historic perfumery creates and manufactures its own perfumes, using the scents of Bermuda's flowers and citrus trees as inspiration. New perfumes are constantly being created, but try out Coral and Lili for women and Navy, 32 North, and Somers for men. You can also tour the facilities to learn about perfume making, and visit a small museum. Sweet P on the premises offers a cash-only afternoon tea on Wednesday and Saturday afternoons, with finger sandwiches, various pastries, and tea. The Perfumery opened the Lili Bermuda Boutique in Hamilton at 67 Front Street where you can also test out and purchase all of the scents. ⊠ *Stewart Hall, 5 Queen St.,*

St. George's ☎ 441/293-0627 ⊕ www.
lilibermuda.com ⊗ Closed Sun.

Salt Spray Soap Co.
PERFUME/COSMETICS | These brightly
colored chunks of soap are handmade
on-site using locally sourced seawater,
as well as natural ingredients such as
coconut oil and shea butter. Island-inspired scents like pink colada and sunrise
mimosa make them an extra special treat
to take home. Moisturizers and exfoliat-
ing salt scrubs in complementary scents
are another option. ✉ 7 Water St., St.
George's ☎ 441/707-6449.

CRAFTS
Adventures at Sea
CRAFTS | The spicy smell of cedar is the
first thing to greet you in this shop,
where owner Kersley Nanette handcrafts
teak and cedar model ships. The focus is
on tall ships of the 17th and 18th centuries, but other handcrafted cedar gifts are
also available. Prices range from $150 to
$5,000. Models of the *Sea Venture* and
Deliverance are especially popular. ✉ 3
Penno's Dr., St. George's ☎ 441/297-
2143 ⊗ Closed Sun.

FOOD
Somers Supermarket
FOOD/CANDY | Despite its small size,
Somers has a large selection, with hot
food, salads, and sandwiches made fresh
daily. It offers delivery service within St.
George's, and it's open daily. ✉ 41 York
St., St. George's ☎ 441/297-1177.

JEWELRY AND ACCESSORIES
★ Davidrose
JEWELRY/ACCESSORIES | Focusing on one-
of-a-kind and specially designed jewelry,
husband-and-wife-team David and Avrel
Zuill can create anything you dream up.
The St. George's design studio is filled
with their unique statement pieces and,
with a view over St. George's Harbour,
is the perfect place to find inspiration
for your next fine piece of jewelry.
There's also a location in the City of
Hamilton. ✉ 20 Water St., St. George's

☎ 441/293-7673 ⊕ www.davidrosestu-
dio.com ⊗ Closed Sun.

NOVELTIES AND GIFTS
Paradise Gift Shop
GIFTS/SOUVENIRS | You can find every
permutation of gift in this shop—from
"Bermuda" T-shirts to plates to funky
knickknacks. ✉ 7 King's Sq., St. George's
☎ 441/297-0670.

★ Robertson's Drug Store
FOOD/CANDY | This is so much more than
a pharmacy, as it's crammed full of goodies. It stocks great greeting cards, many
toiletries, and beauty products. One of
the best selections of unusual toys can
be found downstairs. ✉ 24 York St., St.
George's ☎ 441/297-1828.

Trustworthy Gift Shop at The Globe Hotel
GIFTS/SOUVENIRS | Proceeds from the
sales of Bermuda-inspired coffee-table
books, key chains, serving trays, spoons,
ceramics, pens, and bags at this gift
shop benefit the Bermuda National Trust.
Look out for their specially designed
bluebird boxes. This is where you can find
some of the most upscale gifts to take
back home. ✉ The Globe Hotel, 32 Duke
of York St., St. George's ☎ 441/297-1423
⊕ www.bnt.bm ⊗ Closed Sun.

WINES AND SPIRITS
Bermuda Duty Free Shop
WINE/SPIRITS | Before you head home, this
airport store invites you to put together
your own package of Bermuda liquors
at duty-free prices. Gosling's Black Seal
Rum and rum cakes are among the local
products. ✉ L. F. Wade International
Airport, 3 Cahow Way, St. George's
☎ 441/293-2870 ⊕ bermudaairport.com.

🏃 Activities

St. George's might be small, but there
are plenty of activities to keep you busy,
from biking to horseback riding to yoga.

For Love of Cricket

The Oval and Lords are names of English cricket grounds that evoke memories of Britain long ago, a time of cucumber sandwiches and tea poured from china pots—but the cricket scene in Bermuda is definitely Caribbean. The *thwack* of leather on willow is the same, but overcast skies and frequent breaks as the ground staff move quickly to put the rain covers in place are not for these players. The fans, gathered on grassy knolls and open terraces, are also far removed from those back in England, where the game originated.

Polite clapping and hearty hurrahs are not to be heard here. Instead the air is filled with chanting, and the grandstands reverberate to the sound of music. Allegiances are clearly defined, though few miles separate the opposing factions—mothers, fathers, sons, and daughters all cheering on their favorites. As the match comes to a conclusion, the setting sun falls low behind the clubhouse, and players and fans mingle to await the dawn of another day of runs, catches, and cries of "Howzat."

BIKING

Pedego Electric Bikes

BICYCLING | Looking for an easy way to explore St. George's and beyond? Opt for an electric bicycle to get the freedom of riding a bike with a little extra assistance. Pedego offers several different styles of bikes as well as tour packages. Locks and helmets are included in the price. ⊠ *19 York St., St. George's* ☎ *441/533–8687* ⊕ *pedegoelectricbikes.com/dealers/bermuda* 🖾 *From $20 per hour, $40 per day.*

BOWLING

Strykz Bowling Lounge

BOWLING | You can make bowling a social event with Strykz's energetic party atmosphere, upbeat music, and big-screen TVs. Walk-ins are welcome, but reservations are recommended, especially on weekends. ⊠ *27 Southside Rd., St. David's Island* ☎ *441/297–2727* 🖾 *From $9.*

CRICKET

Bermuda Cricket Board

CRICKET | The board was founded in 1938 and is in charge of scheduling, game regulations, and player development. Visit the BCB's website to learn more about its history, review past and upcoming events, and much more. ☎ *441/292–8958* ⊕ *www.cricket.bm.*

★ Cup Match

CRICKET | Among Bermuda cricket aficionados, Cup Match in late July or early August is *the* summer sporting event, played over two days. The top players from around the island compete in two teams: the East End team and the West End team. Although the match is taken very seriously, the event itself is a real festival, complete with plenty of Bermudian food and music. Cup Match coincides with two national holidays, Emancipation Day and Somers' Day. Emancipation Day is the celebration of the passing of the Slavery Abolition Act in 1834, which freed Bermuda's slaves, and Somers' Day celebrates Admiral Sir George Somers discovering Bermuda, which led to its settlement in 1609. Cup Match is Bermuda's only venue for legal gambling: the Crown & Anchor tent is pitched at the field. Thousands of picnickers and partiers show up during the two-day match. Fans wear colors to support their team—light blue on dark blue represents the East End, and navy on red represents the West End. General

admission tickets are available each day at the stadium entrance.

The venue alternates each year between the St. George's Cricket Club and the Somerset Cricket Club in Sandys Parish. See ⊕ *www.gotobermuda.com* for Match Cup information. ⊠ *St. George's Cricket Club, 56 Wellington Slip Rd., St. George's* ☎ *441/297–0374* ⊕ *www.sgcc.bm.*

FISHING

From casting a handline off the rocks or nearby dock to trawling the deep for sport fish like marlin, Bermudians take their fishing excursions very seriously.

Atlantic Spray Charters

FISHING | Half-day and full-day year-round charters are available on Atlantic's 40-foot *Tenacious.*Serious anglers can enjoy the challenge of reeling in sport fish like mahimahi, blue and white marlin, and yellowfin tuna. Rates include all the equipment you need, soda and water, and, most important, the knowledge of an experienced captain to help you catch the big fish. Charters are child friendly, and lunch can be provided at an extra cost. ⊠ *Chapel of Ease La., St. George's* ☎ *441/735–9444* ⊠ *From $1,175.*

GOLF

Mid Ocean Club

GOLF | The elite Mid Ocean Club is a 1921 Charles Blair Macdonald design revamped in 1953 by Robert Trent Jones Sr. *Golf Digest* ranks it among the top 100 courses outside the United States. The club has a genteel air and a great sense of history. Even though it's expensive, a round of play is worthwhile, as you walk with a caddy to savor the traditional golf experience and the scenery. There are many holes near ocean cliffs, but you'll want to linger on the back tee of the last hole, where the view up the coast is spectacular. Overlooking the 18th hole and the south shore, the Mid Ocean's pink clubhouse is classically Bermudian down to the interior cedar trim. The pro shop offers a range of golfing goodies. The Clubhouse is open

Taxi to Tee

If you bring your own clubs, budget for taxis to get you to the various courses. It's dangerous to carry your golf bag on a scooter, and clubs are not allowed on public buses. Taxis are expensive, but most rides are relatively short.

to visitors for breakfast, lunch, dinner, or drinks before or after their round of golf. Nonmembers can play midweek; be sure to reserve your tee time early as the calendar books up months in advance. Caddies, club rentals, and shoe rentals are all available. ⊠ *1 Mid Ocean Dr., Tucker's Town* ✛ *Off South Shore Rd.* ☎ *441/293–1215* ⊕ *www.themidocean-club.com* ⊠ *$275 for nonmembers ($32 for cart); $65 for caddy* ⏱ *18 holes, 6548 yards, par 71.*

HORSEBACK RIDING

Moran Meadows

HORSEBACK RIDING | For a different way to sightsee, take in the views and the coast around scenic St. George's on horseback during personalized trail rides. Start the day with a breathtaking sunrise beach excursion or spend a few hours exploring St. George's, with part of the ride taking you through the Old Town. ⊠ *9 Cut Rd., St. George's* ☎ *441/537–0400* ⊕ *www. bermudahorsetrailride.com* ⊠ *From $150 for 1-hour coastal ride, $220 for 90-minute sunrise trail ride.*

YOGA

Just Breathe

AEROBICS/YOGA | Situated above Water Street in a spacious and airy room with views of St. George's Harbour, this yoga studio offers drop-in yoga, with classes offered morning and evening. ⊠ *32 Water St., St. George's* ☎ *441/707–5001* ⊕ *www.justbreatheyoga.bm* ⊠ *$20 for 1-hour class.*

Chapter 6

EASTERN PARISHES

Updated by
Melissa Fox

👁 Sights	🍴 Restaurants	🛏 Hotels	🛍 Shopping	🍸 Nightlife
★★★★☆	★★★☆☆	★★☆☆☆	★☆☆☆☆	★☆☆☆☆

ISLAND SNAPSHOT

TOP EXPERIENCES

■ **Blue Hole Park:** Hike through this lovely park from its entrance by the causeway to its exit by Tom Moore's Tavern.

■ **Swizzle Inn:** Swagger out of Swizzle Inn after sampling a rum swizzle.

■ **Crystal Cave:** Explore the history and natural beauty of the cave, including a bridge across a subterranean lake, before treating yourself to ice cream at Bailey's.

■ **Bermuda Aquarium, Museum & Zoo:** Learn all about Bermuda's marine and land animals as you view a coral reef and interactive exhibits.

■ **Shelly Bay Beach:** Relax at this perfect family spot for picnics, swimming, and play.

■ **Bermuda Railway Trail:** Go biking or walking along the scenic Railway Trail on the north shore.

GETTING HERE

If you enjoy scenic views, take them in from the north shore as you travel along the Railway Trail. If you don't rent a scooter and don't want to travel by taxi (the cost can add up), you can reach most hot spots in the eastern parishes by taking local transit. From Hamilton, Buses 1, 3, 10, and 11 on the local "pink and blue" will get you where you need to go.

PLANNING YOUR TIME

Crystal and Fantasy Caves in Bailey's Bay are open until 5 pm every day. The real heart of the eastern parishes is Flatts Village, with a handful of restaurants catering to most tastes and the Bermuda Aquarium, Museum & Zoo for the kids. Although it's a relatively busy area, it tends to slow down come nightfall; if you want to watch the tide go in or out, time your visit for low or high tide. You may want to avoid taking an evening stroll along these winding streets because there are no sidewalks and the area is not well lit.

QUICK BITES

■ **Bailey's Ice Cream.** If you've got kids in tow—or are driving a scooter—you may want to skip the rum and stick to Bailey's—Bailey's Ice Cream, that is. The popular parlor, across from the Swizzle Inn, dishes up some two dozen flavors of homemade all-natural ice cream, plus low-fat frozen yogurts and fat-free sorbets. It's cash only. ✉ 2 Blue Hole, Bailey's Bay, Hamilton Parish ☎ 441/293–8605 Ⓜ Bus 10 or 11.

■ **Buzz N Go.** With friendly staff and a multitude of options like the standard burgers, fries, and shakes, along with heart-healthy options (smoothies are particularly popular) and locally brewed coffee, you can enjoy breakfast and lunch on the go at this spot at the Crawl Hill Esso Tigermarket. ✉ 122 North Shore Rd., Smith's Parish ⊕ buzzcafe.bm Ⓜ Bus 10 or 11.

■ **Jamaican Grill.** At this grill by the Bailey's Bay Cricket Club, satisfy your craving for spicy cuisines from farther south. ✉ 1 Ducks Puddle Dr., Bailey's Bay, Hamilton Parish Ⓜ Bus 10 or 11 to Belvin's Variety; then follow Coney Island Rd. to the Cricket Club.

Circling Harrington Sound and taking in Flatts Village, the eastern parishes are laced with residential streets and clusters of limestone-capped, pastel-color homes. In this area removed from the busy city center, you will find historical and educational sites worth the day trip here, though there is little in the way of dine-in restaurants or evening entertainment.

Scenic hikes and world-class golfing are just a few of the activities of note in this area, not to mention a quick tour of Tucker's Town, where some of the world's most influential individuals come for their own R & R. In the past, these included the late David Bowie and Iman, his wife.

👁 Sights

In addition to St. George's, the east of the island includes the parishes of Smith's and Hamilton. This is probably the quietest corner of the island, so it's a great spot to enjoy tranquil nature trails. Tucked away in Hamilton Parish, however, you'll find two of the island's biggest attractions: Crystal Cave and the Bermuda Aquarium, Museum & Zoo. The East End is also home to some of Bermuda's finest golf courses.

★ Bermuda Aquarium, Museum & Zoo (BAMZ)

ZOO | FAMILY | Established in 1926, the Bermuda Aquarium, Museum & Zoo (BAMZ for short) is one of Bermuda's top attractions, with harbor seals, flocks of flamingos, exhibits on local animals and marine life, and a coastal walkway with stunning water views. In the aquarium the big draw is the North Rock Exhibit, a 140,000-gallon tank that gives you a diver's-eye view of the area's living coral reefs (one of the largest living coral collections in the world) and the colorful marine life it sustains. The museum section has multimedia and interactive displays focusing on native habitats and the impact humans have on them. The island-themed zoo displays more than 300 birds, reptiles, and mammals. Don't miss the Islands of Australasia exhibit with its lemurs, wallabies, and tree kangaroos, or Islands of the Caribbean, a walk-through enclosure that gets you within arm's length of ibises and golden lion tamarins (a type of monkey). Other popular areas include an outdoor seal pool, tidal touch tank, and cool kid-friendly Discovery Room. Take a break at Beastro (part of the popular Buzz café chain), on the zoo grounds, for good food and great views. ✉ 40 North Shore Rd., Flatt's Village ☎ 441/293–2727 ⊕ www.bamz.org 🎫 $10.

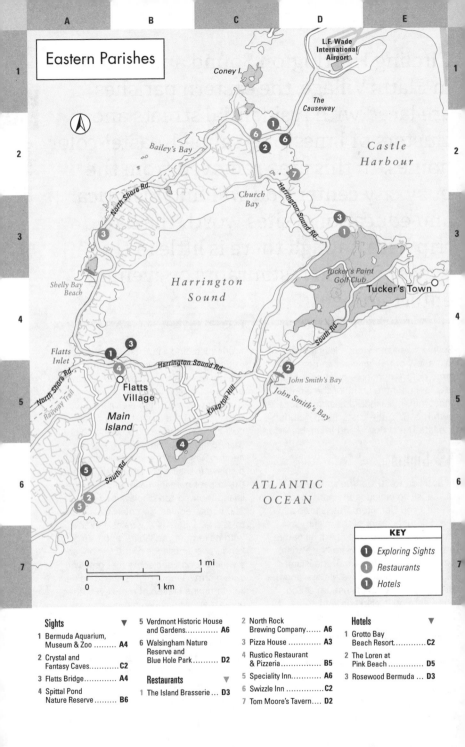

Eastern Parishes

Coney I.

L.F. Wade International Airport

The Causeway

Bailey's Bay

Castle Harbour

Church Bay

Harrington Sound Rd.

North Shore Rd.

Shelly Bay Beach

Harrington Sound

Tucker's Point Golf Club

Tucker's Town

Flatts Inlet

North Shore Rd.

Railway Trail

Harrington Sound Rd.

Flatts Village

South Rd.

Main Island

Knapton Hill

John Smith's Bay

John Smith's Bay

South Rd.

ATLANTIC OCEAN

0   1 mi
0   1 km

KEY

- ① Exploring Sights
- ① Restaurants
- ① Hotels

Sights ▼

1 Bermuda Aquarium, Museum & Zoo **A4**
2 Crystal and Fantasy Caves **C2**
3 Flatts Bridge **A4**
4 Spittal Pond Nature Reserve **B6**
5 Verdmont Historic House and Gardens **A6**
6 Walsingham Nature Reserve and Blue Hole Park **D2**

Restaurants ▼

1 The Island Brasserie ... **D3**
2 North Rock Brewing Company **A6**
3 Pizza House **A3**
4 Rustico Restaurant & Pizzeria **B5**
5 Speciality Inn **A6**
6 Swizzle Inn **C2**
7 Tom Moore's Tavern **D2**

Hotels ▼

1 Grotto Bay Beach Resort **C2**
2 The Loren at Pink Beach **D5**
3 Rosewood Bermuda ... **D3**

★ Crystal and Fantasy Caves

NATURE SITE | As far back as 1623, Captain John Smith (of Pocahontas fame) commented on the "vary strange, darke, and cumbersome" caverns that today are a popular attraction. Nevertheless, it came as a surprise when two boys, attempting to retrieve a lost ball, discovered Crystal Cave in 1907. The hole through which the boys descended is still visible. Inside, tour guides will lead you across a pontoon bridge that spans a 55-foot-deep subterranean lake. Look up to see stalactites dripping from the ceiling or down through the perfectly clear water to see stalagmites rising from the cave floor. Amateur spelunkers can also journey through geologic time at Crystal's smaller sister cave, Fantasy. Set aside 30 minutes to see one cave; 75 minutes if you plan to take in both. ■TIP→ **More than a few people have lost important items to the depths of the caves by accidentally dropping them over the edge. Keep items tucked away safely.** ⊠ *8 Crystal Caves Rd.* ⊹ *Off Wilkinson Ave.* ☎ *441/293–0640* ⊕ *www. caves.bm* ⊠ *One cave $24; combination ticket $35* Ⓜ *Bus 1, 3, 10, or 11.*

Flatts Bridge

BRIDGE/TUNNEL | Just west of the Bermuda Aquarium, Museum & Zoo, Flatts Bridge spans Flatts Inlet, connecting Hamilton and Smith's Parish. The inlet provides an entry point for much of the seawater that flows into Harrington Sound. While the bridge itself is fairly nondescript, it's what goes on underneath that's worth a stop. The strong tidal current that rushes beneath the bridge is pretty spectacular, especially if you catch a Spotted Eagle Ray surfing the current, and Harrington Sound is one of its favorite habitats. ⊠ *North Shore Rd., Flatt's Village.*

★ Spittal Pond Nature Reserve

NATURE PRESERVE | **FAMILY** | This Bermuda National Trust park has 64 acres for roaming, though you're asked to keep to the well-marked walkways that loop through the woods and along the spectacular shoreline. More than 30 species of waterfowl—including herons, egrets, and white-eyed vireos—winter here between November and May, making the reserve a top spot for birders. Get your timing right and you may be able to spy migrating whales too.

History buffs may be more interested in climbing the high bluff to Portuguese Rock. Early settlers found this rock crudely carved with the date 1543 along with other markings that are believed to be the initials "RP" (for *Rex Portugaline*, King of Portugal) and a cross representing the Portuguese Order of Christ. The theory goes that after a Portuguese ship was wrecked on the island, its sailors marked the occasion before departing on a newly built ship. The rock was removed to prevent further damage by erosion, and a bronze cast of the original stands in its place. A plaster-of-paris version is also on display at the Museum of the Bermuda Historical Society in Hamilton. ⊠ *South Rd.* ☎ *441/236–6483* ⊕ *www. bnt.bm/spittal-pond* ⊠ *Free.*

Verdmont Historic House and Gardens

HOUSE | **FAMILY** | Opened as a museum in 1956, this National Trust property is notable for its Georgian architecture, but what really sets this place apart is its pristine condition. Though the house was used as a residence until the mid-20th century, virtually no structural changes were made to Verdmont since it was erected around 1710. Former owners never even added electricity or plumbing (so the "powder room" was strictly used for powdering wigs).

The house is also known for its enviable collection of antiques. Some pieces—such as the early-19th-century piano—were imported from England. Most are 18th-century cedar, however, crafted by Bermudian cabinetmakers. Among the most interesting artifacts are the pint-size furnishings and period toys that fill Verdmont's upstairs nursery. A china

The North Rock Exhibit at the Bermuda Aquarium, Museum & Zoo houses one of the largest living coral collections in the world.

coffee service, said to have been a gift from Napoléon to U.S. President James Madison, is also on display. The president never received it, though, since the ship bearing it was seized by a privateer and brought to Bermuda. Verdmont also has its share of resident ghosts: among them, an adolescent girl who died of typhoid there in 1844. ⊠ *6 Verdmont La.* ⚓ *Off Collector's Hill* ☎ *441/236–7369* ⊕ *www.bnt.bm* ✉ *$5; $10 combination ticket with Bermuda National Trust Museum in Globe Hotel and Tucker House* ⊙ *Closed Thurs. and Sat.–Tues.*

★ Walsingham Nature Reserve and Blue Hole Park

NATURE PRESERVE | FAMILY | It's said that Irish poet Tom Moore (1779–1852) wrote several of his most famous poems while residing in Bermuda, and the lovely parkland just past the causeway has been dedicated to his memory. Known locally as "Tom Moore's Jungle," the Walsingham Nature Reserve and Blue Hole Park encompass 12 acres of nearly unspoiled forest with a secluded and shallow beach, canopied trails, pristine grottoes, and caves. The area is popular for swimming, snorkeling, and rock climbing, as well as viewing marine life from parrotfish to the occasional nurse shark. A highlight, however, is the crystal-clear pond near Tom Moore's Tavern, one of the island's oldest establishments. ⊠ *Blue Hole Hill* ✉ *Free* Ⓜ *Bus 1, 3, 10, or 11 from Hamilton.*

Beaches

Bermuda's beaches are characterized by gently rolling waves and soft, pink sand. The few coves and inlets that line the island's northern shore have protected shores that are ideally suited to families with small children, while the popular south shore beaches pose more of a challenge, particularly when the wind picks up and waters get a bit rougher. Only a handful of beaches have lifeguards during the summer months, so swimmers should exercise caution when heading out into the waves.

John Smith's Bay

BEACH—SIGHT | FAMILY | Just past Spittal Pond Nature Reserve, this beach consists of a pretty strand of long, flat, open sand. The presence of a lifeguard in summer makes it an ideal place to bring children. The only public beach in Smith's Parish, John Smith's Bay is also popular with locals. Groups of young folks like to gather in the park area surrounding the beach for parties, especially on weekends and holidays. If you're not in the mood for a festive bunch with music and plenty of beer, this may not be the place for you. Lots of scooter parking is available, as is the occasional local food vendor. **Amenities:** lifeguards; parking (free). **Best for:** partiers; snorkeling; swimming. ⊠ *South Shore Rd.* Ⓜ *Bus 1 from Hamilton.*

Shelly Bay Beach

BEACH—SIGHT | FAMILY | Known for its sandy bottom and shallow water, Shelly Bay is a good place to take small children. It also has shade trees, a rarity at Bermudian beaches. A large playground behind the beach attracts hordes of youngsters on weekends and during school holidays. There's also a nearby soccer and cricket practice field and a public basketball court. Keep an eye out for the food truck that often stops in the parking lot behind the beach. There are no public changing rooms, but a bathroom facility is by the upper parking lot. **Amenities:** parking (free); toilets. **Best for:** partiers; swimming. ⊠ *Off North Shore Rd.* Ⓜ *Bus 10 or 11 from Hamilton.*

 **Restaurants**

The east of the island is best known for the Swizzle Inn, and it's probably the one place that most people have heard of before they even arrive. Its reputation is legendary, and it doesn't disappoint. Other restaurants are quite spread out from Flatts Village to St. David's, but they are well worth the trek. Your efforts will be rewarded with the freshest of

Did You Know? 👁

An 80-foot harbor mural by Eurasian artist Gerard Henderson winds around the Rosewood Bermuda's Island Brasserie. Originally hung in the Pan Am offices in Manhattan, the impressive artwork brings a little piece of history to Bermuda.

ingredients (there's an abundance of fisherfolk at this end of the island) away from the crowds.

The Island Brasserie

$$$ | STEAKHOUSE | The signature restaurant of the Rosewood Bermuda resort, Island Brasserie is a classic steak house with a modern colonial atmosphere that captures the historic vibe of the island. The menu is a celebration of international cuisine, with a large focus on steak, of course (one of their classic plates is a delectable chateaubriand that serves two), as well as locally sourced seafood. **Known for:** stunning views of Harrington Sound; classic cocktails; iconic Henderson mural. Ⓢ *Average main: $36* ⊠ *Rosewood Bermuda, 60 Tucker's Point Dr.* ☎ *441/298–4077* ⊕ *www.rosewood-hotels.com.*

North Rock Brewing Company

$$ | BRITISH | The copper and mahogany tones of the handcrafted beers and ales are reflected in the warm interior of this casual bar and restaurant, Bermuda's only brewpub. North Rock offers an extensive selection of seafood and pub favorites, plus locally made ales from Dockyard Brewing Company to accompany your meal. **Known for:** fish-and-chips; Bermuda-made beers; indoor and outdoor seating. Ⓢ *Average main: $28* ⊠ *10 South Shore Rd.* ⊹ *Near Collector's Hill* ☎ *441/236–6633.*

The Dish on Local Dishes

Shark hash, made of minced shark meat sautéed with spices, may not sound too appetizing, but it's a popular Bermudian appetizer, usually served on toast.

Bermudians love **codfish cakes** made of salted cod mashed with cooked potatoes and fresh thyme and parsley, and then shaped into patties and panfried. They taste great topped with a zesty fruit salsa and a side of mesclun salad or—a Bermudian favorite—served on a hot cross bun with cheese.

The island's traditional weekend brunch is a huge plate of **boiled or steamed salt cod** with boiled potatoes, onions, and sliced bananas, all topped with a hard-boiled egg or tomato sauce and, sometimes, avocado slices.

Cassava pie—a savory blend of cassava, eggs, sugar, and either pork or chicken—is a rich, flavorful dish (formerly reserved for Christmas dinner) often offered as a special side. It's served with a healthy dollop of chowchow (pickles in mustard sauce). More common is **mussel pie**, made of shelled mussels, potatoes, and onions, and seasoned with thyme, parsley, and curry. The dish is loaded into a flaky, sweet crust and baked.

As for Bermudian desserts, **bananas** baked in rum and brown sugar are to die for, and **loquat or banana crumble** is sweet and rich.

Pizza House

$ | PIZZA | FAMILY | Cheesy pizza, hefty sandwiches, fried chicken, local baked goods: Pizza House, with several locations, is more than just a pizza joint, offering a diverse menu of items for the whole family. Dine in or take out (you can order online) from the Shelly Bay location, which is about a 15-minute walk from Shelly Bay Beach. **Known for:** good pizza by the slice or whole pie; popular local chain; good value for money. $ Average main: $20 ⊠ 110 North Shore Rd. ☎ 441/293–8465 ⊕ www.pizzahouse.bm.

Rustico Restaurant & Pizzeria

$$ | ITALIAN | FAMILY | At Rustico, you can dine on colorful Italian specialties and appreciate the beauty of the quaint village of Flatts, across from the Bermuda Museum, Aquarium & Zoo. Start with stylish cocktails at the bar before settling in for some of Bermuda's best thin-crust pizza. **Known for:** thin-crust pizza and homemade pastas; alfresco dining on patio, but call to reserve; popular with groups. $ Average main: $30 ⊠ 38 North Shore Rd., Flatts Village ☎ 441/295–5212 ⊕ www.bermuda-dining.com/rustico.

Speciality Inn

$ | AMERICAN | FAMILY | You may have to wait in line a few minutes to snag a table, but you can't beat Speciality Inn for satisfying, reasonably priced meals. With its cozy tables and a handful of booths, this cheerful place is a favorite of locals and families.The large, no-frills menu features everything from pizza to burgers to sushi. **Known for:** home-style family cooking; good-value food from breakfast through dinner; Saturday's codfish and potato breakfast. $ Average main: $18 ⊠ Collectors Hill, 4 South Shore Rd. ☎ 441/236–3133 ⊕ www.specialityinn. bm ⊗ Closed Sun.

★ Swizzle Inn

$ | AMERICAN | Swizzle Inn created one of Bermuda's most hallowed drinks, the rum swizzle: gold and black rum, triple sec, orange and pineapple juices, and bitters. This place is a local landmark, with a warm and welcoming atmosphere,

Grotto Bay Beach Resort offers Bermuda's only all-inclusive supplement option.

friendly staff, and plenty of decent, affordable pub fare. **Known for:** pitchers of rum swizzle; business cards and names on the walls; quiz nights and live music. $ *Average main: $20* ⊠ *87 Blue Hole Hill, Bailey's Bay* ☎ *441/293–1854* ⊕ *www. swizzleinn.com.*

★ Tom Moore's Tavern

$$$ | FRENCH | Tucked away from Middle Road, one of the island's oldest restaurants occupies a 17th-century Bermuda cottage with historical charm. Tom Moore was an Irish poet who lived and wrote on Bermuda in the early 19th century, but whether you're a fan of literature or not, the sophisticated, French-influenced menu and dreamy setting amid the Walsingham Nature Reserve offer an experience to remember. **Known for:** fish chowder; decadent dessert soufflés; over-the-top service. $ *Average main: $38* ⊠ *Tom Moore's Jungle, 7 Walsingham La., Bailey's Bay* ☎ *441/293–8020* ⊕ *www.tommoores.com* ⊙ *No lunch.*

🛏 Hotels

This is the perfect hideaway spot that's off the beaten track. One of the less populated areas of the island, it really isn't geared toward tourists, but there are hotels in the lovely Castle Harbour area, which offers great water views and water sports opportunities. If you opt for this location, you're in for a peaceful and relaxing getaway.

Grotto Bay Beach Resort

$$$$ | RESORT | FAMILY | The ocean is never far from sight at this popular resort best known for its two on-site caves; you can treat yourself to a spa treatment in one, then go for a relaxing swim in the other. **Pros:** kids' program in summer; on-site aquatic activities; all-inclusive available for extra charge. **Cons:** small beach; can get crowded with package tour groups due to all-inclusive option; airport noise. $ *Rooms from: $550* ⊠ *11 Blue Hole Hill, Bailey's Bay* ☎ *441/293–8333, 855/447–6886* ⊕ *www.grottobay.com* ⇌ *212 rooms* ❘○❘ *No meals.*

The Rosewood Bermuda offers guests access to the Tucker's Point Beach and Tennis Club.

The Loren at Pink Beach

$$$$ | **HOTEL** | One of Bermuda's most luxurious resorts, the Loren at Pink Beach blends the natural beauty of a spectacular oceanfront setting with elegant European-inspired architecture, modern and high-end finishes, and an intimate vibe. **Pros:** amazing ocean views; elegant and private, but close to airport; near Mid Ocean and Tucker's Point golf courses. **Cons:** isolated from populated parts of island; limited dining options. Ⓢ *Rooms from: $1100* ⊠ *116 South Shore Rd., Tucker's Town* ☎ *441/293–1666, 844/384–3103 in U.S.* ⊕ *www.theloren-hotel.com* ⇆ *45 suites* ⊠ *No meals.*

★ Rosewood Bermuda

$$$$ | **RESORT** | Dramatically perched above Castle Harbour, the immaculately furnished and spacious rooms at this luxurious escape have picture-perfect water views. **Pros:** amazing ocean views; excellent spa and amenities on-site; tastefully modern rooms. **Cons:** hotel is a substantial distance from its separate beach club; secluded area of the island; service can be slow. Ⓢ *Rooms from: $1,300* ⊠ *60 Tucker's Point Dr., Hamilton* ☎ *441/298–4000, 888/767–3966* ⊕ *www.rosewoodhotels.com/en/bermuda* ⇆ *88 rooms* ⊠ *No meals.*

🍸 Nightlife

The East End is the quietest corner of the island, but that isn't to say you won't find anything going on; you may just have to look a little harder. Your best bet is to head to the Swizzle Inn for a rowdy night of singing with strangers. The nightly entertainers are more than happy to welcome people to the stage.

BARS AND LOUNGES

North Rock Brewing Company

BARS/PUBS | As well as being a relaxed and traditional pub and restaurant, the North Rock Brewing Company is one of only a few places on the island to get a genuine Bermuda-brewed ale. Try a sampler for a taste of all six of North Rock's famous beers—ranging from the sharp St. David's Light Ale to the head-spinning

Whale of Wheat. The relaxed outdoor seating area is the perfect place for a breather if the pub gets too noisy. ✉ *10 South Shore Rd.* ☎ *441/236–6633.*

★ Swizzle Inn
BARS/PUBS | Proudly bearing the motto "Swizzle Inn, swagger out," this busy and unique spot is a must-see for visitors. Business cards, exotic money, photos of friends, and even love notes completely cover the walls, ceilings, and doors. Even the tables are scratched with messages and signatures. As the name suggests, it's the best place on the island for a jug of rum swizzle. Entertainment in the summer includes live bands, pub quizzes, and barbecues. The Bailey's Bay venue proved so successful that the owners have set up a sister bar close to the south shore beaches in Warwick. ✉ *3 Blue Hole Hill, Bailey's Bay* ☎ *441/293–1854* ⊕ *www.swizzleinn.com.*

🛍 Shopping

There are a handful of stores in Flatts Village, a possible stop if you're on your way to the Bermuda Aquarium, Museum & Zoo.

CLOTHING
Flatts Men's Wear
CLOTHING | Owner Mick Adderley runs this popular shop selling men's clothing, shoes, and accessories, including Dickies work clothes. It also has a small selection of specially made clothes in big-and-tall sizes. ✉ *13 North Shore Rd., Flatt's Village* ☎ *441/292–0360.*

FOOD
Harrington Hundreds
FOOD/CANDY | A family-owned supermarket, Harrington Hundreds is a must for those observing special diets or seeking unusual ingredients. As well as all your usual groceries and prepared foods, it has the island's best selection of wheat-free foods, including gluten-free pastas, breads, and cookies. It's within walking distance of Spittal Pond. ✉ *99 South Shore Rd.* ☎ *441/293–1635* ⊕ *www.harringtonhundreds.bm.*

Shelly Bay MarketPlace
FOOD/CANDY | Often called the Piggly Wiggly by locals, the MarketPlace is an island-wide grocery store chain offering a wide selection of necessities. At the Shelly Bay location you will find an in-store bakery, as well as authentic Portuguese and Filipino products. An additional location—A1 Smith's—is at the bottom of Collector's Hill in Smith's Parish. ✉ *110 North Shore Rd.* ☎ *441/293–0966* ⊕ *www.marketplace.bm.*

Shelly Bay MarketPlace
FOOD/CANDY | This branch of the MarketPlace chain is the only large grocery store on North Shore Road. It stocks everything you could need. There's also a huge parking lot and a handful of other stores nearby. ✉ *110 North Shore Rd., Hamilton* ☎ *441/293–0966.*

NOVELTIES AND GIFTS
Regali by Luxury Gifts Bermuda
GIFTS/SOUVENIRS | Located in the lobby of Rosewood Bermuda, this boutique is more than just a hotel gift shop. There is a gorgeous selection of flowy summer dresses, bathing suits, cover-ups, and hats on one side with a selection of high-end gifts from Jonathan Adler as well as specialty spa and beauty products on the other. Men can pick up shirts from local menswear line Coral Coast Clothing, and there is a lovely selection of clothing and gifts for babies and toddlers. The shop also stocks a small selection of travel necessities and snacks. ✉ *Rosewood Bermuda, 60 Tucker's Point Dr.* ☎ *441/298–6095* ⊕ *luxury.bm/regali.*

SPAS
Sense, a Rosewood Spa
SPA/BEAUTY | At this spa inspired by the culture of the island, indulge yourself with a luxurious signature treatment like the Cedar Warming Massage, which uses juniper and cedar essential oils to induce a state of pure relaxation, or join

in a mindful yoga or tai chi practice on the expansive hotel lawn with its breathtaking ocean views. The treatment menu at Sense is comprehensive and guaranteed to leave you feeling pampered and refreshed, though prices are high. There's also a hair salon, and aquatic therapy is available. ⊠ *Rosewood Bermuda, 60 Tucker's Point Dr.* ☎ *441/298–4000* ⊕ *www.rosewoodhotels.com.*

🏃 Activities

The eastern parishes offer visitors scenic beauty, but bear in mind that most shops and agencies close early—around 5 pm—and the area is relatively quiet after hours. Be sure to plan outings and excursions during the day, when the narrow, winding streets and secluded trails are well lit and well traveled.

BIKING

When referencing "bikes" in Bermuda, locals will almost always automatically think of mopeds or scooters, speedy little vehicles that are propelled by engines and not your feet. If you prefer pedal power, however, several agencies across the island offer off road or mountain bikes for a reasonable fee. Even on a hot day, biking around **Harrington Sound** can be a rewarding way to experience the island at your own pace.

The **Bermuda Railway Trail** (⊕ *www.bermudarailway.net*) may snake its way from one end of the island to the other, but this walking and biking path along the former railway was, for a long time, broken in several places. A pedestrian bridge, the first of many reconstruction efforts by the Friends of the Bermuda Railway Trail, was constructed over Gibbons Bay in Hamilton Parish, reconnecting a section of trail and providing a safer path. Along this lovely north shore stretch, you're likely to see fish, manta rays, turtles, and the occasional octopus.

Oleander Cycles

BICYCLING | Pick up a mountain bike from the location in Grotto Bay (by Grotto Bay Beach Resort) or in St. George's for a scenic tour of the island's secluded East End. ⊠ *Grotto Bay Beach, 11 Blue Hole Hill, Bailey's Bay* ☎ *441/293–1010 Grotto Bay, 441/297–4425 St. George's Club* ⊕ *www.oleandercycles.bm* 🎫 *From $40 for 2-hr rental.*

BIRD-WATCHING

With over 400 species of bird that either pass by or call Bermuda their home throughout the year, avid bird-watchers are sure to fill at least a page in their books at the "twitcher" hot spots in the eastern parishes. Stretching placidly over 60 acres of preserved parkland, **Spittal Pond** is easily the most accessible area for viewing up to 30 kinds of shorebirds. Semipalmated sandpipers are perhaps the most abundant. In winter, herons and egrets roost serenely in the shallow water. Don't forget your camera if you take one of the great coastal nature trails. **Blue Hole Park** in Blue Hill also provides the perfect habitat for local and visiting birds, including the still-as-a-statue herons that land before dusk. Visit the Bermuda Audubon Society online (⊕ *www.audubon.bm*) for detailed information on local bird-watching and a Bermuda bird-watching checklist, or contact the Bermuda National Trust (⊕ *www.bnt.bm*) for more information or assistance planning your own self-guided tour.

H. T. North Nature Reserve and Mangrove Lake

BIRD WATCHING | A reserve maintained by the Bermuda National Trust, Mangrove Lake lies on the border of Hamilton and Smith's Parishes and provides an ideal woodland spot for migrating thrushes and warblers, as well as the northern water thrushes that hide among the dense mangrove trees. If you're keeping a list, watch for pied-billed grebes, lesser scaups, buffleheads, and hooded

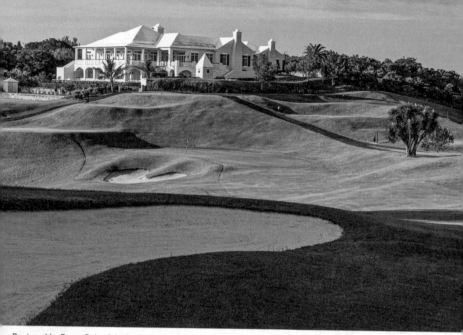

Designed by Roger Rulewich, the Tucker's Point Golf Club was built in 2002 on the site of the old Castle Harbour Golf Club.

mergansers. ⊹ *Access via Judkin La. off Somersall Rd.* ⊕ *www.bnt.bm.*

BOATING

Ana Luna Adventures

TOUR—SPORTS | The *Ana Luna* is a 45-foot catamaran that provides snorkeling cruises, scuba diving trips, and sunset tours as well as a host of other marine adventures. The regularly scheduled sailing charters depart daily from Grotto Bay during the summer months and tour Bermuda's northern coastline. Panoramic views of forts, railway artifacts, old docks, and an array of marine life await. There are also romantic sunset voyages and bioluminescent glowworm tours. Planning something extra special? Speak to Captain Nathan to schedule a private adventure aboard the *Ana Luna.* ✉ *Grotto Bay Beach Resort, 11 Blue Hole Hill, Bailey's Bay* ☎ *441/504–3780* ⊕ *www.analunaadventures.com* ✉ *From $70.*

Blue Hole Watersports

WATER SPORTS | Based out of the Grotto Bay Beach Resort, Blue Hole has you covered for water sports in the East End.

Cruise the waters and soak up some rays in a Fun Cat, a low-powered floating deck chair, or rent a single or double kayak. Blue Hole also offers windsurfing and Sunfish sailboat rentals (experience required) and paddleboards. You can rent a motorboat for prices starting for two hours plus fuel costs. Reservations are recommended. There's a gorgeous sheltered beach with a small wreck sunk just offshore for snorkelers (rental gear available). ✉ *Grotto Bay Beach Resort, 11 Blue Hole Hill, Bailey's Bay* ☎ *441/293–2915* ⊕ *www.blueholebermuda.com* ✉ *From $8 for snorkeling gear rental, $20 for kayak, $30 for windsurfer, sailboat, or paddleboard, $120 for motorboat.*

GOLF

★ Tucker's Point Golf Club

GOLF | Roger Rulewich, a former senior designer for the late Robert Trent Jones Sr., mapped out a stunning site layout for the old Castle Harbour Golf Club in 2002, making the most of elevation changes and ocean views. On many holes, you tee off toward the crest of a hill, not

Secrets from a Golf Pro

Golf courses elsewhere are often designed with the wind in mind—long downwind holes and short upwind holes. Not so in Bermuda, where the wind is anything but consistent or predictable. **Quirky air currents** make play on a Bermudian course different every day. The wind puts a premium on being able to hit the ball straight and grossly exaggerates any slice or hook.

The **hard ground** of most Bermudian courses means you must abandon the strategy you use on heavily watered tracks. Your ball will run a lot in the fairway, so don't overestimate the distance to hazards. Around the greens, it's wise to run the ball to the hole rather than chipping. Not only will you find it difficult to get under the ball on the firm fairways, but your shot will be subject to the vagaries of the wind. If you're in the clinging Bermuda grass rough, your club face is likely to turn if you try to swing through it.

How should you prepare for a Bermuda trip? Practice **run-up shots** from close-cropped lies using a 5- or 6-iron—or a putter from just off the green. Use midirons to practice **punching shots** from the rough, angling back into the fairway rather than trying to advance the ball straight ahead and risk landing in the rough again. Putting surfaces are often undulating and grainier than bent grass, so putts will break less than you expect. They'll also die much more quickly unless you use a firm stroke.

knowing what lies beyond. Topping the rise reveals the challenge, often involving a very elevated, sculpted green with a scenic vista. If you're not a guest at the Rosewood Bermuda, you must have an introduction (your hotelier can do this) for playing and dining privileges. Walking is reserved for members; carts are recommended for nonmembers. The par-4 17th is one of the most picturesque in Bermuda, with sweeping views of Tucker's Town and the Castle Islands. A rival is hole 13, where the perspective is the north coast and the Royal Navy Dockyard on the island's western tip. ⊠ *60 Tucker's Point Dr., off Harrington Sound Rd.* ☎ *441/298–6970* ⊕ *www.tuckerspoint. com* ✉ *Member guest $125; nonmember $210 for 18 holes, $130 for 9 holes (cart included); hotel guest $195* ⚑ *18 holes, 6500 yards, par 70.*

TENNIS
Grotto Bay Tennis Club

TENNIS | A little more than a stone's throw from the L. F. Wade International Airport, Grotto Bay has four Plexipave cork-based courts, two of which are equipped with lights for nighttime play. Resident tennis pros offer lessons (individual and small group) for adults and juniors. Tennis attire is required. ⊠ *11 Blue Hole Hill, Bailey's Bay, Flatt's Village* ☎ *441/293–3420* ⊕ *www.grottobaytennis.com* ✉ *From $10 for hourly bookings; lessons from $30 per half hour.*

Chapter 7

WEST END

Updated by
Melissa Fox

7

⊙ Sights	🍴 Restaurants	🛏 Hotels	🛍 Shopping	🍸 Nightlife
★★★★★	★★★★☆	★☆☆☆☆	★★★★☆	★★★☆☆

ISLAND SNAPSHOT

TOP EXPERIENCES

■ **Royal Naval Dockyard:** This former British naval stronghold has forts, museums, shops and restaurants, and water activities to keep everyone entertained.

■ **Bermuda National Museum:** Learn about the history of this tiny, seafaring nation by touring the extensive collection of artifacts and exhibits.

■ **Dolphin Quest:** Dolphins may not be native to Bermuda waters, but visitors and islanders alike have come to love the experiences offered here.

■ **Fish chowder at Somerset Country Squire:** When in Bermuda, eat like the locals and enjoy fish chowder with a side of sherry pepper sauce and Gosling's Black Seal Rum, along with a view of Mangrove Bay.

■ **Fort Scaur trails:** A special trip to hike the well-preserved grounds of Fort Scaur (pack sturdy walking shoes) will take you on trails above and below ground for historical insight and picturesque views.

GETTING HERE

Comprised of a string of interconnected islands, Sandys Parish—home to Somerset and the Royal Naval Dockyard—lies at the "tip of the fishhook," so to speak, and is easily accessible by scooter, bus, or ferry. From Hamilton, hop on Bus 7 or 8 toward Somerset. Buses depart roughly every 15 minutes, and it takes about an hour to reach Dockyard via South or Middle Road. If you're in a hurry, the blue line ferry will take you directly to the Dockyard from Hamilton, and you can bring your scooter (extra charge). If you're visiting during the summer months, a high-speed ferry can take you from St. George's to Dockyard in 35 minutes (weekdays only). Before setting out, check public transit schedules (online at ⊕ www.gov.bm). Are you planning to scoot about on one of the ubiquitous red mopeds? Give yourself plenty of room on these narrow, winding streets.

PLANNING YOUR TIME

■ Allow a full day for exploring this area. You'll need an hour or two in the Royal Naval Dockyard, which offers opportunities for local shopping and dining, along with historic sights, the National Museum of Bermuda, and outdoor attractions. You can avoid the crowds on the south shore's pink-sand beaches at Somerset Long Bay, with its gentle surf and crystalline water. Families can find excitement and water sports at Snorkel Park Beach or the floating water park at X20 Adventures near Somerset Village.

QUICK BITES

■ **Nannini's.** Cool off with smooth and creamy Häagen-Dazs ice cream, sorbet, and frozen yogurt. ⊠ *Clock Tower Shopping Mall, Dockyard* ☎ 441/234-2474.

■ **Misty's Takeout.** From "simple" fish sandwiches to full dinner platters, Misty's is the ultimate in Bermudian comfort food. ⊠ 54 *Somerset Rd., Somerset Village* ☎ 441/234-2449.

■ **Mr. Chicken.** One of several local fast-food chains, Mr. Chicken opened a Somerset location in 2019, offering its signature chicken and sides for dine in or take out. ⊠ 23 *Somerset Rd.*

Bermuda is denser than you might imagine. But in contrast to Hamilton and St. George's, the island's West End seems positively pastoral. Many of the top sites here are natural ones: namely the wildlife reserves, wooded areas, and beautiful waterways of Sandys Parish. The notable exception is Bermuda's single largest tourist attraction—the Royal Naval Dockyard.

Its story begins in the aftermath of the American Revolution, when Britain suddenly found itself with neither an anchorage nor a major ship-repair yard in the western Atlantic. Around 1809, just as Napoléon was surfacing as a serious threat and the empire's ships were becoming increasingly vulnerable to pirate attack, Britain decided to construct a stronghold in Bermuda. Dubbed the "Gibraltar of the West," the Dockyard operated as a shipyard for nearly 150 years. The facility was closed in 1951, although the Royal Navy maintained a small presence here until 1976 and held title to the land until 1995.

Today the redeveloped Dockyard has trees and shrubs where once there were vast stretches of concrete. Private yachts calmly float where naval vessels once anchored, and cruise ships dock at the terminal. Historic structures—like the Clocktower and Cooperage buildings—house restaurants, galleries, and shops carrying everything from locally made goods to souvenirs imported from all over the world. A strip of beach has been turned into a snorkel park. At the center of it all are the National Museum of Bermuda and Dolphin Quest, two popular facilities that share a fortified 6-acre site.

Outside the Dockyard, Sandys is just a short bus ride away. You'll notice that Sandys (pronounced Sands) is made up of several islands, all connected by bridges, including the smallest drawbridge in the world. It's in this parish that you'll also find Somerset Village, a popular spot for swimming and fishing.

◉ Sights

If the pace of island life is slow, things get just a little slower the farther you go from the city of Hamilton. Although technically Sandys Parish and Hamilton are rather close, as they share the Great Sound, a visit to Sandys provides a very different experience. While you'll find more attractions in the central parishes, Sandys offers unique insight into life on the island, as well as a few popular and historical attractions you won't want to miss.

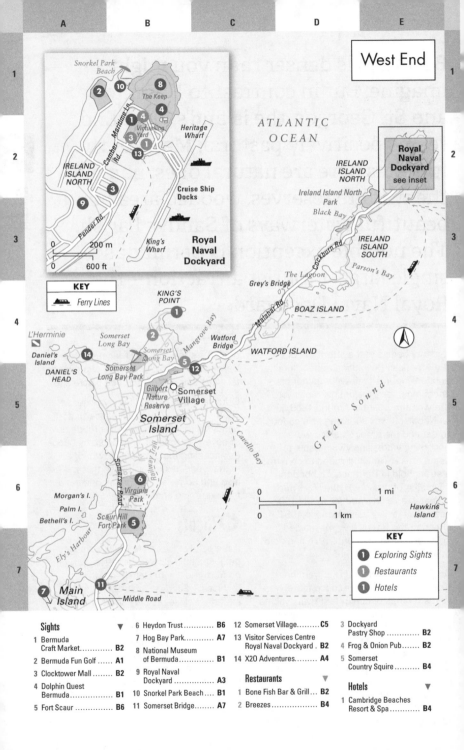

West End

ATLANTIC OCEAN

Royal Naval Dockyard (see inset)

IRELAND ISLAND NORTH

Ireland Island North Park

Black Bay

IRELAND ISLAND SOUTH

Parson's Bay

Cockburn Rd.

The Lagoon

Grey's Bridge

Malabar Rd.

BOAZ ISLAND

WATFORD ISLAND

Watford Bridge

Mangrove Bay

KING'S POINT

Somerset Long Bay

Somerset Long Bay

Somerset Long Bay Park

DANIEL'S HEAD

Daniel's Island

L'Herminie

Gilbert Nature Reserve

Somerset Village

Somerset Island

Cavello Bay

Great Sound

Hawkins Island

Morgan's I.

Palm I.

Bethell's I.

Virginia Park

Scaur Hill Fort Park

Somerset Rd.

Railway Trail

Ely's Harbour

Main Island

Middle Road

Inset — Royal Naval Dockyard

Snorkel Park Beach

The Keep

IRELAND ISLAND NORTH

Maritime Ln.

Camber Rd.

Victualling Yard

Heritage Wharf

Pender Rd.

Cruise Ship Docks

King's Wharf

Royal Naval Dockyard

0 — 200 m
0 — 600 ft

KEY
Ferry Lines

KEY
1 Exploring Sights
1 Restaurants
1 Hotels

The Bermuda Railway ◉

The history of the Bermuda Railway—which operated on the island from 1931 to 1948—is as brief as the track is short. Bermuda's Public Works Department considered proposals for a railroad as early as 1899, and Parliament finally granted permission in 1922 for a line to run from Somerset to St. George's. But laying tracks was a daunting task, requiring the costly and time-consuming construction of long tunnels and swing bridges. By the time it was finished, the railway had cost investors $1 million, making it, per mile, the most expensive railway ever built.

"Old Rattle and Shake," as it was nicknamed, began to decline during World War II. Soldiers put the train to hard use, and it proved impossible to obtain the necessary maintenance equipment. At the end of the war the government acquired the distressed railway for $115,000. Automobiles arrived in Bermuda in 1946, and train service ended in 1948, when the railway was sold in its entirety to British Guiana (now Guyana). Then, in the 1980s, the government gave new life to the ground it had covered by converting the tracks into multiuse recreational trails.

Today the secluded 18-mile Bermuda Railway Trail runs the length of the island, offering fabulous coastal views along the way. Restricted to pedestrians, horseback riders, and cyclists, the trail is a delightful way to see the island away from the traffic and noise of main roads. You might want to rent a bike if you plan to cover the entire trail, as many enthusiastic travelers do. Do note, though, that many portions of the trail are isolated—so you should avoid setting out alone after dark. Regardless of when you go, it's wise to first pick up a free copy of the Bermuda Railway Trail Guide available at Visitor Services Centres.

Bermuda Craft Market

STORE/MALL | Inside this former barrel-making factory, you can find the Bermuda Craft Market—arguably the island's largest and best-priced crafts outlet. It showcases the wares of more than 60 craftspeople, including quilters, candle makers, toy makers, and wood carvers. Also in the building is the Bermuda Arts Centre, a member-run art gallery that displays innovative high-end work in changing exhibits. ■TIP→ **A half-dozen artists at the Bermuda Arts Centre also maintain studios on the premises, so leave some time to watch them at work.** ⊠ *4 Maritime La., Dockyard* ☎ *441/234–3208 Craft Market, 441/534–2809 Arts Centre* ⊕ *bermudacraftmarket.com* ⊠ *Free.*

Bermuda Fun Golf

SPORTS VENUE | FAMILY | The design team had a bit of fun with these minilinks: featuring 18 holes representing the best golf courses from around the world—including Augusta National and St. Andrews—it'll challenge even the most experienced minigolfers. ■TIP→ **Surprisingly, Bermuda Fun Golf is one of the best places to watch the sunset with uninterrupted views.** There's also a bar serving cold drinks and snacks. ⊠ *9 Sally Port La., Dockyard* ☎ *441/400–7888* ⊕ *www. fungolf.bm* ⊠ *$15.*

Clocktower Mall

STORE/MALL | A pair of 100-foot towers makes it impossible to miss the Clocktower Mall, where the 19th-century building that held the Royal Navy's

administrative offices now is home to distinctly Bermudian boutiques—including specialty shops and branches of Front Street favorites. Observant folks will note that one tower features a standard clock, the other a tide indicator. The shops are particularly popular on Sunday because most stores outside the Dockyard area are closed. ⊠ *6 Clock Tower Parade, Dockyard* ☎ *441/234–1709* ⊕ *www. dockyardbermuda.com* ⌖ *Free.*

Dolphin Quest Bermuda

ZOO | **FAMILY** | After immersing yourself in maritime history at the National Museum of Bermuda, you can immerse yourself—literally—in the wonderful world of dolphins. Dolphin Quest offers a range of in-water programs that allow adults and children ages five or older to pet, play with, and swim alongside its eight Atlantic bottlenose dolphins in the historic Keep Pond. There are even specially designed sessions, conducted from a submersible bench, for younger kids. Since entry to the Dolphin Quest area is free with museum admission, anyone can watch the action. Participation in the actual programs, however, ranges in price, and advance booking is recommended. For $725 you can be a dolphin trainer for the day. ⊠ *15 The Keep, Dockyard* ☎ *441/234–4464* ⊕ *www. dolphinquest.com/bermuda* ⌖ *Free with admission to National Museum of Bermuda ($15); programs from $49.*

Fort Scaur

MILITARY SITE | The British chose the highest hill in Somerset for the site of this fort, built in the late 1860s and early 1870s, not for the lovely panoramas but to defend the flank of the Dockyard from possible American attacks. British troops were garrisoned here until World War I, and American forces were, ironically, stationed at the fort during World War II. Today its stone walls are surrounded by 22 acres of pretty gardens, and the view of the Great Sound and Ely's Harbour from the parapet is unsurpassed. Be sure

to check out the early-Bermuda Weather Stone, billed as a "perfect weather indicator." A sign posted nearby solemnly explains all. There is also access to the Bermuda Railway Trail. ⊠ *107 Somerset Rd., Dockyard* ☎ *441/236–5902* ⌖ *Free* Ⓜ *Bus 7 or 8 from Hamilton.*

Heydon Trust

CITY PARK | A reminder of what the island was like in its early days, this blissfully peaceful 44-acre preserve remains an unspoiled open space, except for a few flower gardens. Pathways with well-positioned park benches wind through it, affording some wonderful water views. If you continue along the main path, you'll reach rustic Heydon Chapel. Built in the early 1600s, it's Bermuda's smallest church. Weddings can be arranged by prior appointment. ⊠ *16 Heydon Dr., off Somerset Rd., Dockyard* ☎ *441/234–1831* ⌖ *Free* ⊙ *Chapel closed Sun.* Ⓜ *Bus 7 or 8.*

Hog Bay Park

NATIONAL/STATE PARK | Near their starting points, trails in this park are dominated mostly by agricultural land; however, once you trek past rows of vegetables, you'll find one of the best views along the western part of south shore. Outside of the arable land, there are 32 acres to explore via trails covered with endemic spice trees, as well as the remains of cedar trees that were affected by the blight in the 1940s and '50s that destroyed much of the island's cedar tree population. But the standout is the steep coastal path that leads to the shallow shoreline. If your timing is just right, you'll find a small beach. But regardless, there are tide pools to explore, and the shallow waters mean there are plenty of opportunities to spot hog fish and brightly colored parrot fish. ⊠ *Middle Rd., across from Overplus Ln.*

★ National Museum of Bermuda

MUSEUM | **FAMILY** | Ensconced in Bermuda's largest fort, the museum displays its collections of maritime and historical

Did You Know?

The Clock Tower Mall used to hold the Royal Navy's administrative offices; it's now filled with popular Bermuda shops (and it's open on Sunday).

artifacts in old munitions warehouses that surround the parade grounds and Keep Pond at the Dockyard. Insulated from the rest of the Dockyard by a moat and massive stone ramparts, it is entered by way of a drawbridge. At the Shifting House, right inside the entrance, rooms hold relics from some of the 350-odd ships wrecked on the island's reefs. Other buildings are devoted to seafaring pursuits such as whaling, shipbuilding, and yacht racing.

More displays are in the 19th-century Commissioner's House, on the museum's upper grounds. Built as both home and headquarters for the Dockyard commissioner, the house served as a World War I barracks and was used for military intelligence during World War II. Today it contains exhibits on Bermuda's social and military history. A must-see is the Hall of History, a mural of Bermuda's history covering 1,000 square feet. Painting it took local artist Graham Foster more than 3½ years. You'll also want to photograph the sheep that graze outside the building, mowing the grass. Mind your feet! They're very good at their work. ✉ *The Keep, Maritime La., Dockyard* ☎ *441/234–1418* ⊕ *www.nmb. bm* ✑ *$15; includes admission to Dolphin Quest Bermuda.*

★ Royal Naval Dockyard

HISTORIC SITE | Once a military stronghold that played a role in conflicts from the War of 1812 to World War II, the restored buildings of the sprawling Royal Naval Dockyard offer a full day of history with plenty of shopping and dining, and some adventure as well. The centerpiece is the National Museum of Bermuda, with exhibits on local maritime history and more in an imposing stone fortress; it has stunning ocean views from its highest points. The Old Cooperage holds the Bermuda Craft Market and the Bermuda Arts Centre; you can also shop in the Clocktower Mall, in another historic building. Dolphin Quest, an interactive

experience, and Snorkel Park Beach are other diversions. The Dockyard has plenty of places to eat, such as British pub fare and locally brewed beer at the Frog & Onion, or a quick latte and flaky baked goods at the Dockyard Pastry Shop. Note that a cruise terminal is on King's Wharf, making this a busy spot. ✉ *5 Freeport Drive.*

Snorkel Park Beach

SPORTS—SIGHT | FAMILY | Both beautiful marine life and evidence of the Dockyard's impressive naval legacy can be viewed at this protected inlet, accessed through a stone tunnel adjacent to the National Museum of Bermuda. Beneath the water's surface lie cast-iron cannons dating from 1550 to 1800, plus an antique anchor and gun-carriage wheel. The true attractions, however, are colorful fish (you might see more than 50 varieties) and other sea creatures including anemones, sea cucumbers, and assorted species of coral. Thanks to amenities like floating rest stations, snorkeling and scuba diving couldn't be easier. Everything is available to rent, including kayaks, pedalos, Jet Skis, and underwater scooters. This is a family beach by day, catering mainly to cruise ship passengers, and a nightclub by night, with beach parties and island barbecues. ✉ *7 Maritime La., Dockyard* ☎ *441/234–6989* ⊕ *www. snorkelparkbeach.com* ✑ *$5.*

Somerset Bridge

BRIDGE/TUNNEL | The West End is connected to the rest of Bermuda by Somerset Bridge, and once you have crossed over it, you're no longer, according to local lingo, "up the country." More than marking a boundary, Somerset Bridge is something of an attraction in its own right because it's reputed to be the world's smallest drawbridge. It opens a mere 18 inches, just wide enough to accommodate the mast of a passing sailboat. ✉ *Between Somerset and Middle Rds., Dockyard.*

The National Museum of Bermuda is housed in what was once Bermuda's largest fort, a centerpiece of the Royal Navy Dockyard.

Somerset Village

TOWN | Its position on Mangrove Bay once made it a popular hideout for pirates, but judging by Somerset Village's bucolic appearance, you'd never guess that now. The shady past has been erased by shady trees, quiet streets, and charming cottages. As far as actual attractions go, this quaint one-road retreat has only a few eateries and shops—most of them offshoots of Hamilton stores. Nevertheless, it provides easy access to Springfield and the Gilbert Nature Reserve (29 Somerset Rd. ⊕ www.bnt.bm), a 5-acre woodland with paths that connect to some of the most scenic portions of Bermuda's Railway Trail. ⊠ Somerset Ⓜ Bus 7 or 8, or ferry to Watford Bridge.

Visitor Services Centre Royal Naval Dockyard

INFO CENTER | The information center, adjacent to the cruise ship pier, the ferry terminal, and a bus stop, has helpful staff, plenty of information about sights and itineraries, and booking monitors so you can arrange activities and tours of all kinds. ⊠ Royal Naval Dockyard, 2 Dockyard Terr., Dockyard ☎ 441/542–7104 ⊕ www.gotobermuda.com.

X20 Adventures

CITY PARK | **FAMILY** | For those not content to sunbathe on the island's pink beaches or splash in the surf (especially kids), there is this seasonal floating water-themed park on a beach in Somerset. Waterslides, floating loungers, paddleboards, and other equipment can keep the family entertained for hours. Pack plenty of sunscreen, as no one is going to want to get out of the water. ⊠ Daniel's Head Beach Park ⊹ Somerset Island ☎ 441/704–4082 ⊕ www.x2oadventures. com ⊠ $25 ⊘ Closed Sept.–late May.

🏖 Beaches

The beaches that line the south shore of the West End of the island are just as picturesque but not nearly as crowded as the popular stretches of sand in the central parishes. Spend a relatively serene

afternoon in the sun and then stop off at a local watering hole for a bite before you head home for the night.

Snorkel Park Beach

BEACH—SIGHT | FAMILY | This is a popular spot for tourists as well as local families who like to treat their children to a sheltered white-sand beach and pristine views of the water. Enjoy local and American cuisine while sipping a frozen cocktail at the beach's Hammerheads Bar and Grill; on-site water-sport and beach equipment rentals are available for kids and parents. A playground outside the park features a 70-foot, wooden green moray eel and a replica of St. David's Lighthouse. Snorkel Park Beach is just a short walk from the Dockyard cruise terminal, so it attracts many cruise passengers. Before you leave, stop in the Clocktower Mall and the Bermuda Craft Market to pick up a souvenir or two. Also nearby are restaurants, the Dockyard Ferry Terminal, and an ATM.

At night, Snorkel transforms into a lively nightclub area, especially on Monday and Thursday when live DJs spin top 40, soca, reggae, and dancehall hits. **Amenities:** food and drink; parking (free); toilets; water sports. **Best for:** partiers; snorkeling; sunset; swimming. ⊠ *7 Maritime La., Dockyard* ☎ *441/234–6989* ⊕ *www. snorkelparkbeach.com* ⊠ *$5; check website for special-event prices* Ⓜ *Bus 7 or 8 from Hamilton.*

Somerset Long Bay

BEACH—SIGHT | Popular with Somerset locals, this beach is on the quiet northwestern end of Bermuda, far from the bustle of Hamilton and major tourist hubs. In keeping with the area's rural atmosphere, the beach is low-key and great for bird-watching. Undeveloped parkland shields the beach from the light traffic on Cambridge Road. The main beach is long by Bermudian standards—nearly ¼ mile from end to end. Although exposed to northerly storm winds, the bay water is normally calm and

Some Assembly Required ◉

Though it may appear to be yet another stalwart stone building, the Commissioner's House, now part of the National Museum of Bermuda at the Dockyard, is actually an engineering landmark. Designed by a naval architect, it was the world's first prefabricated residence. The component parts—made of cast iron rather than standard wood—were constructed in England between 1823 and 1827, then shipped to Bermuda, where they were assembled and sheathed in local limestone.

shallow—ideal for children. The bottom, however, is rocky and uneven, so it's a good idea to put on water shoes before wading. **Amenities:** parking (free). **Best for:** solitude; swimming; walking. ⊠ *Cambridge Rd., Somerset* ⊠ *Free* Ⓜ *Bus 7 or 8 from Hamilton.*

🍴 Restaurants

Though dining options are not as plentiful in Sandys Parish as elsewhere, this end of the island is not without stellar cuisine. Fresh seafood and burgers are popular options, particularly at neighborhood favorites like the Frog & Onion, but you'll find other cultures represented here as well: Italian, French, and British, to name a few, with the food most often accompanied by a stellar ocean view.

Bone Fish Bar & Grill

$$ | SEAFOOD | Though service isn't exactly speedy, the happy, friendly vibe and huge, covered patio make Bone Fish a local and tourist favorite; the breezy dining room offers respite from the heat too. Choose from Bermuda-style catch of the day (or local lobster in season),

A Tour of Dockyard and the West End ◉

To make the most of your visit to the West End, plan to combine sea and land transportation. Transit tokens, tickets, and passes work on both ferries and buses, allowing you to hop on and off wherever you please. If you have a bicycle or scooter, you can bring it on the ferry; however, you'll be charged an extra adult fare to take the latter. Once you arrive, the Dockyard itself can be covered easily on foot. Other sights are rather far apart, so plan to take a taxi, bus, or ferry if you're continuing on to Somerset or elsewhere.

The logical place to begin a tour is the Royal Naval Dockyard. Start your day by visiting the **National Museum of Bermuda** and **Dolphin Quest**, which are housed together in a stone fortress built between 1837 and 1852. To the left of the entrance is the **Snorkel Park Beach**, a small protected reef where you can get up close to marine life. Across from the museum entrance, the tempting art gallery and permanent **Bermuda Craft Market** in the Old Cooperage Building also warrant a visit. To the west are a pottery shop, glassblowing center, and other businesses that occupy attractive old military warehouses; just south is the **Clocktower Mall**, where you can find

still more shops. The Visitor Services Centre is close to the ferry stop. Finish your tour here, or continue via ferry to Somerset Island.

For an interesting change of pace, opt for the slow boat (not the one heading directly to Hamilton) out of the Dockyard. You'll pass by Boaz and Watford islands on your way to Somerset Island, fringed on both sides with beautiful secluded coves, inlets, and bays. Getting off the ferry at Watford Bridge, you can make a quick jaunt into **Somerset Village**, which consistently ranks among Bermuda's prettiest communities.

The next sights, reached via Somerset Road, are best visited by bus or scooter. About 2 miles east of Somerset Village, opposite the Willowbank Hotel, is the entrance to the **Heydon Trust**, which has gardens and a tiny 1616 chapel. Around the bend on your left is **Fort Scaur**, a serene spot with sweeping views of the Great Sound. Linking Somerset Island with the rest of Bermuda is **Somerset Bridge**, built in 1620 and reputedly the smallest working drawbridge in the world. Across the bridge, Somerset Road becomes Middle Road, which leads into Southampton Parish.

fish-and-chips, rib-eye steaks, and tasty homemade pastas, and chat with Italian owner Livio Ferigo, who loves to mingle with diners. **Known for:** social patio seating; live music; colorful cocktails. ⑤ *Average main: $30* ⊠ *6 Dockyard Terr., Dockyard, Somerset* ☎ *441/234–5151* ⊕ *www.bonefishbermuda.com.*

Breezes

$$$ | **CARIBBEAN** | The flavorful, island-inspired menu and location of Breezes

are simply perfect—these beachfront views and ocean breezes are what a Bermudian vacation is all about. With a table under the stars or on the covered patio, you'll want to time your dinner for sunset: For out-of-this-world romance, reserve a table right on the beach. **Known for:** reservations required, especially for sunset; superb fish choices; live music. ⑤ *Average main: $35* ⊠ *Cambridge Beaches Resort, 30 Kings Point Rd., Somerset* ☎ *441/234–0331* ⊕ *www.*

Bermudian Architecture

The typical Bermudian building is built of limestone block, usually painted white or a pastel shade, with a prominent chimney and a tiered, white roof that Mark Twain likened to "icing on the cake." More than just picturesque, these features are proof that "necessity" really is "the mother of invention." Limestone, for instance, was a widely available building material—and far better able to withstand hurricane-force winds than the old English-style wattle and daub.

The distinctive roof, similarly, was not developed for aesthetic reasons. It's part of a system that allows Bermudians to collect rainwater and store it in large tanks beneath their houses. The special white roof paint even contains a purifying agent. If your visit includes some rainy days, you may hear the expression, "Good day for the tank!" This is rooted in the fact that Bermuda has no fresh water. It relies on rain for drinking, bathing, and cooking water, as well as for golf-course and farmland irrigation, so residents are careful not to waste the precious liquid. The island has never run out of water, though the supply was stretched during World War II, when thousands of U.S. soldiers were stationed in Bermuda.

Moongates are another interesting Bermudian structural feature, usually found in gardens and walkways around the island. These Chinese-inspired freestanding stone arches, popular since the late 18th century, are still often incorporated into new construction. Thought to bring luck, the ring-shaped gates are favored as backdrops for wedding photos.

Other architectural details you may notice are "welcoming arms" stairways, with banisters that seem to reach out to embrace you as you approach the first step, and "eyebrows" over window openings. Also look for butteries: tiny, steep-roofed cupboards, separate from the house, and originally built to keep dairy products cool in summer. If you wonder why, in this warm climate, so many houses have fireplaces in addition to air conditioners, come in January, when the dampness makes it warmer outside than in.

---

cambridgebeaches.com ⊘ Closed Oct.–May.

Dockyard Pastry Shop
$ | **BISTRO** | When you want a quick coffee or a gourmet sandwich in Dockyard, this is the place to stop, just across from the Visitor Services Centre. Focusing on simple, familiar dishes and delectable house-made pastries, the charming little bistro offers afternoon tea (add champagne if you wish) under the golden Bermuda sunshine. **Known for:** croissants and danishes; afternoon tea with scones, sandwiches, and petit fours; cocktail and beer options. ⑤ Average main: $18 ⊠ 12 Dockyard Terr., Dockyard ☎ 441/232–2253 ⊕ www.thedockyardpastryshop.com ⊘ No dinner.

Frog & Onion Pub
$$ | **BRITISH** | **FAMILY** | Housed in the former Royal Naval Dockyard warehouse, this nautical-themed restaurant is loved locally for its good, satisfying food, craft beers, and lively atmosphere. The menu caters to every palate and includes juicy burgers, hearty house-made pub pies, and a selection of fresh local fish plates. **Known for:** lively spot with games area

Offering a sheltered cove for snorkeling, Snorkel Park Beach is very popular with families and cruise passengers.

in back; flights of local Bermuda beers; music in summer. $ *Average main: $21* ⊠ *The Cooperage, 4 Freeport Rd., Dockyard* ☎ *441/234–2900* ⊕ *www.irg.bm/ frog-and-onion.*

Somerset Country Squire

$$ | BRITISH | FAMILY | Overlooking Mangrove Bay, this well-worn tavern is all dark wood and good cheer, with a great deal of malt and hops in between. The food is simple, but a few items stand out: the Bermuda fish chowder, panfried rockfish, and steak sandwich are all delicious. **Known for:** scenic beach and bay views; covered patio seating; summertime barbecues. $ *Average main: $22* ⊠ *10 Mangrove Bay Rd., Somerset* ☎ *441/234–0105.*

🛏 Hotels

The western tip of the island has a lot going for it, having been energized with an increase in bars, restaurants, and stores. The Royal Naval Dockyard combines the old with the new; it's steeped

in history and also plays home to two cruise-ship terminals. In the summer this place is packed with cruise-ship passengers. This is a nice spot, just not for peace and quiet. Rentals are a common form of accommodation here.

★ Cambridge Beaches Resort & Spa

$$$$ | RESORT | No other Bermuda resort uses its privileged setting better—the resort's 30 acres on a peninsula near the western end of the island creates a sense of meandering expansiveness at this luxurious cottage colony. **Pros:** private and refined, with excellent spa; wide range of room and cottage options; beautiful grounds and beaches. **Cons:** far removed from rest of island; not family-friendly; older facilities could use modernizing. $ *Rooms from: $600* ⊠ *30 King's Point Rd., Somerset* ☎ *441/234– 0331, 800/468–7300 in U.S.* ⊕ *www. cambridgebeaches.com* ⇆ *94 rooms* ⏹ *Breakfast.*

The Bermuda Triangle Demystified

Long before the myth of the Bermuda Triangle became legend, Bermuda had already earned a reputation as an enchanted island. It was nicknamed "The Devil's Island" by early sea travelers, frightened by the calls of cahow birds and the squeals of wild pigs that could be heard onshore. But perhaps the most damning tales were told by sailors terrified of being wrecked on Bermuda's dangerous reefs. The island's mystical reputation is believed to have inspired Shakespeare's *The Tempest*, a tale of shipwreck and sorcery in "the still-vexed Bermoothes."

The early origin of the Triangle myth stretches as far back as Columbus, who noted in his logbook a haywire compass, strange lights, and a burst of flame falling into the sea. Columbus, as well as other sailors after him, also encountered a harrowing stretch of ocean now known as the Sargasso Sea. Ancient tales tell of sailboats stranded forever in a windless expanse of water, surrounded by seaweed and the remnants of other unfortunate vessels. It's true that relics have been found in the Sargasso Sea—an area of ocean between Bermuda and the Caribbean—but the deadly calm waters are more likely the result of circular ocean currents sweeping through the North Atlantic rather than paranormal activity.

In the past 500 years at least 50 ships and 20 aircraft have vanished in the Triangle, most without a trace—no wreckage, no bodies, nothing. Many disappeared in reportedly calm waters, without having sent a distress signal. Among the legends is that of Flight 19. At 2:10 on the afternoon of December 5, 1945, five TBM Avenger Torpedo Bombers took off from Fort Lauderdale, Florida, on a routine two-hour training mission. Their last radio contact was at 4 pm. The planes and 27 men were never seen or heard from again. The official navy report said the planes disappeared "as if they had flown to Mars."

The bizarre disappearances attributed to the Triangle have been linked to everything from alien abduction to sorcery. Although the mystery has not been completely solved, there are scientific explanations for many of the maritime disasters that have occurred in the Triangle. The most obvious answers are linked to extreme weather conditions with which any Bermudian fisher would be well acquainted. "White squalls"—intense, unexpected storms that arrive without warning on otherwise clear days—are probable culprits, along with waterspouts, the equivalent of sea tornadoes. The most recent scientific theory on the infamous Triangle suggests that the freakish disappearance of ships and aircraft could be the result of large deposits of methane gas spewing up from the ocean floor. Huge eruptions of methane bubbles may push water away from a ship, causing it to sink. If the highly flammable methane then rises into the air, it could ignite in an airplane's engine—causing it to explode and disappear.

Fact or fiction, the Triangle is a part of local lore that won't disappear anytime soon. But don't let it scare you away—this myth isn't the only thing that makes Bermuda seem so magical.

🍸 Nightlife

There are a handful of nightspots—most are bars with live entertainment—to keep you entertained in Dockyard. You should head to Snorkel Park Beach if you want to party until the early hours.

BARS AND LOUNGES
Frog & Onion Pub
BARS/PUBS | This place serves a splendid variety of down-to-earth pub fare in a dark-wood, barnlike setting. If you're spending the day at Dockyard, it's a great place to get out of the sun and try a Bermuda rum swizzle or sample a flight of Bermudian-brewed beers. There's a weekly quiz night as well as live performances on Monday night, and karaoke starts at 10 pm on Thursday. ✉ *The Cooperage, 4 Freeport Rd., Dockyard* ☎ *441/234–2900* ⊕ *www.irg.bm/ frog-and-onion.*

Somerset Country Squire
BARS/PUBS | An unpretentious bar with down-to-earth bar staff, this spot also has great views of the water. It's a decent spot for a quiet pint in the West End thanks to its outdoor terrace. Pull up a chair and appreciate a true Bermudian watering hole at one of the summertime barbecues. ✉ *10 Mangrove Bay, Somerset* ☎ *441/234–0105.*

MUSIC AND DANCE CLUBS
Club Aqua—Snorkel Park Beach
DANCE CLUBS | Up your vacation vibes at this popular club right on the beach. Monday, Wednesday, and Thursday nights are particularly lively, with barbecue beach bashes, Dark 'n' Stormy nights, rocking DJ sets, and even foam parties. The party often goes strong until 3 am, but if you're a cruise passenger, you won't be far from your bed, as the ship pier at Dockyard is just a stone's throw away. Admission is usually $10, more if there's a special event. ✉ *7 Maritime La., Dockyard* ☎ *441/234–6989* ⊕ *www. snorkelparkbeach.com.*

🛍 Shopping

New stores continue to spring up as the West End begins to threaten Hamilton as a shopping hot spot. Dockyard is the place to go for those quirky gifts you won't be able to find anywhere else. Don't miss the Bermuda Craft Market, Bermuda Glassworks, and Bermuda Rum Cake Company; in addition, just around the corner you have the Clocktower Mall with its quaint indoor selection of little stores and boutiques. A few miles along the road is the village of Somerset, which has a few stores to browse.

ART GALLERIES
Bermuda Arts Centre at Dockyard
ART GALLERIES | Sleek and modern, with well-designed displays of local art, this gallery is in one of the stone buildings of the former Royal Naval Dockyard. The walls are adorned with paintings and photographs, and glass display cases contain exquisitely crafted ceramics, jewelry, and wood sculptures. Exhibits change every month. Several artists' studios inside the gallery are open to the public. Much of the work on show is for sale, and a small shop sells prints and art-related gifts. ✉ *4 Maritime La., Dockyard* ☎ *441/234–2809* ⊕ *www.artbermuda.com.*

★ Carole Holding Print & Craft Shops
ART GALLERIES | Prices for artist Carole Holding's watercolors of Bermuda's scenes and flowers range from $12 for small prints to more than $5,000 for framed originals. The artist's prints can also be found on linen, china, and clothing, including T-shirts and aprons, and she has her own line of jams, chutneys, and rum cakes. Works by Carole and other local arists can be found at Dockyard's Clocktower Mall or at Heritage Wharf near the cruise ship terminal. The wharf location is open only when cruise ships are in port. ✉ *Clocktower Mall, Clocktower Parade, Dockyard* ☎ *441/535–4000* ⊕ *www.caroleholding.com.*

CLOTHING

Crown & Anchor

CLOTHING | Housed in a former ship captain's home, the nautically designed shop with whitewashed exposed wooden beams and model sailboats is the perfect showcase for the nautically inspired clothing. Find polos and khaki shorts for men and striped T-shirt dresses and colorful beach dresses that can be easily dressed up or down for women. ⊠ Royal Naval Dockyard, 4 Dockyard Terr., Dockyard ☎ 441/296–9558.

Island Outfitters

CLOTHING | This shop has everything you need for your beach vacation, from hats to flip-flops to cover-ups. Bermuda-inspired dresses, shorts, and hats from local children's clothing designer Aqua Designs are carried here. You can also buy island souvenirs. ⊠ 6 Dockyard Terr., Dockyard ☎ 441/238–4842.

CRAFTS

Bermuda Craft Market

CRAFTS | The island's largest permanent craft outlet is in the Dockyard's old Cooperage building, which dates from 1831. Dozens of artists show their work here, and this is the place to go to find that unusual gift, from Bermuda-cedar hair clips to Bermuda chutneys and jams. Hand-painted glassware, sterling silver jewelry, handmade toys, and sand sculptures are also among the pretty offerings. ⊠ The Cooperage, 4 Maritime La., Dockyard ☎ 441/234–3208 ⊕ www. bermudacraftmarket.com.

Jon Faulkner Gallery

CRAFTS | Customized house-number and name plaques and tableware are among the brightly painted pottery pieces created in this little shop in Dockyard. Faulkner's salt-fired pottery and porcelain fare are some of the standout pieces. There's also a walk-in Paint Your Own Pottery Studio where you can create your own masterpieces. ⊠ 7 Camber Rd., Dockyard ☎ 441/234–5116 ⊕ www. jonfaulknergallery.com.

FOOD AND CANDY

GROCERY STORES

Somerset MarketPlace

FOOD/CANDY | The largest grocery store on the island's western end is convenient to Cambridge Beaches Resort, but take a moped or taxi. ⊠ 48 Somerset Rd., Somerset ☎ 441/234–0626 ⊕ www. marketplace.bm.

NOVELTIES AND GIFTS

★ Dockyard Glassworks and Bermuda Rum Cake Company

GIFTS/SOUVENIRS | Pull up an armchair and watch as artists turn molten glass into vases, plates, miniature tree frogs, and other collectibles. Afterward help yourself to the rum-cake samples. Flavors include traditional black rum, chocolate, coconut, rum swizzle (with tropical fruit juices), coffee, banana, and ginger. You can buy the cakes duty-free or pick up a specially presented cake in a tin. Black rum fruitcake and loquat cakes are also sold. If you buy glassware, the company will pack the purchase and deliver it to your hotel or cruise ship for a small fee. ⊠ Bldg. No. 9, 1 Maritime La., Dockyard ☎ 441/234–4216 ⊕ www.dockglass.com.

Littlest Drawbridge Gift Shop

GIFTS/SOUVENIRS | Bermuda-cedar treasures, such as bowls, candle holders, and letter openers, are the highlight of this closet-size shop. Resort wear, handcrafted pottery, pens, and incense cones are also for sale. ⊠ Clocktower Mall, 6 Clock Tower Parade ☎ 441/234–6214 ⊕ littlest-drawbridge.01.free.bm.

SPAS

Cambridge Beaches Ocean Spa

SPA/BEAUTY | Sunlight dapples the indoor swimming pools at the Cambridge Beaches Ocean Spa, inside a traditional Bermudian cottage with pink-stucco walls and a ridged roof. The glass dome that covers the pool is opened in warm weather, allowing salt-tinged ocean breezes to drift into the villa. Ocean Spa caters to both men and women, and offers a wide variety of choices: from

wraps and facials to massages and nail treatments, using high quality products from the United Kingdom. Ocean Spa also features a whirl pool, sauna, and top-notch fitness center. ⊠ *Cambridge Beaches Resort & Spa, 30 King's Point Rd., Somerset* ☎ *441/234–3636* ⊕ *www. cambridgebeaches.com.*

🏃 Activities

Although it's far from the bustle of activity in Bermuda's central parishes, there is adventure to be had in the West End. The narrow, winding streets are ideal for cycling enthusiasts, or you can take a Segway tour of Dockyard. Whether you prefer a leisurely cruise or a fishing charter, whether you are PADI-certified or a helmet diver looking for action, Sandys Parish offers countless opportunities to enjoy the island's clear waters.

BIKING

Because it's one of the few areas of the island where elevation remains relatively constant, biking in Somerset poses a fun challenge for anyone interested in viewing the area at a slow and steady pace. Bring plenty of water and a camera: the views of the north shore and the rest of the island can be pretty stunning from Watford Bridge.

Oleander Cycles

BICYCLING | The agency rents both motor scooters and bicycles and has a handy branch in the Dockyard. ⊠ *9 Camber Rd., King's Wharf, Dockyard* ☎ *441/234–2764* ⊕ *www.oleandercycles.bm* ⊠ *From $41 for 2 hours.*

BOATING

No island visit is complete without spending at least part of your day on the water, especially if it means you can play captain. Rentals are available at reasonable prices, and veteran sailors can point you in the direction of the best spots to drop anchor. If your trip coincides with summer's national Cup Match holiday (a four-day extravaganza celebrating

emancipation from slavery), book your rental in advance and join the hundreds of locals who "raft up" in Mangrove Bay near Somerset for the party of the year.

Bermuda Waterski and Wakeboard Center

WATER SPORTS | FAMILY | International competitor Kent Richardson represented Bermuda at nine World Championships and the Pan Am games. He also took a trick skiing bronze medal at the Latin American games, but don't be intimidated—Kent is a patient teacher. His business operates at the same location as Somerset Bridge Watersports at Robinson's Marina from May to September. You can take your pick from waterskiing (regular and barefoot), wakeboarding, cliff jumping, or tubing, or mix it up with a bit of everything. Kent charges by the hour and can take up to six people at a time, ages five and older. ⊠ *Robinson's Marina, Somerset Bridge, Somerset* ☎ *441/335–1012* ⊕ *bermudawaterski.com* ⊠ *$250 per hour, regardless of number of people.*

H2O Sports

WATER SPORTS | Located on the shore of Mangrove Bay in Somerset, H2O offers just about everything there is to do on the water: sailing, boat rentals, kayaking, as well as instruction from experienced mariners. You can rent 17-foot-long motorboats, and adventurous explorers and independent anglers can take out a 17-foot sailboat; 90-minute sailing lessons are available if you need a refresher. See the island at speed with a guided 75-minute Jet Ski tour or snorkel (gear is available for rent) at your own pace. The staff will happily point out the best snorkeling spots and what marine life to look out for. ⊠ *Cambridge Beaches Resort, 2 Cambridge Rd.* ☎ *441/234–3082* ⊕ *www. h2osportsbermuda.com* ⊠ *From $80 for first hour of sailboat rental, $100 for first hour of motorboat rental; Jet Ski tour $135.*

KS Watersports

BOATING | This is the one and only place to go for WildCat (a type of catamaran) adventure tours, Jet Ski safaris, and sailboat rentals. Its Dockyard location, right next to the ferry stop, is open year-round and specializes in water sports excursions. For a more low-key day in the sun, check out the KS Watersports locations in King's Square, St. George's, and Pitts Bay Road, Hamilton; they offer pontoon and Boston Whaler boat rentals and private charters. All three locations run Jet Ski tours, starting with a 75-minute thrilling adventure. ⊠ *Dockyard Watersports Center, 6 Dockyard Terr., Dockyard* ☎ *441/238–4155 Dockyard, 441/232–4155 Hamilton, 441/297–4155 St. George's* ⊕ *www.kswatersports.com* ⊠ *From $145 for Jet Ski tour.*

Restless Native Tours

BOATING | **FAMILY** | What is billed as the only Bermudian-built catamaran has a full bar, huge music library, iPod dock, and onboard souvenir shop, ensuring that everyone will enjoy cruising on this family-owned and-operated charter vessel. Restless Native is unique in its educational approach to chartering—it offers a crash course on Bermuda's fish and a guided snorkeling trip. The 50-by-30-foot pink boat is excellent for dinner charters, evening cocktail cruises, birthday parties, and weddings. Excursions meet near the cruise ship terminal in Dockyard, but pickup can be arranged at any wharf on the island; charters are available year-round for two to five hours and up to 50 guests. ☎ *441/531–8149* ⊕ *www.restlessnative.bm* ⊠ *$75 for 3½-hour snorkel and cruise; $55 for 1½-hour sunset swizzle cruise.*

Rising Son II Catamaran

TOUR—SPORTS | The *Rising Son II* is a beautiful, 60-foot, 75-passenger catamaran with a full bar, roomy shaded cockpit, and multiple trampolines. Besides offering sailing, swimming, and snorkeling trips, Captain Steve "Squid" Smith and the accommodating crews can arrange for private cocktail parties and even catering. You can also book one of the popular cruises, such as the Ultimate Catamaran Sail and Snorkel, which anchors off a quiet sandy bay for snorkeling and kayaking. Keep your eyes peeled for marine life as turtles are often spotted. ⊠ *King's Wharf, North Arm, Dockyard* ☎ *441/236–1300* ⊕ *www.risingsoncruises.com* ⊠ *From $75 for cruises.*

Somerset Bridge Watersports

WATER SPORTS | Located right next to the Somerset Bridge, this West End outfitter rents 13- and 15-foot Boston Whalers. Rates increase slightly on bank holidays, and you must pay for gas. You can also take a speed tour of the western end of the island on a Jet Ski. The tour will take you flying over crystal clear waters, weaving through coral reefs, and under the world's smallest drawbridge. Prices include a paid taxi ride to or from Dockyard; be aware that groups are kept small, so big parties may need to split up. Single and double kayaks are also available for rent. ⊠ *Robinson's Marina, Somerset Bridge, Somerset* ☎ *441/234–0914, 441/234–3145* ⊕ *www.bdawatersports.com* ⊠ *From $95 for 2-hour boat rental, $145 for 4 hours, $260 for 8 hours; $125 for Jet Ski tour; kayak rentals from $25 per hour.*

CRICKET

It may take a little time to get the hang of the rules of cricket, the island's national game, but after a few rowdy runs, you'll be cheering in the stands like everyone else: howzat!

Somerset Cricket Club

CRICKET | Home of the Somerset Cricket Team and occasional venue for the annual Cup Match cricket game, the club is where devout local fans catch games of cricket or football (soccer), as this club also plays host to the parish's football team, the Somerset Trojans. ⊠ *6 Cricket La., Somerset.*

World Cup

Bermuda's angling competitions attract top fishers from all over the world. The Bermuda Billfish Blast tournament over the Fourth of July weekend coincides with the World Cup—where anglers across the globe compete to land the largest fish on the planet between 8 am and 4:30 pm. Each year more and more boats descend on Bermuda over the holiday weekend. The biggest local tournament is the Bermuda Big Game Classic, with many of the World Cup participants sticking around to take part in the three-day festival. The dates vary depending on when the weekend falls, but it's usually around July 15. The lure of monster marlin in excess of 1,000 pounds keeps them coming for the third leg of the Bermuda Triple Crown, the Seahorse Anglers Club tournament, the following week. Marlin season is what a lot of Bermuda's sport fishers live for. "It's the biggest, baddest fish in the ocean—there's no feeling like landing a marlin," explains Sloane Wakefield of Atlantic Spray Charters. The **Bermuda Game Fishing Association** (☎ 441/292–7131) and the **Bermuda Angler's Club** (⊕ www.bermudaanglersclub.com) are good sources of information about tournaments.

FISHING

Jolly Roger Bermuda

FISHING | FAMILY | If you're interested in a family-friendly fishing excursion, note that the *Jolly Roger* features a large, air-conditioned cabin and full snack bar. You visit the crew's favorite spots to drop a line and land fish like snappers, groupers, porgies, and jacks. The *Jolly Roger* can hold up to 40 passengers, and bait and tackle are included in the price. Charters leave from King's Wharf in Dockyard. Private charters can be arranged for the weekend. ☎ 441/234–2193, 441/333–2204 cell phone ⊕ jollyrogerbermuda.com ✉ From $100 for 4 hours.

Overproof

FISHING | Skipper Peter Rans is a regular in the big-game classic and a master at hooking monster marlin. He navigates a fully equipped 42-foot vessel to the very best spots to help you reel in whatever game fish is in season. His rates include equipment, bait, and beverages. ✉ 136 Somerset Rd. ☎ 441/238–5663, 441/335–9850 cell ⊕ www.overprooffishing.com ✉ From $1,000 for half day to $1,400 for 8 hours.

HELMET DIVING

A different, less technical type of diving popular in Bermuda is helmet diving, offered between April and mid-November. Although helmet-diving cruises last three hours or more, the actual time underwater is about 25 minutes, when underwater explorers walk along the sandy bottom in about 10 to 12 feet of water (depending on the tide), wearing helmets that receive air through hoses leading to the surface. Underwater portraits are available for an extra charge. A morning or afternoon tour includes wet suits when the water temperature is below 80°F.

Hartley's Under Sea Adventures

SCUBA DIVING | FAMILY | The Hartleys schedule two diving trips per day, usually at 9 am and 1:30 pm during high season. Nondivers (who pay about half of what helmet divers do) are not allowed to snorkel or swim in the same area as the divers, the theory being that fish that are used to helmet divers and approach them may endanger themselves by becoming used to snorkelers, swimmers, and eventually fisherfolk. Underwater

tours typically last between 30 and 40 minutes in a maximum depth of 8 to 12 feet. ⊠ *Heritage Wharf, at cruise ship terminal* ☎ *441/234–3535* ⊕ *www.hartleybermuda.com* ✉ *$108 per diver; $50 per rider.*

KITEBOARDING

Island Winds Bermuda

WATER SPORTS | You can sign up with Bermuda's "board sports specialists" for lessons or rent equipment for water sports including kiteboarding, paddleboarding, windsurfing, wakeboarding, and kayaking. ⊠ *Daniel's Head Beach Park, Scott's Hill, Somerset* ☎ *441/234–1111* ⊕ *www.islandwindsbermuda.com.*

SCUBA DIVING

There is another world beneath the waves, one vastly more complex than anything the native foliage of Bermuda may have to offer. Submerge yourself in sunken wrecks and coral reefs that are home to a host of multicolor creatures. Keep your eyes peeled for stingrays, parrotfish, nurse sharks, groupers, and the beautiful but poisonous lionfish, whose presence threatens the balance of the island's delicate reef system. Point them out to your tour operator or instructor: Bermudians are on a mission to eradicate the deadly fish.

Blue Water Divers and Watersports

SCUBA DIVING | The major operator for wrecks on the western side of the island, Blue Water Divers offers lessons, tours, and rentals. The lesson-and-dive package for first-time divers includes equipment and one tank or two. Prices for dives include all necessary equipment. With two tanks—the more commonly offered package—you can explore two or more wrecks in one four-hour outing. Discounts are offered for dive packages that range from two to five days. This operator is not to be confused with Dive Bermuda, despite the Web address. ⊠ *Robinson's Marina, Somerset Bridge* ☎ *441/234–1034* ⊕ *www.divebermuda.*

com ✉ *From $90 for one tank, $130 for two tanks; $210 for lesson package.*

SEGWAY TOURS

Take a step off the beaten path and explore Dockyard in a whole new way: the Segway. During this popular alternative to walking and bicycling tours, you tool around the town on your motorized two-wheeled steed—after a quick lesson on how to make it go, of course.

Segway Tours Bermuda

TOUR—SPORTS | Rent a Segway, a two-wheeled upright power scooter, and take a tour around historic Dockyard. Pick yours up at the old-fashioned double-decker bus across from Dockyard Glassworks and Bermuda Rum Cake Company. Tours are 1½ hours long, and the cost includes Segway training. Times are 10 am, noon, 2 pm, and 4 pm during summer months. ⊠ *Corner of Camber Rd. and Dockyard Terr., Dockyard* ☎ *441/236–1300* ⊕ *www.segway.bm* ✉ *$80 tour.*

SNORKELING CRUISES

Snorkeling cruises, offered from April to November, are a less expensive albeit less personal way to experience the underwater world. One of the area's most interesting snorkeling spots is the wreck of the HMS *Vixen.* Much like an iceberg, the bow of this gunboat, which was sunk on purpose off Daniel's Head in 1896, crests the surface; the body of the ship lies beneath, proving a suitable home for a local sea life. Look but don't touch! You may be tempted to snap a selfie at the boat's apex, but this landmark is protected. Snorkeling is allowed, but scuba diving requires a permit. *Also see the Boating section in Activities, since other boats can offer snorkeling.*

★ Captain Kirk's Coral Reef Adventures

SNORKELING | Pick your adventure with Captain Kirk's Coral Reef Adventures, but regardless of which option you want, prepare for memorable hours with a wide option of boats and tours. Depending on

Wreck Diving

If you've heard the stories of the Bermuda Triangle, then you won't be surprised to hear that there are more than 20 ships wrecked off the island. Actually it's got more to do with the craggy reefs that surround the island than that old myth, but each wreck has a story, and most dive operators here know it. Graham Maddocks, a veteran of Bermuda's waters and owner of Triangle Diving, gave us a history lesson on five of Bermuda's most interesting wrecks.

Constellation. Jaws author Peter Benchley based his follow-up novel *The Deep,* set in Bermuda, around the *Constellation* wreck. A cargo ship bound for Venezuela during World War II, she was carrying building materials, morphine, and 700 bottles of whiskey when her hull was broken apart on the reef. Some of the building materials remain, but the rest of her cargo is long gone.

The Cristobel Colon. This massive Spanish cruise liner is the biggest of Bermuda's shipwrecks, at 499 feet long. It crashed into the reefs off the north shore in 1936 after its captain mistook an offshore communications tower for the Gibbs Hill Lighthouse. It was crewed by Spanish dissidents from the civil war in Puerto Rico. (They were eventually rounded up and hanged for treason in Spain.) The *Cristobel* sat in Bermuda's waters for several years, and many of its furnishings can be found in Bermudian homes today. The British eventually sank its empty shell by using it for target practice during World War II.

The Hermes. Probably the most popular wreck dive in Bermuda, the *Hermes* remains fully intact sitting in 80 feet of water off the south shore. It's one of the few wrecks that you can actually get inside and explore. It arrived in Bermuda with engine trouble and was ultimately abandoned by its crew. The Bermuda government took possession of the 165-foot steel-hulled ship and sank it as a dive site in the early 1980s.

The Pelinaion. This 385-foot Greek cargo steamer was another victim of World War II. The British had blacked out the lighthouse in a bid to stop the Germans from spying on Bermuda. The captain had a perfect record, had sailed past Bermuda many times, and was months away from retirement when he made this journey from West Africa to Baltimore in 1940, carrying a cargo of iron ore. Without the lighthouse to guide him, he couldn't find the island until he struck the reef off St. David's. You can still see the ship's steam boiler and engine as well as some of the cargo of iron ore.

The Xing Da. A modern-day pirate ship, the *Xing Da* was carrying a "cargo" of Chinese immigrants to be smuggled into the United States in 1996. Crewed by members of the Chinese mafia, the Triad, it had arranged to meet a smaller boat 145 miles off Bermuda for the immigrants to be transferred and taken into the United States. Instead, they found themselves surrounded by U.S. marines. The boat was given to the government as a dive site in 1997.

the weather, you can choose to stop at two of three exciting locations: a ship-wreck, a secluded island beach, or one of Bermuda's beautiful coral reefs. Or book a day out fishing on the *Jolly Roger*. Snorkeling equipment, masks, and vests are provided; plus you can peer into the turquoise waters right through the glass bottom of some of the boats. The 31-foot *Pisces* holds up to 20 people and departs from Dockyard. ⊠ *Royal Naval Dockyard, North Arm, Dockyard* ☎ *441/236–1300* ⊕ *www.kirksadventures.com* ⊠ *From $50.*

Fantasea Bermuda

WATER SPORTS | You're spoiled for choice with this one-stop recreational company with snorkeling tours, diving, sightseeing cruises, glass-bottom boat trips, and even banana-boat rides. You can choose a three-hour Catamaran Coral Reef Snorkel aboard a luxury catamaran or a 90-minute rum-tasting sunset sail. The whale-watching tours in March and April are immensely popular, when you can get close to the majestic humpbacks as they migrate north. Take your pick of a cruise-and-kayak or boat-and-bike ecotour for a closer look at some of the prettiest spots on the island. Most tours depart from Dockyard, near the cruise ship ter-minal. ⊠ *Dockyard Watersports Center, North Arm, Dockyard* ☎ *441/234–3483* ⊕ *fantasea.bm* ⊠ *From $60 for sunset sail; $70 for 3-hour snorkel sail.*

Chapter 8

CRUISING TO BERMUDA

8

Updated by
Melissa Fox

● Sights 🍴 Restaurants 🛏 Hotels ● Shopping Y Nightlife

Wouldn't you like to arrive in Bermuda relaxed, unpacked, and already in vacation mode? Bermuda is an island paradise just a hop, skip, and a jump away from the East Coast by plane, but there's nothing quite as stylishly traditional, or gracious, as an arrival by sea.

Cruising to Bermuda is one of the best ways to enjoy the turquoise waters of this 22-square-mile (57-square-km) island, where white limestone roofs and pastel-painted buildings stand in dramatic contrast to the lush green foliage. Your choice of ships that berth at one of Bermuda's ports is extensive, with more than 15 cruise lines putting Bermuda on their yearly schedules. While many mainstream cruise lines visit Bermuda, only a handful feature vessels small enough to squeeze through the narrow channels into the harbors at St. George's and Hamilton, meaning that popular mega-ships are able to dock only at King's Wharf in the Royal Naval Dockyard. This doesn't mean you'll miss out on any of the island's great attractions: Take a shore excursion or tour the island on your own by taxi, moped, public bus, or high-speed ferry, all of which are available at each end of the island.

The island is accessible from many departure points along the Eastern Seaboard, including Baltimore, Boston, New York, Norfolk, and Philadelphia. Your best bet is to check with the cruise line or your travel agent to find the most convenient port for you. Running parallel to the island's summer, cruise season begins in mid-April and runs through mid-November, although the occasional

ship has been known to dock during off-season months.

Increasingly popular are round-trip itineraries originating in northeastern embarkation ports that include a single day or overnight port call in Bermuda before continuing south to the Bahamas or Caribbean. In addition to these Bermuda/Bahamas and Bermuda/Caribbean itineraries, "special" voyages or one-way ship-repositioning cruises are often available at the beginning or end of the usual Bermuda season, when cruise lines move their ships to the Caribbean for winter months.

Choosing a Cruise

Your choice of cruise line to Bermuda is narrowed by the government's firm control over the annual number of cruise ships and visitors to the island. That figure has increased in recent years, allowing more passengers to experience all Bermuda has to offer while still receiving the best service and hospitality. Although most ships to Bermuda are big, floating-resort-type vessels, each has its own personality, determined by its amenities, theme, and, of course, passengers.

Your cruise experience will be shaped by several factors. To decide whether a

particular ship's style will suit you, you need to consider your lifestyle and vacation expectations and then do a bit of research: Is there a full program of organized activities each day? What happens in the evening? What kind of entertainment is offered after dark? How often will you need to dress up for dinner? Are there facilities for kids and teens?

Space and passenger-to-crew ratios are equally important. The latter indicates the number of passengers served by each crew member—the lower the ratio, the better the level of service. The space ratio (the gross tonnage of a ship divided by its passenger capacity) allows you to compare ships' roominess. The higher the ratio, the more spacious the vessel feels: at 40:1 or higher a ship will feel quite roomy. Less than 25:1 will cramp anyone's style.

Best Bets for Cruise Passengers

- Climb up Gibbs Hill Lighthouse for an expansive view of the inlets and harbors.
- Absorb Bermuda's nautical and military history at the National Musem of Bermuda.
- Ride on the ferries to rub shoulders with Bermudians.
- Attend the summertime street festival called Harbour Nights, held every Wednesday in Hamilton.
- Marvel as ships gingerly inch through the cuts at Hamilton's harbor with very little room to spare.

Cabins

In years gone by, cabins were almost an afterthought. The general attitude of both passengers and the cruise lines used to be that a cabin is a cabin—used only for changing clothes and sleeping. That's why the cabins on most older cruise ships are skimpy in size and short on amenities.

Most cabin layouts on a ship are identical or nearly so. Commanding views fetch higher fares, but you should know that cabins on the highest decks are also more susceptible to side-to-side movement; in rough seas you could find yourself tossed right out of bed. On lower decks, you'll pay less and find more stability, particularly in the middle of the ship—even upper-level cabins in the middle of the ship are steadier.

Some forward cabins have a tendency to be oddly shaped, as they follow the contour of the bow. They are also likely to be noisy; when the ship's anchor drops, you won't need a wake-up call. In rough

seas you can feel the ship's pitch (its upward and downward motion) more in the front. Should you go for the stern location instead? You may feel the pitch there, too, and possibly some vibration. You're also more likely to hear engine and machinery noise, and depending on the ship, you might find soot on your balcony railings. However, many passengers feel the view of the ship's wake (the ripples it leaves behind as its massive engines move it forward) is worth any noise or vibration they might encounter there.

Above all, don't be confused by all the categories listed in cruise-line brochures; price levels are more likely to reflect cabin location than any physical differences in the cabins themselves. Shipboard accommodations fall into four basic configurations: inside cabins, outside cabins, balcony cabins, and suites.

INSIDE CABINS
An inside cabin has no window or porthole. These are always the least expensive cabins and are ideal for passengers who would rather spend their vacation funds on excursions or other

incidentals than on upgraded accommodations. Inside cabins are generally just as spacious as the lowest category of outside cabins, and decor and amenities are similar. Parents sometimes book an inside cabin for their older children and teens, while they stay across the hall in an outside cabin with a window or balcony. On some newer ships, inside cabins have "virtual" windows that show a picture of the outside of the ship, giving the illusion you aren't completely inside.

OUTSIDE CABINS

A standard outside cabin has either a picture window or porthole. To give the illusion of more space, these cabins might also rely on the generous use of mirrors for an even airier feeling. Two twin beds can be joined together to create one large bed. Going one step further, standard and larger outside staterooms on modern ships are often outfitted with a small sofa or loveseat with a cocktail table or small side table. Some larger cabins may have a combination bathtub-shower instead of just a shower.

BALCONY CABINS

A balcony (or veranda) cabin is an outside cabin with floor-to-ceiling glass doors that open onto a private deck. Although the cabin may have large expanses of glass, the balcony is sometimes cut out of the cabin's square footage (depending on the ship). Balconies are usually furnished with two chairs and a table for lounging and casual dining outdoors. However, you should be aware that balconies are not always completely private; sometimes your balcony is visible from those next door and from above. The furnishings and amenities of balcony cabins are otherwise much like those in standard outside cabins.

SUITES

Suites are the most lavish accommodations afloat, and although they are always larger than regular cabins, suites do not always have separate rooms for sleeping. They almost always have amenities that standard cabins do not have. Depending on the cruise line, you may find a small refrigerator or minibar stocked with complimentary soft drinks, bottled water, and the alcoholic beverages of your choice. Top suites on some ships include complimentary laundry service and complex entertainment centers with large flat-screen TVs, in-cabin espresso or cappucino makers, and iPhone docks. An added bonus to the suite life is the extra level of services many ships offer—for example, afternoon tea and evening canapés delivered to your suite and served by a white-gloved butler.

Although "minisuites" on most contemporary ships have separate sitting areas with a sofa, chair, and cocktail table, don't let the marketing skill of the cruise lines fool you: so-called minisuites are usually little more than slightly larger versions of standard balcony cabins and seldom include the extra services and elaborate amenities you can get in regular suites. They're still generally a good value for the price, if space matters.

ACCESSIBILITY ISSUES

All major cruise lines offer a limited number of staterooms designed to be wheelchair- and scooter-accessible. Booking a newer vessel will generally ensure more choices. On newer ships, public rooms are generally more accessible, and more facilities have been planned with wheelchair-users in mind. Auxiliary aids, such as flashers for the hearing impaired and buzzers for visually impaired passengers, as well as lifts for swimming pools and hot tubs, are sometimes available. However, more than the usual amount of planning is necessary for smooth sailing if you have special needs.

For example, when a ship is unable to dock—as is the case in Grand Cayman—passengers are taken ashore on tenders that are sometimes problematic even for the able-bodied to negotiate. Some people with limited mobility may find it difficult to embark or disembark the ship

when docked because of the steep angle of the gangways during high or low tide. In some situations, crew members may offer assistance that involves carrying guests, but if the sea is choppy when tendering is a necessity, that might not be an option.

Passengers who require continuous oxygen or have service animals will have further hurdles to overcome. You can bring both aboard a cruise ship, but you should be prepared to present up-to-date records for your service animal if requested.

Cruise Costs

The average daily price for Caribbean itineraries varies dramatically depending on several circumstances. The cost of a cruise on a luxury line such as Silversea or Seabourn may be three to four times the cost of a cruise on a mainstream line such as Carnival or even premium lines like Princess. *When* you sail will also affect your costs: published brochure rates are usually highest during the peak summer season and holidays. When snow blankets the ground and temperatures are in single digits, a Caribbean cruise can be a welcome respite and less expensive than land resorts, which often command top dollar in winter months.

Solo travelers should be aware that single cabins have virtually disappeared from cruise ships, with the exception of Norwegian Cruise Line's *Norwegian Epic*, *Breakaway*, and *Getaway*, and some single cabins on Cunard Line, Royal Caribbean, and Holland America Line ships. Taking a double cabin can cost twice the advertised per-person rates (which are based on double occupancy). Some cruise lines will find same-sex roommates for singles; each then pays the per-person, double-occupancy rate.

TIPS
One of the most delicate—yet frequently debated—topics of conversation among cruise passengers involves the matter of tipping. Whom do you tip? How much? What's "customary" and "recommended"? Should parents tip the full amount for children, or is just half adequate? Why do you have to tip at all?

When transfers to and from your ship are a part of your air-and-sea program, gratuities are generally included for luggage handling. In that case, do not worry about the interim tipping. However, if you take a taxi to the pier and hand over your bags to a stevedore, be sure to tip him. Treat him with respect and pass along at least $5.

During your cruise, room-service waiters generally receive a cash tip of $1 to $3 per delivery. A 15% to 18% gratuity will automatically be added to each bar bill during the cruise. If you use salon and spa services, a similar percentage might be added to the bills there as well. If you dine in a specialty restaurant, you may be asked to provide a one-time gratuity for the service staff.

Nowadays, tips for cruise staff generally add up to about $12 to $22 per person per day, depending on the category of your accommodations. You tip the same amount for each person who shares the cabin, including children, unless otherwise indicated. Most cruise lines now either automatically add gratuities to passengers' onboard charge accounts or offer the option.

EXTRAS
Cruise fares typically include accommodations, onboard meals and snacks, and most onboard activities. Not normally included are airfare, shore excursions, tips, soft drinks, alcoholic drinks, or spa treatments. Some lines now add a room service fee; for instance Norwegian Cruise Line charges $7.95 for all room service, with the exception of suites, and

DECIPHER YOUR DECK PLAN

LIDO DECK

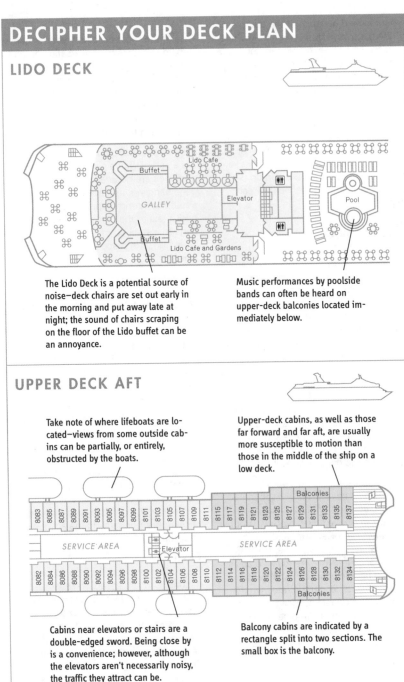

The Lido Deck is a potential source of noise—deck chairs are set out early in the morning and put away late at night; the sound of chairs scraping on the floor of the Lido buffet can be an annoyance.

Music performances by poolside bands can often be heard on upper-deck balconies located immediately below.

UPPER DECK AFT

Take note of where lifeboats are located—views from some outside cabins can be partially, or entirely, obstructed by the boats.

Upper-deck cabins, as well as those far forward and far aft, are usually more susceptible to motion than those in the middle of the ship on a low deck.

Cabins near elevators or stairs are a double-edged sword. Being close by is a convenience; however, although the elevators aren't necessarily noisy, the traffic they attract can be.

Balcony cabins are indicated by a rectangle split into two sections. The small box is the balcony.

MAIN PUBLIC DECK

Cabins immediately below restaurants and dining rooms can be noisy. Late sleepers might be bothered by early breakfast noise, early sleepers by late diners.

Theaters and dining rooms are often located on middle or lower decks.

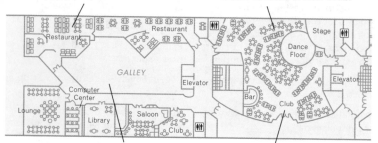

The ship's galley isn't usually labeled on deck plans, but you can figure out where it is by locating a large blank space near the dining room. Cabins beneath it can be very noisy.

Locate the ship's show lounge, disco, children's playroom, and teen center and avoid booking a cabin directly above or below them for obvious reasons.

LOWER DECK AFT

Cabins designated for passengers with disabilities are often situated near elevators.

Interior cabins have no windows and are the least expensive on board.

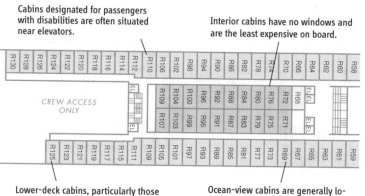

Lower-deck cabins, particularly those far aft, can be plagued by mechanical noises and vibration.

Ocean-view cabins are generally located on lower decks.

8

Cruising to Bermuda CHOOSING A CRUISE

Recommended Gratuities by Cruise Line ◉

Each cruise line has a different tipping policy. Some allow you to add tips to your shipboard account, and others expect you to dole out the dollars in cash on the last night of the cruise. Here are the suggested tipping amounts for each line covered in this book. Gratuity recommendations are often higher if you're staying in a suite with extra services, such as a butler.

Azamara Club Cruises: No tipping expected

Carnival Cruise Lines: $12.95–$13.95 per person per day

Celebrity Cruises: $14.50–$18 per person per day

Costa Cruises: $13.50–$16.50 per person per day

Crystal Cruises: No tipping expected

Cunard Line: $11.50–$13.50 per person per day

Disney Cruise Line: $12 per person per day

Holland America Line: $13.50–$15 per person per day

MSC Cruises: $12.50 per person per day

Norwegian Cruise Line: $14.50–$17.50 per person per day

Oceania Cruises: $16–$23 per person per day

Ponant: No tipping expected

Princess Cruises: $13.50–$15.50 per person per day

Regent Seven Seas Cruises: No tipping expected

Royal Caribbean International: $14.50–$17.50 per person per day

Seabourn Cruise Line: No tipping expected

Seadream Yacht Club: No tipping expected

Silversea Cruises: No tipping expected

Star Clippers: $8 per person per day

Viking Ocean Cruises: $15 per person per day

Windstar Cruises: $13.50 per person per day

Royal Caribbean adds a $3.95 fee for late-night orders. Port fees, fuel surcharges, and sales taxes are generally added to your fare at booking but are often included in quoted rates.

The Bermuda Cruise Fleet

To avoid overcrowding, the Bermudian government limits the number of regular cruise-ship visits to the island. Cruise lines with weekly or monthly sailings are Norwegian Cruise Line, Carnival Cruise Lines, Celebrity Cruises, and Royal Caribbean International. In addition, cruise lines such as AIDA Cruises, Azamara Club Cruises, Cunard Line, Disney Cruise Lines, Holland America Line, Marella Cruises, Oceania Cruises, P&O Cruises, Princess Cruises, Saga Cruises, Seabourn Cruises, Silversea Cruises, MSC Cruises, Regent Seven Seas Cruises, and Viking Ocean Cruises may have a Bermuda port call on their schedules.

Booking Your Cruise

As a rule, the majority of cruisers still plan their trips 9–12 months ahead of time, though the booking window has narrowed over time. It follows, then, that a longer booking window should give you the pick of sailing dates, ships, itineraries, cabins, and flights to the port city. If you're looking for a standard itinerary and aren't choosy about the vessel or dates, you could wait for a last-minute discount, but they are more difficult to find than in the past.

If particular shore excursions are important to you, consider booking them when you book your cruise to avoid disappointment later.

Using a Travel Agent

Whether it is your first or 50th sailing, your best friend when booking a cruise is a knowledgeable, experienced travel agent. The last thing you want when considering a costly cruise vacation is an agent who has never been on a cruise, calls a cruise ship "the boat," or—worse still—quotes brochure rates. The most important steps in cruise-travel planning are research, research, and more research. Booking a cruise is a complex process, and it's seldom wise to try to go it alone, particularly the first time. But how do you find a cruise travel agent you can trust?

The most experienced and reliable agent will be certified as an Accredited Cruise Counselor (ACC), Master Cruise Counselor (MCC), or Elite Cruise Counselor (ECC) by the Cruise Lines International Association (CLIA). These agents have completed demanding training programs, including touring or sailing on a specific number of ships. Your agent should also belong to a professional trade organization. In North America, membership in the American Society of Travel Agents

(ASTA) indicates that an agency has pledged to follow the code of ethics set forth by the world's largest association for travel professionals. In the best of all worlds, your travel agent is affiliated with both ASTA and CLIA.

Contrary to what conventional wisdom might suggest, cutting out the travel agent and booking directly with a cruise line won't necessarily get you the lowest price. According to Cruise Lines International Association (CLIA), 7 out of 10 cruise bookings are still handled through travel agents. In fact, cruise-line reservation systems simply are not capable of dealing with tens of thousands of direct calls from potential passengers. Without an agent working on your behalf, you're on your own. Do not rely solely on Internet message boards for authoritative responses to your questions—that is a service more accurately provided by your travel agent.

BOOKING YOUR CRUISE ONLINE

In addition to local travel agencies, there are many hardworking, dedicated travel professionals working for websites. Both big-name travel sellers and mom-and-pop agencies compete for the attention of cyber-savvy clients; and it never hurts to compare prices from a variety of these sources. Some cruise lines even allow you to book directly with them through their websites or toll-free reservation call centers.

As a rule, Internet-based and toll-free brokers will do a decent job for you. They often offer discounted fares, though not always the lowest, so it pays to check around. If you know precisely what you want and how much you should pay to get a real bargain—and you don't mind dealing with an anonymous voice on the phone—make your reservations when the price is right. Just don't expect the personal service you get from an agent you know. Also, be prepared to spend a lot of time and effort on the phone if something goes wrong.

Before You Book

If you've decided to use a travel agent, ask yourself these 10 simple questions, and you'll be better prepared to help the agent do his or her job.

1. Who will be going on the cruise?

2. What can you afford to spend for the entire trip?

3. Where would you like to go?

4. How much vacation time do you have?

5. When can you get away?

6. What are your interests?

7. Do you prefer a casual or structured vacation?

8. What kind of accommodations do you want?

9. What are your dining preferences?

10. How will you get to the embarkation port?

TRAVEL AGENT PROFESSIONAL ORGANIZATIONS American Society of Travel Agents. (*ASTA*) ⊕ *www.travelsense.org.*

CRUISE LINE ORGANIZATIONS Cruise Lines International Association. (*CLIA*) ⊕ *www.cruising.org.*

Before You Go

To expedite your preboarding paperwork, most cruise lines have convenient forms on their websites. As long as you have your reservation number, you can provide the required immigration information, reserve shore excursions, and even indicate special requests from the comfort of your home. Less "wired" cruise lines might mail preboarding paperwork to you or your travel agent for completion after you make your final payment and request that you return the forms by mail or fax. No matter how you submit them, be sure to make copies of any forms you fill out and to bring them with you to the pier to shorten the check-in process.

Travel Documents

After you make the final payment to your travel agent, the cruise line will issue your cruise tickets and vouchers for airport-to-ship transfers, or you may be able to print them yourself from the line's website. Depending on the airline, and whether you have purchased an air-sea package, you may receive your flight reservations or e-ticket vouchers at the same time; you may also receive vouchers for shore excursions, although cruise lines generally issue these aboard ship. Should your travel documents not arrive when promised, contact your travel agent or call the cruise line.

Children under the age of 18 who are not traveling with both parents almost always require a letter of permission from the absent parent(s). Airlines, cruise lines, and immigration agents can deny minor children initial boarding or entry to foreign countries without proper proof of identification and citizenship *and* a permission letter from absent or noncustodial parents. Your travel agent or cruise line can help with the wording of such a letter.

A WORD ABOUT PASSPORTS

It is every passenger's responsibility to have proper identification. If you arrive at the embarkation port without it, you will not be allowed to board, and the cruise line will issue no fare refund. Most travel agents know the requirements and can guide you to the proper agency to obtain what you need if you don't have it.

What to Pack

Cruise wear falls into three categories: casual, informal, and formal. Cruise documents should include information indicating how many evenings fall into each category. You will know when to wear what by reading your ship's daily newsletter—each evening's dress code will be prominently announced.

Time spent ashore touring and shopping calls for shorts topped with T-shirts or polo shirts and comfy walking shoes. In summer, forget denim, which is too hot, and concentrate on lighter fabrics that will breathe in the heat. Winter months tend to be windy and rainy, so pack a jacket. If you plan to hit the beach, we recommend bringing at least two swimsuits so that you can wear one while the other is drying back in your cabin. Cruises typically allow you to take towels off the boat, but you'll want a coverup as well as sandals or flip-flops. At night, casual means khaki-type slacks and polo or sport shirts for men and sundresses, skirts, or casual pants outfits for women. Golfers should be aware that many golf courses also have dress codes.

Informal dress—sometimes called "resort casual" or "country club casual"—is a little trickier. It applies only to evening wear and can mean different things depending on the cruise line. Informal for women is a dressier dress or pants outfit; for men it almost always includes a sport coat, and a tie is optional. Check your documents carefully.

Formal night means dressing up, but these days even that is a relative notion. You'll see women in everything from simple cocktail dresses to elaborate, glittering gowns. A tuxedo (either all black or with white dinner jacket) or dark suit is required for gentlemen. For children, Sunday best is entirely appropriate.

Men can usually rent their formal attire from the cruise line, and if they do so, it will be waiting when they board. Be sure to make these arrangements in advance; your travel agent can get the details from the cruise line. But if you're renting a tux, buy your own studs: a surefire way to spot a rented tuxedo is by the inexpensive studs that come with it.

An absolute essential for women is a shawl or light sweater. Aggressive air-conditioning can make public rooms uncomfortable, particularly if you're sunburned from a day at the beach.

Put things you can't do without—such as prescription medication, spare eyeglasses, toiletries, a swimsuit, and a change of clothes for the first day—in your carry-on. Most cruise ships provide soap, shampoo, and conditioner.

Insurance

It's a good idea to purchase travel insurance, which covers a variety of possible hazards and mishaps—including trip interruptions, lost or delayed baggage, medical emergencies, and other disruptions—when you book a cruise. Preexisting medical conditions are often covered only if you buy a policy at the time or within a few days of the initial booking. Any policy should insure you for travel and luggage delays. A travel policy will ensure that you can get to the next port of call should you miss your ship, or reimburse you for unexpected expenditures. Several travel insurance providers offer faster reimbursement for covered disruptions via mobile apps. Save your

receipts for all out-of-pocket expenses to file your claim, and be sure to get an incident report from the airline at fault.

Insurance should also cover you for unexpected injuries and illnesses. The medical insurance program you depend on at home might not extend coverage beyond the borders of the United States. Medicare assuredly will not cover you if you are hurt or sick while abroad. It is worth noting that all ships of foreign registry are considered to be "outside the United States" by Medicare.

Nearly all cruise lines offer their own line of insurance. Compare the coverage and rates to determine which is best for you. Keep in mind that insurance purchased from an independent carrier is more likely to include coverage if the cruise line goes out of business before or during your cruise. Although it is a rare and unlikely occurrence, you do want to be insured in the event that it happens.

U.S. TRAVEL INSURANCE Allianz Travel Insurance. ☎ *866/884–3556* ⊕ *www.allianztravelinsurance.com.* **Generali Global Assistance.** ☎ *800/874–2442* ⊕ *www.generalitravelinsurance.com.* **GeoBlue Travel Health Insurance.** ☎ *610/254–5850, 855/481–6647* ⊕ *www.geobluetravelinsurance.com.* **Travelex Insurance.** ☎ *800/228–9792* ⊕ *www.travelexinsurance.com.* **Travel Guard International.** ☎ *800/826–5248* ⊕ *www.travelguard.com.* **Travel Insured International.** ☎ *800/243–3174* ⊕ *www.travelinsured.com.*

On Board

Check out your cabin to make sure that everything is in order. Try the plumbing and set the thermostat to the temperature you prefer. Your cabin may feel warm while docked but will cool off when the ship is underway. You should find a copy of the ship's daily schedule in the cabin. Take a few moments to look it over—you will want to know what time the lifeboat (or muster) drill takes place (a placard on the back of your cabin door will indicate directions to your emergency station), as well as meal hours and the schedule for various activities and entertainment.

Bon voyage gifts sent by your friends or travel agent will be delivered sometime during the afternoon. Be patient if you are expecting deliveries, particularly on megaships. Cabin stewards participate in the ship's turnaround and are extremely busy, although yours will no doubt introduce themselves at the first available opportunity. It may also be a while before your checked luggage arrives (possibly not until late afternoon), so your initial order of business is usually the buffet, if you haven't already had lunch. Bring along the daily schedule to check over while you eat.

While making your way to the lido buffet, no doubt you'll notice bar waiters offering trays of colorful bon voyage drinks, often in souvenir glasses that you can keep. Beware—they are not complimentary! If you choose one, you will be asked to sign for it. Like the boarding photos, you are under no obligation to purchase.

Do your plans for the cruise include booking shore excursions and indulging in spa treatments? The most popular tours sometimes sell out, and spas can be busy during sea days, so your next stops should be the Shore Excursion Desk to book tours and the spa to make appointments, if you didn't already book your spa visits and excursions in advance.

Dining room seating arrangements are another matter for consideration. If you aren't happy with your assigned dinner seating, speak to the maître d'. The daily schedule will indicate where and when to meet with him. If you plan to dine in the ship's specialty restaurant, make those reservations as soon as possible to avoid disappointment.

Paying for Things on Board

A cashless society prevails on cruise ships, and during check-in either an imprint is made of your credit card or you must make a cash deposit for use against onboard charges. Most expenditures are charged to your shipboard account (via a swipe of your key card) with your signature as verification, with the exception of some casino gaming.

You'll get an itemized bill listing your purchases at the end of the voyage, and any discrepancies can be discussed at the purser's desk. To save time, check the balance of your shipboard account before the last day by requesting an interim printout of your bill from the purser to ensure accuracy. On some ships you can even access your account on your stateroom television.

Dining

All food, all the time? Not quite, but it's possible to literally eat away the day and most of the night on a cruise. A popular cruise directors' joke is, "You came on as passengers, and you will be leaving as cargo." Although it's meant in fun, it does contain an element of truth. Food—tasty and plentiful—is available 24 hours a day on most cruise ships, and the dining experience at sea has reached almost mythical proportions. Perhaps it has something to do with legendary midnight buffets, the absence of menu prices, or maybe it's the vast selection and availability.

RESTAURANTS

Every ship has at least one main restaurant and a lido, or casual, buffet alternative. Increasingly important are specialty restaurants. Meals in the primary and buffet restaurants are included in the cruise fare; on most ships there's also 'round-the-clock room service (sometimes with a charge), midday tea and snacks, and late-night buffets. Most mainstream cruise lines levy a surcharge for dining in alternative restaurants that may also include a gratuity (fees are also not uncommon now for room service deliveries), although there generally is no additional charge on luxury cruise lines.

You may also find a pizzeria or a specialty coffee bar on your ship—increasingly popular favorites cropping up on ships old and new. Although pizza is usually complimentary (though on some ships it is not, when delivered by room service), expect an additional charge for specialty coffees at the coffee bar and, quite likely, in the dining room as well. You will also likely be charged for sodas and drinks other than iced tea, regular coffee, tap water, and fruit juice during meals.

There is often a direct relationship between the cost of a cruise and the quality of its cuisine. The food is sophisticated on some (mostly expensive) lines, among them Regent Seven Seas and Silversea. In the more moderate price range, Celebrity Cruises has always been known for its fine cuisine, and Oceania Cruises scores high marks as well. The trend toward featuring specialty dishes and even entire menus designed by acclaimed chefs has spread throughout the cruise industry; however, on most mainstream cruise lines the food is of the quality that you would find in any good hotel banquet—perfectly acceptable but certainly not great.

SPECIALTY RESTAURANTS

A growing trend in shipboard dining is the emergence of sophisticated specialty restaurants that require reservations and frequently charge a fee. From as little as $29 per person for a complete steak dinner to $200 per person for an elaborate gourmet meal including fine wines paired with each course, specialty restaurants offer a refined dining option that cannot be duplicated in your ship's main restaurants. If you anticipate dining in your ship's intimate specialty restaurant, make

Fodor's Cruise Preparation Time Line 👁

4–6 Months Before Sailing

■ Check with your travel agent or the State Department for the identification required for your cruise.

■ Gather the necessary identification you need. If you need to replace a lost birth certificate, apply for a new passport, or renew one that's about to expire, start the paperwork now. Doing it at the last minute is stressful and often costly.

60–75 Days Before Sailing

■ Make the final payment on your cruise fare. Though the dates vary, your travel agent should remind you when the payment date draws near. Failure to submit the balance on time can result in the cancellation of your reservation.

■ Make a packing list for each person you'll be packing for.

■ Begin your wardrobe planning now. Try things on to make sure they fit and are in good repair (it's amazing how stains can magically appear months after something has been dry cleaned). Set things aside.

■ If you need to shop, get started so you have time to find just the right thing (and perhaps to return or exchange just the right thing).

■ Make kennel reservations for your pets. (If you're traveling during a holiday period, you may need to do this even earlier.)

■ Arrange for a house sitter.

If you're cruising, but your kids are staying home:

■ Make childcare arrangements.

■ Go over children's schedules to make sure they'll have everything they need while you're gone (gift for a birthday party, supplies for a school project, permission slip for a field trip).

30 Days Before Sailing

■ If you purchased an air-and-sea package, call your travel agent for the details of your airline schedule. Request seat assignments.

■ If your children are sailing with you, check their wardrobes now (do it too early and the really little kids may actually grow out of garments).

■ Make appointments for any personal services you wish to have before your cruise (for example, a haircut or manicure).

■ Get out your luggage and check the locks and zippers. Check for anything that might have spilled inside on a previous trip.

■ If you need new luggage or want an extra piece to bring home souvenirs, purchase it now.

2–4 Weeks Before Sailing

■ Receive your cruise documents through the travel agent or print them from the cruise line's website.

■ Examine the documents for accuracy (correct cabin number, sailing date, and dining arrangements); make sure names are spelled correctly. If there's something you do not understand, ask now.

■ Read all the literature in your document package for suggestions specific to your cruise. Most cruise lines include helpful information.

■ Pay any routine bills that may be due while you're gone.

■ Go over your personalized packing list again. Finish shopping.

1 Week Before Sailing

■ Finalize your packing list and continue organizing everything in one area.

- Buy film or digital media and ensure your digital devices are in good working order; buy back-up chargers to be safe.

- Refill prescription medications with an adequate supply.

- Make two photocopies of your passport or ID and credit cards. Leave one copy with a friend and carry the other copy separately from the originals.

- Get cash and/or traveler's checks at the bank. If you use traveler's checks, keep a separate record of the serial numbers. Get a supply of one-dollar bills for tipping baggage handlers (at the airport, hotel, pier, etc.).

- You may also want to put valuables and jewelry that you won't be taking with you in the safety deposit box while you're at the bank.

- Arrange to have your mail held at the post office or ask a neighbor to pick it up.

- Stop newspaper delivery or ask a neighbor to bring it in for you.

- Arrange for lawn and houseplant care or snow removal during your absence (if necessary).

- Leave your itinerary, the ship's telephone number (plus the name of your ship and your stateroom number), and a house key with a relative or friend.

- If traveling with young children, purchase small games or toys to keep them occupied while en route to your embarkation port.

3 Days Before Sailing

- Confirm your airline flights; departure times are sometimes subject to change.

- Put a card with your name, address, telephone number, and itinerary inside each suitcase.

- Fill out the luggage tags that came with your document packet, and follow the instructions regarding when and how to attach them.

- Complete any other paperwork that the cruise line included with your documents, either hard copy or online (foreign customs and immigration forms, onboard charge application, etc.). Do not wait until you're standing in the pier check-in line to fill them in!

- Do last-minute laundry and tidy up the house.

- Pull out the luggage and begin packing.

The Day Before Sailing

- Take pets to the kennel.

- Water houseplants and lawn (if necessary).

- Dispose of any perishable food in the refrigerator.

- Mail any last-minute bills.

- Set timers for indoor lights.

- Reorganize your wallet. Remove anything you will not need (local affinity cards, department store or gas credit cards, etc.), and put them in an envelope.

- Finish packing and lock your suitcases.

Departure Day

- Adjust the thermostat and double-check the door locks.

- Turn off the water if there's danger of frozen pipes while you're away.

- Arrange to be at the airport a minimum of two hours before your departure time (follow the airline's instructions).

- Have government-issued photo ID and/or your passport ready for airport check-in.

- Slip your car keys, parking claim checks, and airline tickets into your carry-on luggage. Never pack these items in checked luggage.

8

Cruising to Bermuda ON BOARD

Onboard Extras

As you budget for your trip, keep these likely additional costs in mind.

Cocktails: $8–$15

Wine by the glass: $8–$15

Beer: $6–$8

Bottled water: $2.50–$5

Soft drinks: $2.50–$3

Specialty ice cream and coffee: $5–$7

Laundry: $2–$11 per piece (where self-launder facilities are unavailable)

Spa treatments: $145–$265

Salon services: $30–$149

Casino gambling: 1¢ to $10 for slot machines; $5 and up for table games

Bingo: $5–$15 per card for multiple games in each session

reservations as soon as possible to avoid disappointment.

SPECIAL DIETS

Cruise lines make every possible attempt to ensure dining satisfaction. If you have special dietary considerations (for example, low-salt, kosher, or food allergies), be sure to indicate them well ahead of time and check to be certain your needs are known by your waiter once on board. In addition to the usual menu items, so-called spa, low-calorie, low-carbohydrate, or low-fat selections, as well as children's menus, are usually available. Requests for dishes not featured on the menu can often be granted if you ask in advance.

ALCOHOL

On all but the most upscale lines, you pay for alcohol aboard the ship, including wine with dinner. Wine typically costs about what you would expect to pay at a nice lounge or restaurant in a resort or in a major city. Wine by the bottle is a more economical choice at dinner than ordering it by the glass. Any wine you don't finish will be kept for you and served the next night. Gifts of wine or champagne ordered from the cruise line

(either by you, a friend, or your travel agent) can be taken to the dining room. Wine from any other source will incur a corkage fee of approximately $10 to $25 per bottle. Some (though not all) lines will allow you to carry wine aboard when you embark for the first time; most lines do not allow you to carry other alcohol on board (Viking Ocean Cruises being a notable exception).

Entertainment

Real treats are the folkloric shows or other entertainment arranged to take place while cruise ships are in port. Local performers come aboard, usually shortly before the ship sails, to present traditional songs and dances. It's an excellent way to get a glimpse of their performing arts.

Some ships also have a movie theater or offer in-cabin movies, or you may be able to rent or borrow movies to watch on your in-cabin DVD player, if you have one. The latest twist in video programming can be found on many cruise ships—huge outdoor LED screens where movies, music video concerts, news

Drinking and Gambling Ages

Many underage passengers have learned to their chagrin that the rules that apply on land are also adhered to at sea. On most mainstream cruise ships you must be 21 to imbibe alcoholic beverages. There are exceptions—for instance, on cruises departing from countries where the legal drinking age is typically lower than 21. On some cruise lines, a parent who is sailing with his or her son(s) and/or daughter(s) who is between the ages of 18 and 20 may sign a waiver allowing the 18- to 20-year-old to consume alcoholic beverages, generally limited to beer and wine. However, by and large, if you haven't achieved the magic age of 21, your shipboard charge card will be coded as booze-free, and bartenders won't risk their jobs to sell you alcohol.

Gambling is a bit looser, and 18-year-olds can try their luck on cruise lines such as Carnival, Celebrity, Holland America, Norwegian, Royal Caribbean, and Silversea; most other cruise lines adhere to the age-21 minimum.

channels, sports events, and even the ship's activities are broadcast for passengers lounging poolside.

Enrichment programs have also become a popular pastime at sea. Port lecturers on many large contemporary cruise ships offer more information on ship-sponsored shore tours and shopping than insight into the ports of call themselves. If more cerebral presentations are important to you, consider a cruise on a line that features stimulating enrichment programs and seminars at sea. Speakers can include destination-oriented historians, popular authors, business leaders, political figures, radio or television personalities, and even movie stars.

LOUNGES AND NIGHTCLUBS

You'll often find live entertainment in the ship lounges after dinner (and even sometimes before dinner). If you want to unleash your inner American Idol, look for karaoke. Singing along in a lively piano bar is another shipboard favorite for would-be crooners.

Other lounges might feature easy-listening or jazz performances or live music for pre- and postdinner social dancing. Later in the evening, lounges pick up the pace with music from the 1950s, '60s, and '70s; clubs aimed at a younger crowd usually have more contemporary dance music during the late-night hours.

CASINOS

On most ships, lavish casinos pulsate with activity. On ships that feature them, the rationale for locating casinos where most passengers must pass either through or alongside them is obvious—the unspoken allure of winning. In addition to slot machines in a variety of denominations, cruise-ship casinos usually have table games. Casino hours vary based on the itinerary or location of the ship; most are required to close while in port, whereas others may be able to offer 24-hour slot machines while simply closing table games. Every casino has a cashier, and you may be able to charge a cash advance to your onboard account for a fee. And unlike most ship areas, smoking is still allowed in many cruise-ship casinos.

Will I Get Seasick?

Many first-time passengers are anxious about whether they'll be stricken by seasickness, but there is no way to tell until you actually sail. Modern vessels are equipped with stabilizers that eliminate much of the motion responsible for seasickness. On most Caribbean cruises, you will spend most of your time in reasonably calm, sheltered waters, but when your cruise includes time out in the open sea (say, between Miami and Puerto Rico), you may feel the ship's movement. However, today's modern cruise ships—particularly if your ship is a megaliner—provide a remarkably motion-free experience unless the seas are rough. You may feel slightly more movement on a small ship, but not by much, as these ships ply remote bays and coves that are even more sheltered than those traveled by regular cruise ships.

If you have a history of seasickness, don't book an inside cabin. For the terminally seasick, it will begin to resemble a movable coffin in short order. If you do become seasick, you can use common drugs such as Dramamine and Bonine (often handed out free at concierge desks when seas are rough). Some people find anti-seasickness wristbands helpful; these apply gentle pressure to the wrist in lieu of drugs. Worn behind the ear, the Transderm Scop patch dispenses a continuous metered dose of medication, which is absorbed into the skin and enters the bloodstream. Apply the patch four hours before sailing and it will continue to be effective for three days. It can be prescribed by the ship's physician, but it's usually cheaper and easier to get it from your own doctor.

Sports and Fitness

Onboard sports facilities might include a court for basketball, volleyball, tennis—or all three—a jogging track, or even a ropes course high above the ship's top deck. Some ships are even offering innovative and unexpected features, such as rock-climbing walls, bungee trampolines, ziplines, a go-kart track on Norwegian Cruise Line's *Norwegian Bliss,* and surfing pools and bumper cars on some Royal Caribbean ships. For the less adventurous, there's always table tennis and shuffleboard.

Naturally, you will find at least one swimming pool, and possibly several. Cruise-ship pools are generally on the small side—more appropriate for cooling off than doing laps—and the majority contain filtered salt water. But some are elaborate affairs, with waterslides and interactive water play areas for family fun. Princess Grand–class ships have challenging, freshwater "swim against the current" pools for swimming enthusiasts who want to get their low-impact exercise while on board.

Shipboard fitness centers have become ever more elaborate, offering state-of-the-art exercise machines, treadmills, and stair steppers, not to mention free weights and weight machines. As a bonus, many fitness centers with floor-to-ceiling windows have the world's most inspiring sea views. Most ships offer some complimentary fitness classes, but you will also find classes in Pilates, spinning, or yoga (usually for a fee). Personal trainers are usually on board to get you off on the right foot (also for a fee).

Safety at Sea

Safety begins with you, the passenger. Once settled into your cabin, locate your life vests if they are stored there, and review the posted emergency instructions. Make sure the vests are in good condition, and learn how to secure them properly. Make certain the ship's purser knows if you have a physical infirmity that may hamper a speedy exit from your cabin, so that in an emergency he or she can quickly dispatch a crew member to assist you. If you're traveling with children, be sure that child-size life jackets are placed in your cabin.

Before your ship leaves the embarkation port, you'll be required to attend a mandatory lifeboat drill; you may or may not be required to bring your life vest and stand outside on deck near your assigned lifeboat. Do go and listen carefully (ship staff will take attendance and won't dismiss the passengers until everyone is accounted for). If you're unsure about how to use your vest, now is the time to ask. Some cruise lines no longer require you to bring your vest to the muster drill and instead store them near the muster station, but crew members are more than willing to assist if you have questions. Only in the most extreme circumstances will you need to abandon ship—but it has happened. The time you spend learning the procedure may serve you well in a mishap.

In actuality, the greatest danger facing cruise-ship passengers is fire. All cruise lines must meet international standards for fire safety, which require sprinkler systems, smoke detectors, and other safety features. Fires on cruise ships are not common, but they do happen, and these rules have made ships much safer. You can do your part by *not* using an iron in your cabin or leaving fabric items, such as towels, on your balcony, and by taking care to properly extinguish smoking materials. Never throw a lighted cigarette overboard—it could be blown back into an opening in the ship and start a fire (most ships don't allow smoking in cabins or on balconies any longer for this reason).

Spas

With all the usual pampering and service in luxurious surroundings, simply being on a cruise can be a stress-reducing experience. Add to that the menu of spa and salon services at your fingertips and you have a recipe for total sensory pleasure. Spas have also become among the most popular of shipboard areas. While high-end Canyon Ranch has made inroads with the cruise industry by opening spas on an increasing number of ships, Steiner Leisure is still the largest spa and salon operator at sea (the company also operates the Mandara, Elemis, and Greenhouse spa brands), with facilities on more than 100 cruise ships worldwide.

In addition to facials, manicures, pedicures, massages, and sensual body treatments, other hallmarks of Steiner Leisure are salon services and products for hair and skin. Founded in 1901 by Henry Steiner of London, a single salon prospered when Steiner's son joined the business in 1926 and was granted a Royal Warrant as hairdresser to Her Majesty Queen Mary in 1937. In 1956 Steiner won its first cruise-ship contract to operate the salon on board the ships of the Cunard Line. By the mid-1990s Steiner

Leisure began taking an active role in creating shipboard spas offering a wide variety of wellness therapies and beauty programs for both women and men.

Other Shipboard Services

COMMUNICATIONS

Just because you are out to sea does not mean you have to be out of touch. However, ship-to-shore telephone calls can cost $2 to $15 a minute, so it makes more economic sense to use email to remain in contact with your home or office. Most ships have basic computer systems, and some newer vessels offer more high-tech connectivity—even in-cabin hookups or wireless connections for either your own laptop computer or tablet. Expect to pay an activation fee and subsequent charges in the $0.75- to $1-per-minute range for the use of these Internet services. Ships usually offer some kind of package so that you get a reduced per-minute price if you pay a fee up front.

The ability to use your own mobile phone for calls from the high seas is an alternative that is gaining in popularity. It's usually cheaper than using a cabin phone if your ship offers the service; however, it can still cost $2.50 to $5 a minute. A rather ingenious concept, the ship acts as a cell "tower" in international waters—you use your own cell phone and your own number when roaming at sea, and you can even send and receive text messages and email with some smartphones (albeit with a surcharge in addition to any roaming fees). Before leaving home, ask your cell-phone service provider to activate international roaming on your account. When in port, depending on the type of cell phone you own and the agreements your mobile service-provider has established, you may be able to connect to local networks ashore. Most GSM phones are also usable in Bermuda. Rates for using the maritime service, as well as any roaming charges, are established by your mobile service carrier and are worth checking into before your trip. To avoid excessive charges, it's a good idea to turn off your phone's data roaming option while at sea.

LAUNDRY AND DRY CLEANING

Most cruise ships offer valet laundry and pressing services (and some also offer dry cleaning). Expenses can add up fast, especially for laundry, since charges are per item and the rates are similar to those charged in hotels, unless your ship offers a fixed-price laundry deal (all you can stuff into a bag they provide for a single fee, which is common on longer cruises and even some weeklong cruises). If doing laundry is important to you and you do not want to send it out to be done, some cruise ships have a self-service laundry room (which usually features an iron and ironing board in addition to washers and dryers). If you book one of the top-dollar suites, laundry service may be included for no additional cost. Upscale ships such as those in the Regent Seven Seas, Viking Ocean, and Silversea fleets have complimentary self-service launderettes. On other cruise lines, such as Disney, Princess, Oceania, Carnival, and some Holland America ships, you can do your own laundry for about $4 or less per load. None of the vessels in the Norwegian, Royal Caribbean, or Celebrity fleets has self-service laundry facilities.

Tipping

One of the most delicate—yet frequently debated—topics of conversation among cruise passengers involves the matter of tipping. Who do you tip? How much? What's "customary" and "recommended?" Should parents tip the full amount for children or is just half adequate? Why do you have to tip at all?

When transfers to and from your ship are a part of your air and sea program,

Crime on Ships

Crime aboard cruise ships has occasionally become headline news, thanks in large part to a few well-publicized cases. Most people never have any type of problem, but you should exercise the same precautions aboard a ship that you would at home. Keep your valuables out of sight—on big ships virtually every cabin has a small safe. Don't carry too much cash ashore, use your credit card whenever possible, and keep your money in a secure place, such as a front pocket that's harder to pick.

Single women traveling with friends should stick together, especially when returning to their cabins late at night. When assaults occur, it often comes to light that excessive drinking of alcohol is a factor. Be careful about whom you befriend, as you would anywhere, whether it's a fellow passenger or a member of the crew. Don't be paranoid, but do be prudent.

Your cruise is a wonderful opportunity to leave everyday responsibilities behind, but don't neglect to pack your common sense. After a few drinks it might seem like a good idea to sit on a railing or lean over the rail to get a better view of the ship's wake. Passengers have been known to fall. "Man overboard" is more likely to be the result of carelessness than criminal intent.

gratuities are generally included for luggage handling. In that case, do not worry about the interim tipping. However, if you take a taxi to the pier and hand over your bags to a stevedore, be sure to tip him. Treat him with respect and pass along at least $5.

During your cruise, room-service waiters generally receive a cash tip of $1 to $3 per delivery. Depending on the ship, a gratuity, which may range from 15% to 20%, will automatically be added to each bar bill during the cruise. If you use salon and spa services, a similar percentage might be added to the bills there as well. If you dine in a specialty restaurant, it may be suggested that you extend a onetime gratuity for the service staff.

There will be a "disembarkation talk" on the last day of the cruise that explains tipping procedures. If you're expected to tip in cash, which is increasingly rare these days, small white tip envelopes will appear in your stateroom that day. If you tip in cash, you usually give the tip envelope directly to each person on the last night of the cruise. Tips generally add up to anywhere from $14 to $22 per person (including children) per day.

Most lines now either automatically add gratuities to passengers' onboard charge accounts or offer the option. If that suits you, then do nothing further. However, you're certainly free to adjust the amounts up or down to more appropriate levels or ask that the charge be removed altogether if you prefer distributing cash gratuities.

Shore Excursions

Shore excursions are optional tours organized by the cruise line and sold aboard the ship. Most tours last two to four hours and all are meant to optimize your time on the island—the cruise line does the research about what to see and do, and you just go along for the ride. You'll sometimes pay more for these ship-packaged tours than if you booked them independently, either

before you leave home or after arriving in port. However, with only two or three days at your disposal, the convenience, and assurance that a spot on the tour you're looking forward to is available, may be worth the price. Popular tours often sell out and may not be obtainable at any price once you are ashore. Fees are generally $40–$60 per person for walking tours, $45–$85 per person for island tours, $50–$90 for snorkeling trips, and $150–$185 for diving trips. Prices for children are usually less. For exact durations and pricing, consult your cruise line. Also keep in mind that tour fees and time estimates can vary.

Naturally, you're always free to explore on your own. With its excellent taxi service, Bermuda is a good, although pricey, island for hiring a car and driver. Four-seater taxis charge $7.90 for the first mile and $2.75 for each subsequent mile. A personalized taxi tour of the island costs $50 per hour for up to four passengers and $70 an hour for up to seven, excluding tip. If you can round up a group of people, this is often cheaper than an island tour offered by your ship. Tip drivers 5%. Rental cars are prohibited (with the exception of two-person electric cars from Current Vehicles ⊕ *www.currentvehicles.com*), and while you can rent scooters, this can be dangerous for the uninitiated and is not recommended. Public transportation, including buses and ferries, is convenient to all cruise terminals and the sale of all-day passes might even be offered by the shore-excursion desk on your ship. For a full list of transportation options, visit Bermuda Tourism's website at ⊕ *www.gotobermuda.com/what-to-do/transportation*.

Going Ashore

Three Bermuda harbors serve cruise ships: Hamilton (the capital), St. George's, and King's Wharf at the Royal Naval Dockyard. In Hamilton, cruise ships

A Whole New World

Experience a whole different type of Bermuda nightlife—reserve a night snorkel tour from your ship's shore excursion desk. The island's coral reef comes alive when the sun goes down as nocturnal creatures of the deep emerge from the safety of their caves and crevices. Participants are provided with a dive light as well as snorkel gear, but the real treat is when the lights are turned off to reveal the extraordinary effects of bioluminescence—microscopic creatures that create light as you swim through them.

tie up right on the city's main street, Front Street. A visitor information center is next to the ferry terminal, also on Front Street and nearby; maps and brochures are displayed in the cruise terminal itself. St. George's accommodates a handful of smaller cruise ships every year at Penno's Wharf, located just minutes from the heart of the city. A visitor information center is at King's Square, near the Town Hall and within walking distance of the pier. King's Wharf, in the Royal Naval Dockyard at the westernmost end of the island, is the busiest of the three cruise-ship berthing areas, and it is where the largest vessels dock. Although Dockyard appears isolated on a map, it is well connected to the rest of the island by taxi, bus, and ferry. Three visitor information centers can be found along the piers and adjacent to the ferry dock.

Before anyone is allowed to proceed down the gangway, however, the ship must be cleared for landing. Immigration and customs officials board the vessel to examine paperwork and sort through red tape. It may be more than an hour before you're allowed ashore. Your ship ID acts

as your boarding pass, which you'll need to get back on board. You may also be advised to take a photo ID ashore, such as your passport or driver's license.

One advantage of a Bermuda itinerary is that cruise ships remain docked at night, which affords the opportunity to dine ashore and sample the nightlife. There's a downside to onboard life, though. Although most shipboard services—dining, lounges, and the fitness center and spa—continue to hum along as usual, duty-free shops are required by Bermuda government regulations to remain closed when in port. In addition, professional entertainment in the show lounge is curtailed, although a movie might be screened there instead. Some ships offer a "Bermuda Night" tropical-theme deck party.

Returning to the Ship

Cruise lines are strict about sailing times, which are posted at the gangway and elsewhere and announced in the daily schedule of activities. Be sure to be back on board at least a half hour before the announced sailing time or you may be stranded. If you're on a shore excursion that was sold by the cruise line, however, the captain will wait for your group before casting off. That's one reason why many passengers prefer ship-packaged tours.

If you're not on one of the ship's tours and the ship sails without you, immediately contact the cruise line's port representative, whose phone number is usually listed on the daily schedule of activities. You may be able to hitch a ride on a pilot boat, although that is unlikely. Passengers who miss the boat must pay their own way to the next port, and for a Bermuda cruise that means the U.S. disembarkation port (to where you will not be allowed to fly unless you have brought a valid passport).

On the Seashore

For a "free" souvenir, sea glass (broken bits of glass and china that have been tumbled by the sea to make them nice and smooth) is deposited in fairly large quantities by the surf at Alexandra Battery Beach Park. The beach park is easy to find on any local map and only about a mile walk from St. George's.

Disembarkation

All cruises come to an end eventually, and the disembarkation process actually begins the day before you arrive at your ship's final port. During that day your cabin steward delivers special luggage tags to your stateroom, along with customs forms and instructions on some itineraries.

The night before you disembark, you'll need to set aside clothing to wear the next morning when you leave the ship. Many people dress in whatever casual outfits they wear for the final dinner on board, or change into travel clothes after dinner. Also, do not forget to put your passport or other proof of citizenship, airline tickets, and medications in your hand luggage. The luggage tags go onto your larger bags, which are placed outside your stateroom door for pickup during the hours indicated. Your cruise line may offer self-assist disembarkation, and in that case, you do not have to put your luggage outside your stateroom the night before departure and may leave the ship early if you can take all your luggage with you.

A statement itemizing your onboard charges is delivered before you arise on disembarkation morning. Plan to get up early enough to check it over for

accuracy, finish packing your personal belongings, and vacate your stateroom by the appointed hour. Any discrepancies in your onboard account should be taken care of before leaving the ship, usually at the reception desk. Breakfast is served in the main restaurant as well as the buffet on the last morning, but room service usually isn't available. Disembarkation procedures vary by cruise line, but you'll probably have to wait in a lounge or on deck for your tag color or number to be called.

Then you take a taxi, bus, or other transportation to your post-cruise hotel or to the airport for your flight home. If you are flying out the day your cruise ends, leave plenty of time to go through the usual check-in, passport control and customs, and security procedures at the airport.

Customs and Duties

U.S. CUSTOMS

Each individual or family must fill out a customs declaration form, which will be provided before your ship docks. Be sure to keep receipts for all purchases made outside the United States; you may also be asked to show officials the receipts along with what you've bought. After showing your passport to U.S. immigration officials upon disembarkation, you must collect your luggage from the dock.

You're always allowed to bring goods up to a certain value back home without having to pay any duty or import tax. There's also a limit on the amount of tobacco and liquor you can bring back duty-free, and some countries have separate limits for perfumes; for exact figures, check with your customs department. The values of so-called duty-free goods are included in these amounts. When you shop abroad—and in the Caribbean, this means all islands except for Puerto Rico, which is part of the United States—if the total value of your goods is more than the duty-free limit, you'll have to pay a tax (most often a flat percentage) on the value of everything beyond that limit.

Individuals entering the United States from the Caribbean are allowed to bring in $800 worth of duty-free goods for personal use ($1,600 from the U.S. Virgin Islands), including 1 liter of alcohol (2 liters if one was produced in the Caribbean, and 5 liters from the USVI), one carton of cigarettes (or five if four were purchased in the U.S. Virgin Islands), and 100 non-Cuban cigars. Antiques and original artwork are also duty-free.

Index

Photo Credits

Front Cover: Glowimages [Description: Aerial view of canopies on a beach, Bermuda.]. **Back cover, from left to right:** orangecrush/Shutterstock, dbvirago/iStockphoto, Just dance/Shutterstock. **Spine:** Keith Muratori/Shutterstock. **Interior, from left to right:** andykazie/iStockphoto (1), Darryl Brooks/Shutterstock (2). **Chapter 1: Experience Bermuda:** sbonk/iStockphoto (6-7). Fairmont Hotels & Resorts (8). Bermuda Department of Tourism (9). Verena Matthew | Dreamstime.com (9). Walkabout Photo Guides/Shutterstock (10). Batsman by Matteo X, [CC BY 2.0] (10). Cambridge Beach Resort (10). Bermuda Department of Tourism (10). FOTOSEARCH RM/agefotostock (11). John Greim/age fotostock (11). Dark and stormy by Andrew Malone, [CC BY 2.0] (12). CHRIS BURVILLE (12). Bermuda Department of Tourism (12). Bermuda Department of Tourism (12). John Manderson/Bermuda Tourism Authority (13). Russ Hamilton/Shutterstock (13). Bermuda Tourism Authority (18). Gavin Howarth/Howarth Photography Ltd./Bermuda Tourism Authority (18). Rohan Shastri/Bermuda Tourism Authority (18). Bermuda Tourism Authority (19). Challenger Banks/Shutterstock (19). Bermuda Tourism Authority (20). Bermuda Tourism Authority (20). Bermuda Tourism Authority (20). Bermuda Tourism Authority (20). Bermuda Tourism Authority (20). Bermuda Tourism Authority (21). Hamilton Princess & Beach Club (21). Grotto Bay Beach Resort & Spa (21). Bermuda Tourism Authority (21). Fairmont Southampton (21). Bermuda Tourism Authority (21). Fairmont Southampton (22). Bermuda Tourism Authority (22). Tom Moore's Tavern (22). Bermuda Tourism Authority (23). Bermuda Tourism Authority (23). **Chapter 3: City of Hamilton and Pembroke Parish:** Just dance/Shutterstock (65). Rohan Shastri/Bermuda Tourism Authority (70). Victoria Lipov/Shutterstock (73). Nature Lovin' Geek/Shutterstock (74). V J Matthew/Shutterstock (78). Hamilton Princess & Beach Club (86). Bermuda Tourism Authority (86). Ritu Manoj Jethani/Shutterstock (103). **Chapter 4: Central Parishes:** Russ Hamilton/Shutterstock (107). V J Matthew/Shutterstock (114). Andrew Kazmierski/Dreamstime (116). Gavin Howarth/Howarth Photography Ltd. (118-119). Chapter 5: St. George's: Yingna Cai/ Shutterstock (135). Ramunas Bruzas/ Shutterstock (142). Felix Lipov/ Shutterstock (145). **Chapter 6: Eastern Parishes:** JianweiZ/iStockphoto (153). Courtesy_Bermuda Aquarium, Museum and Zoo (158). Grotto Bay Beach Resort & Spa (161). Look Bermuda/Rosewood Hotels & Resorts (162). Rosewood Hotels & Resorts (165). **Chapter 7: West End:** Darryl Brooks/Shutterstock (167). Carolyn Thomas/iStockphoto (173). Trosenow/Dreamstime (175). M S/Dreamstime (179). **Chapter 8: Cruising to Bermuda:** Andres Virviescas/Shutterstock (189). **About Our Writers:** All photos are courtesy of the writers except for the following.

*Every effort has been made to trace the copyright holders, and we apologize in advance for any accidental errors. We would be happy to apply the corrections in the following edition of this publication.

Notes

Notes

Notes

Notes

Fodor's BERMUDA

Publisher: Stephen Horowitz, *General Manager*

Editorial: Douglas Stallings, *Editorial Director;* Jill Fergus, Jacinta O'Halloran, Amanda Sadlowski, *Senior Editors*; Kayla Becker, Alexis Kelly, Rachael Roth, *Editors*

Design: Tina Malaney, *Director of Design and Production*; Jessica Gonzalez, *Graphic Designer;* Mariana Tabares, *Design & Production Intern*

Production: Jennifer DePrima, *Editorial Production Manager;* Carrie Parker, *Senior Production Editor;* Elyse Rozelle, *Production Editor;* Jackson Pranica, *Editorial Production Assistant*

Maps: Rebecca Baer, *Senior Map Editor;* Mark Stroud (Moon Street Cartography) and David Lindroth, *Cartographers*

Photography: Viviane Teles, *Senior Photo Editor;* Namrata Aggarwal, Ashok Kumar, Carl Yu, *Photo Editors;* Rebecca Rimmer, *Photo Intern*

Business and Operations: Chuck Hoover, *Chief Marketing Officer;* Robert Ames, *Group General Manager;* Devin Duckworth, *Director of Print Publishing;* Victor Bernal, *Business Analyst*

Public Relations and Marketing: Joe Ewaskiw, *Senior Director Communications & Public Relations*; Esther Su, *Senior Marketing Manager*

Fodors.com: Jeremy Tarr, *Editorial Director;* Rachael Levitt, *Managing Editor* Teddy Minford, *Editor*

Technology: Jon Atkinson, *Director of Technology;* Rudresh Teotia, *Lead Developer;* Jacob Ashpis, *Content Operations Manager*

Writers: Robyn Bardgett, Melissa Fox

Editors: Linda Cabasin, Douglas Stallings

Production Editor: Carrie Parker

35th Edition

ISBN 978-1-64097-242-1

ISSN 0192–3765

SPECIAL SALES
This book is available at special discounts for bulk purchases for sales promotions or premiums. For more information, e-mail SpecialMarkets@fodors.com.

PRINTED IN CANADA

10 9 8 7 6 5 4 3 2 1

MIX
Paper from responsible sources
FSC® C016245

About Our Writers

Born and raised in Bermuda, **Robyn Bardgett** considers herself a city girl at heart, and while she loves a day spent out on the boat enjoying Bermuda's aquamarine waters, she also has nothing against a cold, gray day exploring her favorite city, London. However, Robyn is fiercely protective of her Bermudian heritage and her beautiful island home. She currently lives in the historic Town of St. George with her family and is a freelance writer.

Melissa Fox was born and raised in Bermuda and has a love for the island's pink sand beaches and hidden nooks and crannies (not to mention the fantastic fish sandwiches). When she's not crafting content for her clients, she spends her time dreaming about traveling to exotic destinations for life-changing adventures and chasing after her two children, five and one-and-a-half.

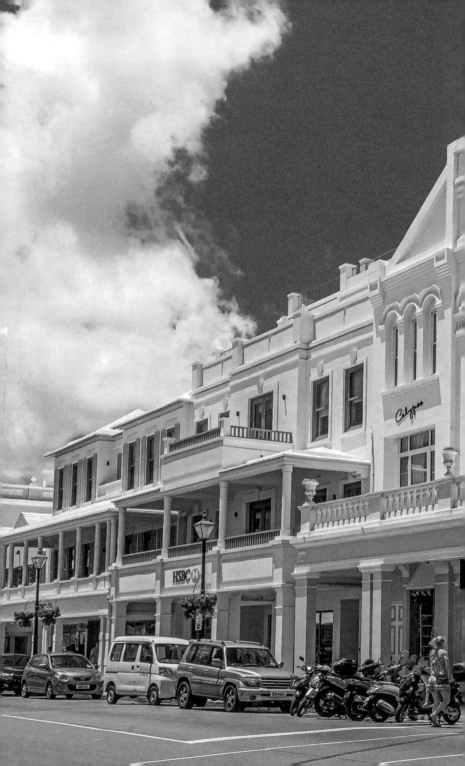

Fodor's

BERMUDA